PRAISE FOR

NOT EXACTLY RETIRED

BY DAVID JARMUL

"David and Champa's story of exploring the world combined with service to others is an inspiring example of how your sixties and beyond can become the most rewarding years of your life. It's a perfect example of how to reinvent retirement (or almost retirement). David's storytelling is engaging and will inspire you to find your own North Star, whether that is more travel or joining the Peace Corps like they did, or striking out for unknown personal territory."

Debbie and Michael Campbell, *The Senior Nomads*

"*Not Exactly Retired* is a fascinating story about the rewards of doing good while seeing the world. It shows how adventure can give new meaning to our lives and make them richer."

Jonathan Look, Jr., *LifePart2*

"I want to be like David Jarmul when I grow up. His story of setting out on an adventure of service in his 60's is a reminder that the itch for adventure can be scratched during any season of life and, as David so perfectly stated, "the important choice is to actually make a choice, to act instead of drifting." His story is the perfect combination of adventure, compassion and love and is sure to stroke the flames of wanderlust in those of us that carry that torch in our chest."

Kim Dinan, *The Yellow Envelope*

"Who in their right mind joins the Peace Corps in their sixties? What were we trying to prove to ourselves or anybody else?" David Jarmul ponders these perplexing questions during an 11,000 mile road-trip across America and his second tour with the Peace Corps, this time in Moldova — explorations that have both personal and historic appeal. He gently teases out a striking contrast between his service in Nepal 35 years ago and in Moldova in the age of Trump."

Marco Werman, Former Peace Corps Volunteer, Togo
Host, 'The World' on public radio

"*Not Exactly Retired* disproves Thomas Wolfe's adage that you can't go home again. The poignant vignettes throughout this remarkably readable book demonstrate that you can serve again after you have "retired" from a rewarding career. Although Peace Corps service after sixty brings challenges including distance from family and friends, learning a foreign language and experiencing cultures vastly different than our own, there are countless opportunities for rewarding service and adventure."

Kevin F. F. Quigley, Former president, National Peace Corps Association

"A delightful and instructive guide to self-renewal from which we all can learn."

Steve Olson, National Book Award nonfiction finalist

"A thoughtful and heart-warming account of love, travel and service to others. As a Moldovan, I found David's observations of my country wise, insightful and encouraging. I am humbled by David and Champa's volunteering in my home country. They will never know how many lives they've touched or changed, or how many young Moldovans will always remember their names."

Stela Brinzeanu, Bessarabian Nights

Not Exactly Retired

Not Exactly Retired

*A Life-Changing Journey on the
Road and in the Peace Corps*

David Jarmul

A PEACE CORPS WRITERS BOOK

Not Exactly Retired:
A Life-Changing Journey on the Road and in the Peace Corps

A Peace Corps Writers Book — an imprint of Peace Corps Worldwide

Printed in the United States of America by Peace Corps Writers of Oakland, California.

For more information, contact peacecorpsworldwide@gmail.com.

Peace Corps Writers and the Peace Corps Writers colophon are
trademarks of PeaceCorpsWorldwide.org

ISBN: 978-1-950444-05-2 (paperback)
ISBN: 978-1-950444-06-9 (e-book)
Library of Congress Control Number: 2019920031

First Peace Corps Writers Edition, April 2020

PCIP data available on WorldCat and on book website.
notexactlyretiredbook.com

Cover and Interior Design: Dania Zafar

For Paula, Maya, Jordan, James, Alina, Malia, and Jackson

CONTENTS

INTRODUCTION

I felt the cold even before I walked out the front door. The previous night's rainfall stretched in a frozen sheet from our alley to the dirt road leading up to the main street. People in dark overcoats there awaited overcrowded minibuses to drive them to the capital. My wife, Champa, had just called to say she'd nearly fallen while walking to school. Now I had to walk past her school to the library where I'd be helping two groups of students program robots for an upcoming "sumo robot" competition.

I covered my boot soles with the orange cleats we'd received from our Peace Corps safety officer, then treaded down the alley, arms out, asking myself anew why I'd left a good job and comfortable life in America to come to this little-known corner of the former Soviet Union. I was freezing. I was sure I was going to slip. Sure enough, as I approached the kindergarten on the next street, I fell hard on my left thigh, which turned black and blue overnight. A few days later, Champa fell near the same spot, bruising her tailbone so badly she could barely sleep for two weeks without painkillers. While she recovered, winter surrounded us, covering our garden with snow. The sun set early. Drab potatoes, beets, and onions filled the shelves of our local grocery. We couldn't drive anywhere for relief since the roads were treacherous and, in any case, we had no car. We were earning less than $750 a month, so we had little money. We missed North Carolina. We missed our children and grandchildren. We missed America.

The library where I worked was a tired cement structure on the edge of town. As I settled beneath its florescent lights into my aging chair that morning, I couldn't focus on my colleagues' conversation, which I could barely understand anyway. I was already thinking about having to walk home again in the evening, as the sun set and the streets refroze. I'd be wearing my daypack to cushion my fall if I tumbled backwards. Once again I wondered: Why had Champa and I left our family and friends back home? Who in their right mind joins the Peace Corps in their sixties? What were we trying to prove to ourselves or anybody else?

I'd been asking myself the same question during the past two years, beginning when I quit my job and we left our North Carolina home to drive 11,000 miles around the perimeter of the United States, from the South Dakota Badlands to the Louisiana bayous. After that we spent nearly two months in Nepal as it recovered from a massive earthquake. Finally, after a short break back home, we left to serve in Moldova, a small country wedged near the Black Sea between Romania and Ukraine. I couldn't have found Moldova on a map before we left our large house, six grandchildren, and American comforts to try to fill something that felt missing in our hearts even though we seemingly had everything we could want. We weren't "retired" now since we both had full-time jobs as Peace Corps volunteers — Champa teaching English, me at the library. But neither were we still employed in the conventional sense of driving to a job, receiving a paycheck, paying bills in our own country. We were redefining this phase of our lives in a new way, what I began to call "not exactly retired." It's the title I gave to a blog I started writing, which ended up attracting readers of all ages who were looking for ideas about how they, too, might pursue new lives combining adventure with service.

I'd liked my job at Duke University, although it wore me down and began to repeat itself. As the head of news and communications, I dealt with everything from the firestorm following the false allegations of our lacrosse players raping a stripper to research discoveries, student protests, and celebrity visits. I could drive in ten minutes from my house to a beautiful campus where I did meaningful work with talented people. Even when Duke's celebrated basketball team fell short of a national championship, or I was awoken at 3 a.m. to deal with a campus crime or an approaching storm, I was engaged with what I was doing.

As I approached and then passed my sixtieth birthday, though, I heard a voice in the back of my head saying, "there's more to your life than this." Another part of myself was now tamped down so far that I wondered whether it still existed. I wanted to be more creative, serve others, and become a citizen of the world again instead of donning a suit every day to promote a university that, for all of the great things it did, was inescapably elite. If I was serious about this instead of deluding myself with a fantasy, the clock was ticking. I needed to act on an idea Champa and I had been discussing for decades – even as we raised our kids and lived the lives of dedicated professionals. She and I had met more than thirty-five years earlier, when I served as a Peace Corps volunteer in Nepal. My first posting there was as an English teacher in Ilam, a town in eastern Nepal known for its beautiful tea plantations. Champa was one of the other teachers. She'd grown up nearby and become one of the first women from her tribal group to graduate from both high school and college. As she and I worked together, we fell in love, marrying at the end of my service and then living for more than two decades in suburban Washington, D.C., where we raised two sons. We moved to Durham in 2001 after Duke recruited me to lead its communications team. Although we never told anyone, we knew Duke might be my last conventional job before we were finally in a position to jump off the career ladder to pursue adventure and service, the same ideals that had brought us together. Champa worked for many of those years as a sonographer for a medical research team at the University of North Carolina at Chapel Hill.

As we entered our early sixties, our two sons were both out of the house and doing well with families of their own. We weren't rich, but we'd paid off our mortgage and become eligible for retirement health care benefits from Duke. Although far from huge, our nest egg was sufficient to support us, especially if we could avoid dipping into it for a few years. We figured we could drop out long enough to travel around the United States and, if that went well, spend time in Nepal. After that, we'd know whether we were ready to make the most significant leap of all and join the Peace Corps, assuming they'd even accept us as volunteers at our age. Each stage of this journey, we figured, would be bigger than the one before it and certainly more substantial than anything we'd done previously as a couple. As a whole, we hoped they would nudge us from our predictable American lives to someplace, well, unpredictable. After doing everything we were supposed to do for so long — waking up to go to work, getting our kids off to school, mowing the grass, paying the mortgage — we were itching to challenge ourselves and find new meaning in our lives. Instead of zigging, we were ready to zag. These three trips could serve as our transition, rewriting the itineraries of our lives.

Our decision shocked many of our family and friends. People who knew how much I enjoyed my job — and being with them — asked why I would walk away when everything was going well. They also wondered how we could afford to do so, probably assuming we were secretly wealthy. Our sons and their wives, who knew about our plans and understood our hearts, supported us, even though it meant we would miss irreplaceable moments with our grandchildren — by far the hardest part of our decision.

By embracing this phase of our lives instead of drifting into retirement, we became part of a growing trend among people in their fifties, sixties, and seventies. My younger sister Nancy had recently published a book called *Second-Act Careers*, which she described as a "semi-retirement handbook." She reassured us we weren't crazy, and said we were doing what more and more people of our generation, as well as younger people, dreamed of doing themselves. On the evening after I announced my decision at Duke, I called her and said, "Nancy, you'd better be right."

In the months and years that followed, we learned we were not alone, even though millions of Americans still hold a more familiar view of retirement as something that starts at an official time and focuses on family, friends, and leisure activities. Some younger Americans have begun overhauling their budgets and career aspirations as part of the FIRE movement — *financial independence, retire early*. Just because we were part of a trend, though, didn't mean it would work out for us. So many things could go wrong. When I'd served in the Peace Corps the first time, I got so sick they had to send me home to the States, twice, the second time for good. Another guy in my group had a mental breakdown. Our oldest member, who didn't seem so old to me now, fell out of a rickshaw and broke several ribs just before she was supposed to swear in as a volunteer. She was sent home, too.

On the other hand, Champa and I knew what it felt like to be outliers. When we wed in 1979, our interracial, international, cross-religious marriage was an oddity. Some of our closest family and friends wondered whether a union between a Jewish boy from Long Island and a Hindu girl from the Himalayas could last, much less thrive. It did. We didn't intend to be pioneers then, nor did we now, but we had learned from experience that we needed to do what felt right to us, regardless of how it appeared to others. And perhaps Nancy was right; maybe we weren't as alone as it seemed.

We knew how lucky we were to be in this position. We'd both had wonderful parents, but now they were gone. Our health was good. Our house was paid off. Our children were financially independent. Most importantly, we loved each other and had always traveled easily together. The time had come to discover where serendipity might lead us, whether it was walking across sheets of ice in a little-known East European country or joining Champa's relatives in a distant Himalayan village to beat drums and say prayers beside a remote mountain stream.

Our suitcases and passports were ready. Over the next three years, we would embark on three trips that would change us forever. For years, the world had called out to us; this time, our hearts were ready to answer.

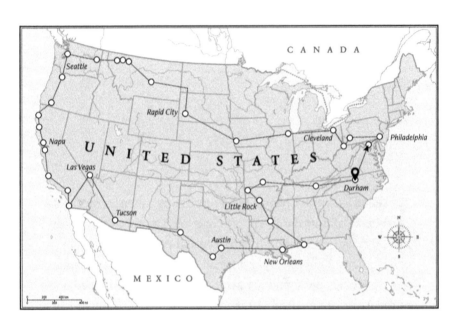

CHAPTER 1

HITTING THE ROAD

I fell in love with Champa as a Peace Corps volunteer in Nepal, but we almost didn't end up together. On my twenty-sixth birthday, several months after she and I agreed to marry, one of the other volunteers, my best friend Mitch, came to Kathmandu to surprise me and found me gasping on my bed. He rushed me to the American medical facility, where the Peace Corps doctor diagnosed me with severe pneumonia. My lung capacity was below thirty percent, and I floated in and out of consciousness.

"Do you know what this means?" the doctor asked when I finally stabilized.

"Yes, I need to cut back on my secondary projects and take better care of myself," I replied.

"No," she said, "you're going home."

Home? I was supposed to marry Champa in a few weeks. My parents were coming from New York. Champa didn't have a visa to go to America. She didn't even have a Nepali passport. I wept beneath my oxygen mask.

Champa was — and is — gorgeous. Several young men wanted to marry her. The braver ones had asked her parents, but Champa wasn't interested. She wanted to teach. By the time I met her, we were both in our mid-twenties. We drank tea together in the teachers' lounge. We chatted. When I learned a student in my 4A English class was her nephew Shankar, I suggested he might benefit from tutoring. Champa served me more tea at her house.

The second time I stopped by, I brought brownies I'd made in a pressure cooker, following a recipe in a Peace Corps cookbook. Shankar enjoyed them. Champa liked them, too, but was more interested in the *Newsweek* magazines I brought the third time. The Peace Corps sent them to me in its weekly mail packages. My only other contact with the outside world were letters and a shortwave radio. I never called home because it was too difficult and expensive. There was no internet.

Months passed. Champa and I spent more time together. No one outside her family knew. Even they didn't suspect we were falling in love. She and I never even kissed.

After my headmaster moved me to an abandoned school building where my room filled with smoke from a man cooking downstairs, my asthma worsened. When I asked the Peace Corps medical office for stronger medication, they ordered me home to see a pulmonologist in Washington. He agreed to let me return if I moved from Ilam to a new school closer to Kathmandu.

As part of my examination, the doctor also checked me for parasites, giving me a stool sample kit to fill and return for analysis. I brought it back in a brown paper bag during a second visit. On my way up to his office on Washington's K Street, the elevator doors opened and in walked one of my journalistic heroes, I.F. Stone, whom I recognized immediately. He smiled and asked, "So, what have you got in the bag?" As the doors opened again, I got off, smiled, and said "shit." This was probably one of the few times anyone in Washington left I.F. Stone speechless.

Before I flew back to Nepal, the Peace Corps let me visit my family on Long Island. I didn't mention Champa. It would freak them out, and I hadn't decided yet what to do.

When I returned to Kathmandu, I asked a close Peace Corps friend for advice. He told me to follow my heart. I traveled back to Ilam to pick up my stuff. When the road washed out, our jeep had to stay overnight at a small roadside lodge. I shared a room with another passenger, a professor at the local community college, who teased me I should marry a Nepali woman. He knew the perfect candidate. When he said her name, I took it as a sign.

I visited Champa's house the next day, a month since I'd left. Champa's face lit up when I returned. "I thought I wasn't going to see you again," she said. I knew then what I wanted. We walked up to her family's sitting room, and I proposed.

She didn't say yes immediately. She prepared a long list of questions about what our life would be like together, then made me meet her sister in Kathmandu. Meena had married a man from another caste, so she would be sympathetic, but she needed to check me out. She and her husband, one of Nepal's most famous singers, took me out for dinner with Champa. They asked about my family. They asked about my plans. They watched the two of us together. Finally, they gave their blessing.

I began teaching at the Lab School near Kathmandu. Champa remained in Ilam, working on her English. We quietly began planning our wedding and future. I finally sent a letter home telling my family. Several weeks later, my Peace Corps mailbox began filling up with letters from relatives urging me to reevaluate my decision.

Then came my birthday and the pneumonia. While the doctor waited for me to regain enough strength to make the long journey home, Mitch raced to Ilam to get Champa. She arrived in time to spend a few distraught days with me before I left.

I returned to Washington to see the same pulmonologist, this time to oversee my discharge. While there, I received a message from a federal official who'd read some articles I'd written as a volunteer. He was the deputy director of the White House office overseeing volunteer agencies, and he wanted to meet me.

After we'd talked for a few minutes, he said his boss, the director, wanted to meet me, too. Sam, who worked for President Carter, and I chatted amiably about the Peace Corps and Nepal for several minutes before he said, "Well, if there's ever anything I can do for you, please don't hesitate to ask."

I didn't hesitate. I told Sam how I'd been sent home before I could make any plans for Champa to get a visa to join me.

"No problem," said Sam. "I'll call Leonel." He meant his friend, the head of the Immigration and Naturalization Service.

Champa got her visa within a few days. When she went to the American Embassy, people there undoubtedly wondered, "Who *is* this woman?"

A few weeks later she arrived at Kennedy Airport, wearing a green sari I'd bought her. Waiting beside me in the terminal was an ABC Eyewitness News television crew. As the crew filmed an elderly Italian woman coming to America to reunite with her brother after decades apart, they had no idea that an even better story was unfolding beside them. The onlookers cheered as the old woman emerged into the lights and her brother's arms, just moments before Champa came more quietly into mine.

My parents embraced Champa, too, after we got home. They realized they weren't going to change my mind, even though they still worried whether others would accept a marriage mixed in so many ways — religion, nationality, ethnicity, language. This was 1979, after the Supreme Court decision making interracial marriages legal but years before they became as common as they are today. My parents opened their hearts to Champa and, in return, got a third daughter, one whose family came to accept me as well.

Within a month, we married in my parents' living room on Long Island. The justice of the peace watched uneasily as we exchanged flower garlands, and I placed red powder in Champa's hair. My grandfather, who brought my mother and her family to New York before the Holocaust, gave a loving toast about the unpredictability of life and the importance of family. Later, Champa changed out of her red wedding sari and into an outfit she'd borrowed from my sister. We drove over the Throg's Neck Bridge to our honeymoon in New England, streamers waving behind our rented car. We spent our wedding night at the Ramada Inn along Interstate 95 in Stamford. It seemed luxurious.

A month later we drove to Washington to begin our married life together. Our first stop was to thank Sam, who became emotional when Champa gave him a colorful mask she'd brought him as a gift from Nepal. "You know, I spend my days testifying before Congress and fighting about the budget," he told us. "When I see the two of you, I know I accomplished at least something."

And now, nearly four decades later, she and I were still together and about to embark on an adventure even greater than the one that brought us together. She still took my breath away.

Champa and I moved to the Washington, D.C. area after we got married in 1979. I'd found a job there with a nonprofit organization that helped developing countries implement "appropriate technology" — low-cost innovations such as fuel-conserving wood stoves, safer latrines, and wind-powered water pumps. Many of my colleagues there had also returned recently from the Peace Corps, and several of them became our friends, as did members of the small local Nepali community and some recent immigrants who shared a special bond with Champa. The organization hired me because of my Peace Corps and journalism experience, even though I knew little about technology. As I worked on its magazine and technical manuals, I discovered to my surprise that I enjoyed writing about technical topics.

After four years at the nonprofit, I moved on to a job at the National Academy of Sciences, which needed someone to launch a nationwide service to place op-ed articles on science-related topics in newspapers across the country. I'd published an op-ed piece in *The New York Times*, and would later publish two more, so they took a gamble on me even though I knew little about science. That job worked out well, expanding to include writing speeches for the Academy's president. Within a few years, I called myself a science writer, and served for a year as the president of the D.C. Science Writers Association.

Champa initially got a job doing secretarial work for a political consulting firm but eventually found a position teaching Nepali to State Department officials and others preparing to serve overseas.

Our first home was a small garden apartment in an aging complex with cockroaches and a neighbor who passed out drunk regularly on our stairwell, but we were young and happy, still not quite believing we were married after meeting halfway around the world.

In the years that followed, we bought our first house in Takoma Park. Later, we moved to Rockville, Maryland, closer to the Howard Hughes Medical Institute, where I took a communications job after nearly a decade at the Academy. We had our first son when we were both thirty, then a second son almost three years later. Champa went back to school to learn sonography and found work performing ultrasound exams at local hospitals. We traded in our bicycles for a car, then two cars. We helped our sons with their school work and science fair projects. We attended their basketball, soccer, baseball, and football games, their graduations, and finally their weddings. After Duke recruited me, we moved to North Carolina, where I worked too many hours and spent more of them than I wanted managing personnel challenges, student protests, and angry telephone calls from Tea Party activists whipped-up by Fox News to complain about happenings on our campus.

The Peace Corps faded into a memory. When I went to gatherings of returned volunteers, I realized I'd become one of those aging members who wore faded shirts from their earlier service. I told the same old stories about teaching in a school with mud floors and meeting Champa there. When I spoke with Duke students interested in the Peace Corps, I wondered whether my experience was relevant anymore. I felt like a well-intentioned, aging alum who does college admissions interviews with applicants younger than their own children.

I could no longer kid myself about still being a Peace Corps volunteer in my heart. I only had to look in the mirror to see the suit I was wearing. I was middle-aged, then was eligible for AARP, calculating how long I had to work until I could qualify for the university's retirement health plan.

Champa felt the passing years as well. When the research funding ended for her ultrasound position at the University of North Carolina at Chapel Hill, she decided to stop working and spend more time gardening, painting, quilting, and caring for our grandchildren.

Even as we settled into respectability, though, the Peace Corps *was* still in my heart. Underneath my starched shirt and silk tie, it called to me, and to Champa as well. We never stopped telling each other we wanted to serve as volunteers once we were in a position to leave our conventional lives. For me, joining the Peace Corps in my sixties would be like adding a second bookend around my career. For Champa, it would bring a new relationship with an organization that had already changed her life. However, we weren't ready to leave our family and country for so long until we were more confident about the idea. Sure, it sounded exciting in the abstract to trade in our traditional lives for serendipity and adventure, but how would we feel after living out of a suitcase for two weeks, or two months, or more than two years? Would we start to miss our American comforts and familiar routines, including things we took for granted like drinking water out of the faucet without boiling and filtering it? Could I just shed a professional identity I'd worked so hard to establish? How long would it take until we tired of the "exotic" aspects of the developing world and began to yearn for smooth roads, air conditioning, or a hamburger?

We'd always wanted to visit Mount Rushmore, Las Vegas, and other places, and to spend time driving through the farms and towns of the heartland. Beginning our big adventure with a trip around the United States would enable us to do this while also exploring our own hearts. It would be a substantial trip on its own terms but also a test run. If it went well, we'd accelerate to the next level and head for Nepal, to places far from the usual tourist destinations. Then we'd reflect and assess again about whether to pursue our Peace Corps dream.

The time leading up to our trip across the United States reminded us of everything we were leaving behind. Four months had passed since I shared my news with my staff, accompanied by my boss, whom I had alerted three months earlier. "I know from working in the news business that you should never 'bury the lede,'" I told them at our weekly meeting. "So I'll get right to the point: I've decided to step down on June 30." I heard gasps and had to look downward to avoid eye contact for a few moments, wanting to hold myself together.

After the meeting ended, I shared my news by e-mail with several hundred other colleagues across the campus, many of whom I'd worked with on stories, projects, and challenges ranging from organizing a speedy press conference to announce a professor's Nobel Prize to explaining to the *Today Show* that, no, we didn't want to chat about our student who became a porn star.

I'd worked hard at Duke to nurture a sense of community among the many communicators across its schools and departments. Now, when things were running smoothly and our team was regularly winning national awards for its work, I was leaving. I also posted my news on Facebook and LinkedIn. Friends across the city, around the country, and beyond sent me messages of congratulations.

My boss organized a big farewell party for me at a small downtown theater he rented for the occasion. There were speeches, gifts, food, and drink, along with a Duke rocking chair bearing a bronze plaque calling it a "hot seat" in my honor. My colleagues surprised me with an emotional video following the storyline of *It's A Wonderful Life*, asking what would have happened to the university and my friends if I had never come there. Since many of them were professional videographers and writers, the video was extraordinary, causing me to blink hard before I rose to say farewell. A few days later, at a party at the Durham Bulls baseball park, I received more gifts, including a fake edition of the campus newsletter filled with funny stories about me, Hawaiian shirts featuring Duke images, and a garden gnome molded to resemble the Duke blue devil.

Several more weeks passed before I officially stepped down, a strange interregnum where I saw meetings proceed without me and e-mail messages in which people made decisions that recently would have required my review. As I packed my books and photos, I could feel myself fading from view. I was still the boss, officially, but everyone was moving on. I was uneasy that some new crisis

— a campus shooting, a scandal, or worse — might erupt before I left. During the previous several months, Duke had been the focus of national stories involving a noose found hanging on a tree, a controversy over whether Muslims should be allowed to sound a "call to prayer" from the iconic Duke Chapel, as well as another championship for Coach K and the basketball team.

As I'd learned over the previous fourteen years, it was impossible to predict what might happen. For someone like me who loves the news business, unpredictability and excitement were among the job's attractions. Now I just wanted to make a graceful exit and let someone else respond to the next breathless inquiry from Fox News.

Fortunately, nothing happened. I managed to leave without any last-minute surprises. Champa and I found a Duke postdoctoral fellow to live in our house and take care of our dog, Bailey, while we were gone. We took my Ford Fusion to our auto repair shop for a checkup before we left a week later. I withdrew money from the bank and compiled a list of bills to track and pay online. I prepared a file with our credit card numbers and other information, in case we lost our wallets. Knowing we'd stay with friends along the way, Champa and I loaded our car trunk with small baskets of North Carolina treats to give as gifts. Since I'd no longer have a phone or computer provided by my office, we also bought a new laptop and smartphones to help us stay in touch and make travel reservations from the road. My new iPhone 6+ had a good camera and synched with my MacBook Pro laptop, enabling me to easily create and maintain a travel blog. Along with Facebook and Twitter, the blog became our main way of sharing our adventures with family, friends, and others.

The rapid transitions from work to trip planning to departure were not an accident. I wanted to leave quickly. If I lingered in

Durham, I would remain connected physically and mentally to my old life. It was better to plunge into something new. For the sake of my colleagues and eventual successor, I also wanted to send a signal to everyone at Duke that I was no longer involved. Over the next several months, I barely communicated with anyone from the university. It wasn't until the staff held its annual holiday party in December, to which my successor, Kristen, generously invited me as a surprise guest, that I began to reengage. By then, she had redecorated my office and settled in.

Just before we left town, Champa and I said goodbye to our younger son, his wife, and our two grandsons, who lived near us in Durham. We'd been seeing them regularly before this, and Champa helped care for both boys when they were little. They were part of our daily lives. Now we wouldn't see them for nearly two months.

On July 8, 2015, we put our overnight bags on the car's back seat since the trunk was already crammed with suitcases, gifts, snacks, and brochures. Although Champa had her own car and drove locally in Durham, she didn't like to drive on the highway. I'd be doing all of the driving until we returned home two months later.

Our first destination was a place we knew well, just four hours north of Durham — Takoma Park, Maryland, where we'd lived for many years. On our way to our friends' house, we stopped at one of the few local attractions we'd never seen -- the National Air and Space Museum center near Dulles Airport in Virginia. At long last, after years of dreaming, months of preparation, and an emotionally draining separation from a job that had defined me for so long, we were on our way.

Starting out in Takoma Park was a reminder of how far we'd already traveled in our lives, and of how other people our age are wrestling with their own issues of identity and meaning as they approach the end of traditional careers.

Located just over the border from Washington, D.C., Takoma Park had become trendy since we left it but remained a progressive outpost within the Beltway. Its hot new restaurant, Republic, reflected the city's reputation as the People's Republic of Takoma Park, albeit one whose fancier homes now cost more than a million dollars. On our first drizzly evening there, graying couples in tie-dyed shirts, Latino immigrant families, and moms with expensive strollers assembled at the local gazebo to beat drums and dance. Obama stickers adorned parked cars nearly three years after his re-election, although some were giving way to Bernie Sanders stickers. In many ways, Takoma Park resembled Durham — a small city known for its ethnic diversity, liberal politics, and funky charm.

We stayed there with friends we'd known since our sons attended pre-school together. The boys had drifted apart, but the four of us remained close, getting together every year or so. After they both retired, Champa and I watched what they were doing, hoping to learn from their experience. Larry began pursuing a new passion as a master gardener, while Linda applied her longtime expertise as a librarian to assist a nonprofit group. Now, as we enjoyed two long dinners together, they told us how they'd handled their emotional transition. They also discussed practical questions we'd never considered much before, such as the choices awaiting us about Medicare and Social Security.

We had a similar conversation the next day with another old friend, Glenda, whom we met downtown at the National Portrait Gallery. She had recently retired from her job at the post office and was getting ready to return to her home country of Grenada, where she'd built a small house in the capital. Glenda told us she planned to return regularly to Washington, where her sister lived, but looked forward to living comfortably in the Caribbean on her pension. She showed us photos of her house near the beach and urged us to visit.

The following morning, the conversation took still another turn as we stopped in a Maryland suburb for breakfast with two other friends. Bob and Karen were a few years younger than us, but they, too, were thinking about their next life stages. Bob had about a year to go in the White House science office, and Karen spent much of her time assisting refugee families through her Catholic parish. Just as Champa and I had viewed Larry, Linda, and Glenda as possible role models for our transition, so were Bob and Karen curious about our upcoming trips. They didn't anticipate doing the same kind of traveling after their youngest child graduated from college, but they were already pondering "what's next?" We'd end up traveling with them at the end of our journey three years later.

Next, we drove to Philadelphia, where our older son and his wife were still adjusting to the birth of twin girls, doubling the two girls they had already. Paul was also racing to complete a renovation of their house botched by a contractor. He did much of the work himself. He and Stephanie strained to hold down full-time jobs and raise four young girls while living atop a construction project. Champa and I wished we lived closer to them, and we now treasured every minute together. As in Durham, it was almost physically painful to say goodbye to our grandchildren when the time came to leave.

It was only the next morning, when we pointed our car west across Pennsylvania, that our trip stopped feeling like a familiar visit with friends and family and became the adventure we'd anticipated. Our next stop would be near Pittsburgh, but we didn't know exactly where. We had deliberately not booked a reservation. We wanted to let the days unfold. We'd been on the clock for the past forty years. We had reservations for an upcoming visit to Glacier National Park and specific dates to stay with friends in Chicago and along the West Coast, but we wanted to resist my usual planning impulse as much as possible and, instead, keep ourselves open to serendipity. If we were so busy racing to Site No. 4 in a city, we figured, we might not spot the charming church fair or local pie stand along the road, much less stop to take a look.

We were so excited to get going that we could barely sleep. We awoke before dawn and quietly slipped out the front door with our overnight bags, leaving a note to express our thanks and say a last goodbye. We drove down the street to the local Wawa, picked up some coffee, then steered onto the highway as the sun rose behind us in the rearview mirror.

We reached Pittsburgh five hours later in a light drizzle. We drove around the city, rode the Monongahela Incline, and marveled at the endless bridges. We ate lunch at Fat Heads, a local saloon that features "headwiches as big as a person's head." Champa ordered the "Bay of Pigs" sandwich and I got the "Mighty Fine Bovine." We could only eat half of each and saved the rest for dinner, a sharp contrast with the vegetarian fare we enjoyed the next day at New Vrindaban, a Hindu temple and retreat in West Virginia.

The complex, which we'd heard about for years from Champa's family and friends, was surrounded by rural residents, many with pickup trucks in their driveways and American flags on their lawns. It was hardly the setting where one would expect to find a Hare Krishna center filled with worshipful devotees, mainly Indian-Americans visiting from neighboring states. But there they were, praying in a large hall adorned with colorful deities, lighting incense, and ringing bells. A seated guru, bald and wearing orange robes, led them in chants. A small gift shop offered prayer scarves, butter lamps, and magnets adorned with Krishna. Peacocks strolled the grounds. Temple staff, who came from as far away as France and Brazil, offered snacks.

In the evening, Champa and I dined in their restaurant, Govinda's, where we enjoyed rice, dal, vegetables, and mango lassi drinks while taking care to not mention our previous day's headwiches. Afterward, we walked the grounds and sat beside a lily pond, gazing on the Palace of Gold. Birds chirped. Frogs croaked. A gentle breeze rustled the tall grass.

I'm not a Hindu or Hare Krishna devotee, and I didn't participate in the prayers, but the generosity and serenity of our hosts enveloped me like the cool night air. At Duke, which I'd left less than two weeks earlier, my life had always been "hurry, hurry". Here, I had no cell phone reception, no wireless connection, and no worries. Already I could feel my life changing. Hare, hare.

In Cleveland, we shifted our attention from food and spirituality to art and culture. We drove there from Wheeling, stopping along the way to tour a candy-making factory in North Canton. We spent several hours at Cleveland's art museum, strolled along Lake Erie, and attended a free outdoor R&B concert in Oval Park. For dinner, we ate pasta and listened to Dean Martin songs at a restaurant in Little Italy. Best of all, we spent nearly an entire day at the Rock and Roll Hall of Fame, engrossed by exhibits and memorabilia ranging from Jerry Garcia's guitars to Michael Jackson's glove.

We drove on through northern Ohio and Indiana towards Aurora, a suburb of Chicago where our nephew and his family live. Champa was entranced as we drove mile after mile through fields of corn and soybeans, punctuated with barns and towns, a scene we'd repeat many times over the next few weeks, the corn giving way to wheat.

She'd grown up on a small farm in Nepal. Her family grew rice and other staples, along with oranges as a cash crop, surrounded by cows, pigs, goats, and chickens. She'd seen large American farms when we'd driven on earlier trips through potato fields in Idaho, almond groves in California, and cherry orchards in northern Michigan. But never before had she driven through the vast farms of America's plains with the aroma of cows and fields wafting through our open windows.

Many years had passed since I'd last been to the heartland myself. I'd driven then from Lincoln, Nebraska to Vermillion, South Dakota and back, visiting projects supported by the philanthropy where I worked before coming to Duke.

We broke up our 400-mile drive from Cleveland to Aurora with a picnic and hike at a nature preserve in Steuben County, which I saw listed in a brochure at a rest stop. I entered its coordinates into our GPS and eventually found its tiny parking lot on a country road. Ours was the only car there, just across from a cornfield and barn, and we had the hiking trail to ourselves. We hadn't thought to apply insect repellant, however, and were attacked by swarms of mosquitoes as we passed a swamp. We accelerated, flapping our arms, but still, they swirled and bit us. As we scurried even faster, I shouted to Champa, "Take a photo of me running, for the blog!"

She replied, "Forget your stupid blog! I'm not stopping!" She relented only after we got down the trail, taking a funny shot with my iPhone, which I posted with a story that evening.

I'd linked our blog to my Facebook page and Twitter site, thereby alerting hundreds of friends and followers whenever we published something. It didn't take long for responses to appear. One of my former colleagues, herself a blogger, cheered for Champa. "Ha!" she wrote, "You know your marriage is working when your spouse takes one for the team and/or the blog." This and other comments made us feel connected to our previous lives even as we settled into our new rhythm on the road.

Back when our two sons were young, we invited our nephew from Nepal to live with us for several years in Takoma Park. He'd attended a local university during the day and helped us take care of the boys in the evening. Pukar graduated at the top of his class with a degree in electrical engineering. He then returned home to work as an engineer at one of Nepal's new television stations, marrying his longtime girlfriend. Together, they had two children and were doing well until things began to unravel in Nepal in the late 1990s. A civil war erupted with Maoist rebels and, in 2001, the crown prince murdered the entire royal family in a palace massacre. Like a growing number of other Nepalis, Pukar and Rekha grew weary of the endless strikes, corruption, and dysfunction. They eventually emigrated near Rekha's sisters outside Chicago. That's where we were headed next.

After we got there, we visited a temple of science and a temple of faith near their house in Aurora, southwest of the city. The temple of science was Fermilab, which I'd written about but never visited during my many years working as a science writer in Washington. For nearly a decade at the National Academy of Sciences, I'd started and run a nationally syndicated service that distributed op-ed articles on science-related topics by prominent authors. One was Leon Lederman, a Nobel Prize-winning former director of Fermilab, who popularized the phrase "God Particle" to describe the mysterious Higgs boson, a subatomic particle whose existence would be confirmed years later. He was among the most interesting of our authors, and I was curious to see where he had worked. Even though it was Saturday and the lab's welcome center was nearly deserted, we had a great time touring the exhibits and grounds, which included a herd of bison.

From Fermilab, we drove to the temple of faith, the Sri Venkateswara Swami (Balaji) Temple, which serves the area's large South Indian community. While we were there, temple members began celebrating Teppotsavam, a colorful ceremony in which devotees carry religious objects from the temple to float on an adjacent pond, making their way with drums, horns, and prayers.

For Champa and me, this juxtaposition between high-tech science and Hindu prayer felt normal. We'd always remained connected to both our American and Asian roots. She had become an American citizen years ago and now followed U.S. politics with a passion. Being married to me, she'd become more American in outlook and habits than many Nepali-Americans who hung out mainly with each other.

Neither of us is very religious, but we'd blended Hindu and Jewish traditions into our cultural mix. When our older son married a woman whose background is Puerto Rican Catholic, and our second son married a woman from a Protestant family, the mixture became even more complex — something we all treasured. We also had many international friends such as Glenda from Grenada and Karen from Trinidad.

I knew of only one other married couple whose husband was a former Peace Corps volunteer and whose wife was from the Limbu ethnic group in Ilam, Nepal. That was Peter and Shashi, friends of ours whom we also visited while near Chicago. Peter served in Nepal several years after me, and Shashi grew up near Champa. Together with Pukar and other guests, we ate a delicious dinner of Nepali *dal-baht* and talked through the evening about our lives and where each of us was heading.

For Champa and me, the answer was simple, at least in the short term. We were heading to Montana.

Our destination was Glacier National Park, 1,500 miles away. This would be one of our longest drives, mainly along rural highways surrounded by fields and pastures, canyons and cowboys.

As we left Chicago for the southwestern part of Illinois, we were surprised to see how much of the state was agricultural, something we'd also seen in Ohio, another state I'd associated with big cities and factories. Then we drove across Iowa, where politicians were already roaming for the upcoming 2016 presidential caucuses. We stopped in Iowa City to see the University of Iowa, Des Moines to visit the beautiful capitol and an outdoor sculpture garden, and Council Bluffs to explore a Lewis and Clark memorial overlooking the Missouri River. On the other side was Omaha, where we enjoyed an outdoor dinner in the Old Market area and then walked along the Bob Kerrey Pedestrian Bridge, which connected the two states. Halfway across, we saw a group of people who looked Nepali — here atop the Missouri River, of all places — and I amused myself by sidling up to them and asking in Nepali where they were going. They stared for a moment and then started laughing at the random white guy speaking their language.

The next day we steered north and west to drive more than 500 miles to Rapid City, stopping en route to visit two of South Dakota's top tourist attractions, the Corn Palace and Wall Drug. Both disappointed us with their kitsch, but we enjoyed Badlands National Park, whose rugged vistas reminded us of the Grand Canyon. Early the next morning, we visited Mount Rushmore, savoring the view before giving way to the daily crush of tourists and vendors selling T-shirts, snow globes, and other modern expressions of patriotism.

As we then headed north from Rapid City towards Montana, we had an important decision to make. Our most direct route was northwest to the national park. If we veered east, we could drive through a bit of North Dakota, adding it to the growing list of states we'd visited. Over the years, we'd traveled to the Four Corners area in the Southwest, the Pacific Northwest, the Upper Midwest, New

England, and elsewhere, often with our sons, bringing our total to 31 states. During the past two weeks, we'd added Ohio, Iowa, Nebraska, and South Dakota, and we expected to add most of the remaining "unvisited states" later in the trip. Indeed, I already had a route in mind that could complete our list except for Hawaii and Alaska. To make that happen, though, we now needed to detour into North Dakota, adding at least a couple of hours to an already long drive, just for the dubious honor of being able to say later we'd done it. Champa and I stared at our map, then at each other, and finally decided to go for it. I programmed the GPS to guide us along Route 85 to Bowman, North Dakota, where we'd turn west onto Route 12, into Montana.

It turned out to be one of the best decisions of our trip. Both roads, especially Route 12, stretched forever — stark, empty ranges with distant horizons, barbed wire fences straddling us, a towering blue sky above. Even as we drove faster than 85 miles per hour, minutes might pass before we saw another vehicle, many of them pickup trucks loaded with hay bales. Champa passed me snacks and water as we drove on and on, eventually reaching the Big Sky Motel in Roundup, Montana. There we ate dinner at the Busy Bee Cafe, a rack of coonskin caps in the lobby and cowboy paintings on the walls. Garth Brooks played in the background. Men wore cowboy hats in the booths. The cashier sold handicrafts from a local Indian tribe. I ordered chicken-fried steak and a beer.

This was why we were traveling — not only to see tourist sites like Mount Rushmore, but to experience realities different from our own. These other worlds had always been there, but our own routines had obscured them. Now we were part of them, at least for a while.

When we arrived the next evening in Shelby, not far from Glacier, we learned that a wildfire had broken out on the park's eastern side. The entrance there was closed, as were many of the hiking trails. The fire had shut down the famous Going-to-the-Sun Road that traverses the park, so we'd have to drive around the park's perimeter to travel from one side to the other — a major detour.

We ended up spending our first day in the park's southeast corner, hiking to an overlook called Aster Park, the mountain air much cooler than back in North Carolina. We stretched out on giant rocks and chatted with a Dutch couple that had been touring the western United States for more than a month. Just before we returned to our car at the bottom of the hill, one of my hiking shoes fell apart, the sole flapping with every step. I'd owned the shoes for years and now said goodbye to them as I tossed them in a trash bin. For the rest of the trip, I'd hike in my sneakers.

We'd come to Glacier mainly because it was fairly close to Yellowstone National Park. Over the years, we'd been fortunate to visit many of our country's natural treasures — Yosemite, the Grand Canyon, the Grand Tetons, the Everglades, Acadia, and more — but Yellowstone was our favorite, with its craggy peaks, alpine lakes, canyons, geysers, and wildlife. Glacier was further north but similar in many respects, and we knew it would be stunning in its own right. We also were eager to return to Montana, whose mountains reminded us of what they call hills in Nepal.

We spent the next two nights in Whitefish, a town near the park's western entrance. After we drank a round of the local brown ale, Moose Drool, at the Buffalo Cafe, I posted a photo on my blog of the restaurant's beer list. It elicited one of the biggest responses I'd gotten so far. People had enjoyed our mountain scenery and tourist pictures but were passionate about commenting on beer.

I shouldn't have been surprised. At Duke, when my colleagues and I had promoted a significant but arcane research discovery, it attracted less attention than a basketball game or a juicy story involving a student. Out here on the road, I still needed to find ways to entertain people if I wanted them to pay attention to what I was posting. Fortunately, I had brought along the gnome.

By now, the most famous member of our traveling team wasn't Champa or me, even though we were the only people in the car. It was the small plastic garden gnome resembling the Duke Blue Devil, which my colleagues had given us at our farewell party at the ballpark. Several people joked then we should bring the gnome with us and take his photo along the way, much as in the Travelocity advertisements or the French film *Amelie*. "Sure thing," I'd said to be polite, but the idea grew on me. Instead of posting predictable photos of Champa and me in front of famous backdrops, I could use the gnome to document our journey.

By the time we reached Pittsburgh, I had settled into the editorial voice I'd use for the rest of the trip. Every day or two, I took a photo of the gnome in front of a local landmark and posted it with a caption, calling the series "GNome Expression," in honor of my previous career as a science writer. I named the gnome "G."

"G is rockin' the Hall of Fame," I wrote in Cleveland. "He's especially enjoyed all of the blues and devil lyrics."

"G visited a sculpture garden in downtown Des Moines. He was too modest to point out that he's pretty sculpted himself."

""G is in Montana, enjoying cowboy country. He is singing 'Gnome on the Range.'"

"G loved Glacier National Park in Montana. He hiked several trails but never broke a sweat."

The captions featured awful jokes and puns — in front of the

Minuteman Missile National Historic Site in South Dakota, I called him radiant — and references to local attractions. For a photo by Seattle's Space Needle, I wrote, "After driving past miles of haystacks, G has found the needle." In Berkeley, I posed him at an angle and said he had "already begun leaning to his left."

A former colleague wrote online: "You are having too much fun."

She was right. For so many years, I'd dressed conservatively and been careful about what I said publicly, especially when I might be seen as speaking for my employer. I'd avoided sharing political views or impertinent thoughts. Now I felt liberated. I could be silly and ridiculous, providing a running commentary about a plastic gnome.

G developed his own audience. Duke's student newspaper, *The Chronicle*, even wrote a story about his travels. People along our route, such as Linda in Takoma Park and Shashi in Chicago, asked me to photograph their gnomes, too. In South Dakota, I held an online contest for readers to submit a caption for a photo of G in front of Mount Rushmore. Some of the entries were hilarious. The winner I picked said, "Who are those knuckleheads who photo-bombed the gnome?"

Both the readers and I began to think of G as a person. I encouraged this, writing that he felt serene at Spokane's Japanese garden but nervous at the Walmart Museum in Arkansas, where he worried he might be marked down.

A friend who is an expert on social media wrote to me how much she enjoyed my shoestring branding campaign. Her message caught me up short. Branding campaign? That's the kind of thing I'd done before. Now I was just having fun. Every new photo was like exhaling old responsibilities and breathing in the fresh air of creativity, which I'd missed more than I realized. Like other Americans who've stepped off their treadmills, I was invigorated by walking in a new direction. It felt good.

Our next stretch took us west from Glacier National Park through Montana, Idaho, and Washington to the Pacific. In Spokane, we visited Riverfront Park, traversing waterfalls that rippled through the city, strolling through a Japanese garden, and riding a cable car. We drove to the Grand Coulee Dam, which lived up to its reputation as an engineering wonder, then on to Wenatchee and Leavenworth, whose main street resembled a Bavarian village. From there, we traversed Stevens Pass and braved the evening rush hour traffic into Seattle. We stayed with friends there in a beautiful condominium overlooking the city, where we visited Pike Place Market, rode the monorail, and toured the new Gates Foundation visitor center.

As we drove through Washington, we passed wheat fields, canyons, cobalt blue lakes, and roadside fruit stands. I'd visited Seattle several times but had never ventured beyond it to sample the state's other attractions, which were a revelation. I found myself thinking back to when we were in Cleveland at the Rock and Roll Hall of Fame, watching a video of Billy Joel singing "New York State of Mind" with Bruce Springsteen. It was Billy Joel's love song to New York State, which is often overshadowed by its giant city. The song now seemed to also apply to Seattle and Washington. To paraphrase it, we were in a Washington state of mind, reminded anew how impressive our country is when you get out and explore it, especially beyond the predictable places.

From Seattle, we turned south and stopped in Olympia to view the capitol and at Mount St. Helens to visit the eruption site and visitor center before continuing on to the Oregon border. We spent the next few days there with the one person with whom I'd traveled even further than Champa, and who had helped the two of us to marry. My old friend Mitch and his wife, Chiyoko, live in the town of Battle Ground, across the river from Portland.

Back in 1975, Mitch and I spent seven months traveling around the world with backpacks and a tiny budget. We'd grown up together on Long Island and remained friends while attending different universities. As graduation approached, neither of us wanted to pursue graduate school or a corporate career, as so many of our classmates were doing. We were only going to be young once, so we decided to blow our modest savings on a journey across Europe, Asia, and Africa, following what was then known as the Hippie Trail.

After spending some time in Greece, we traveled overland to Nepal, passing through Turkey, Iran, Afghanistan, Pakistan, and India. In Nepal, we trekked for three weeks from a village near Kathmandu all the way to an overlook beside the Mount Everest base camp, and then back to a remote airstrip. While waiting for two days there for a small plane to take us back to Kathmandu, we spent several hours talking with one of the few other Americans, who turned out to be the Peace Corps director for Nepal. He encouraged us to return as volunteers — something we were both already considering.

From Nepal, we returned to India for a longer visit and tour. We rode second-class trains from New Delhi to Kolkata, Chennai, and Mumbai, stopping along the way to see sights such as the Taj Mahal in Agra and the funeral ghats in Varanasi. From Mumbai we flew to Kenya, where we took local buses to neighboring Tanzania in the hope of seeing wildlife, which largely eluded us since we couldn't afford a real safari. We headed next to southern Sudan, making the mistake of traveling through Uganda.

Uganda was then under the control of Idi Amin, the crazy dictator who kept the severed heads of political opponents in his refrigerator. Some of his goons in the northern town of Gulu interrogated us, asking whether we were in the CIA. We feared for our lives, so were actually relieved to be taken by men with automatic weapons in a pickup truck to Uganda's remote border with Sudan, where we were allowed to cross.

From there, we traveled several hours on the back of a dump truck along a deeply rutted road to Juba. Now the capital of South Sudan, Juba was then little more than a village with a bar called Victory Gardens. We watched topless men and women dance together while we drank beer and waited for the weekly barge to take us north along the Nile River to the capital, Khartoum.

The journey became even crazier from there as we rode north in both the seats and luggage racks of an ancient train through the Nubian Desert, dust blowing in through the open windows and covering us by the time we reached Wadi Halfa, on the border with Egypt. There we bought cheap tickets on a local boat, trading the desert dust for two days atop a hot metal roof, the sun blazing above us. By the time we reached Aswan, whose majestic temples had just been rescued from rising water, we were dehydrated and exhausted. We bought train tickets to Luxor, whose temples astonished us, and then to Cairo. When we finally reached the pyramids, we treated ourselves to the great luxury of ice cream sundaes at the local Hilton.

A few days later, when we flew to Rome, we were so used to being in the developing world that we began negotiating the price for lasagna at the first cafeteria we visited. The manager looked at us askance until we realized we were back in the West and apologized for the "translation problem."

We returned home a week later, traveling separately through France and Germany before meeting up in Brussels for our flight back to New York. Living as cheaply as we had, the entire trip, airfares included, had cost us each $2,300.

That was only the beginning of my adventures with Mitch. I spent the year after our trip working as a reporter for a small newspaper in San Francisco while he attended graduate school in physics at Berkeley. Our paper covered the local business and maritime industries, so I interviewed corporate executives in swanky hotels during the day and studied meditation and worked on my Peace Corps application in the evening.

I was accepted for Nepal as an English teacher, drawing on the teaching certification I'd earned as a student at Brown, and left again for the Himalayas just over a year after I'd returned from our world tour. Mitch followed a year later after earning a master's degree at Berkeley.

Once in Nepal, he met Champa, to whom I'd just gotten engaged. A year later, Mitch got married, too, to a Japanese nurse who served in Nepal through JOCV, her country's version of the Peace Corps. He used to joke, before it became politically incorrect, that his Jewish parents always wanted him to marry a Jewish American Princess, or JAP. So he did. As the years passed, both of our marriages prospered and the four of us retained a special bond despite seeing each other infrequently.

Our reunion this time was joyful and relaxed, filled with trips to places like Powell's bookstore and Cannon Beach, and capped by Chiyoko's delicious dinners. As always, Mitch and I laughed at the two trips we had taken, amazed in retrospect that we had survived and grateful for how the experiences had broadened our perspectives of the world and ourselves. We'd come home as different people — more worldly, flexible, and confident about following our hearts even when our paths appeared strange to others.

Nearly four decades had passed since we embarked on that first trip. Now I was doing something similar, this time with Champa, and with Mitch and Chiyoko cheering us on.

From Portland, we had several free days before we were scheduled to arrive at my aunt and uncle's home in Berkeley. We headed to Crater Lake, where our view was obscured by the haze from nearby wildfires, then steered west to the coastline of Northern California.

A Duke friend who grew up in Arcata had given us a list of places to visit, from redwood forests to charming coastal towns and distinctive local restaurants. Among his suggestions was Arcata's Los Bagels, which combines Jewish and Mexican cuisine. Its bagel with lox and guacamole proved delicious. Arcata was like traveling back in time to the 1960s, its sidewalks filled with young people with long hair, guitars, and backpacks, openly smoking grass, although they now had cell phones as well. Across town, we took a hike at a wildlife sanctuary located next to a wastewater treatment plant, the marsh providing both a habitat for birds, otters, frogs, and other creatures, and a system to purify the water supply.

At the Jedediah Smith Redwoods State Park, we wandered through groves of giant trees. In Eureka, we shopped in the historic Old Town. In Mendocino, we watched the sun set over a spectacular coastline.

My friend's list provided a great starting point for deciding where to visit. Here and elsewhere, we also relied on free travel materials we'd ordered from the state travel agency. Before we'd left, I'd visited the tourism websites for many of the states and cities we planned to visit. Most offered free printed brochures, which I ordered online. As the brochures arrived at our home, I placed them in a bag in chronological order of when we would need them. Every time we entered a new place, I reached into the bag, pulled out the next brochure, and got ideas about where to go. Most of the brochures — a word I use here to include larger booklets and magazines — were professionally produced and filled with helpful information. California's booklet, for instance, included itineraries for the northern coast, where we were now, and the wine country to the south, which we'd visit next, as well as for places in southern California we planned to explore.

For stretches like this, where we were traveling without reservations, we also used sites such as Trip Advisor and Frommers.com for general information, Yelp and RoadFood for restaurant ideas, and Travelocity, Google, or Hotels.com to book rooms.

I'd typically wait until late in the afternoon to pull out my iPhone and find an inexpensive motel nearby. I'd either book the room online or call to see if we could get a better rate. The only places where we booked a room more than a day in advance were at the New Vrindaban temple in West Virginia and near Glacier National Park, which is crowded during the summer. Even at Glacier, we switched plans for our final night to grab a room that came open at one of the park's stunning lodges.

As someone who spent fourteen years helping to steer a university away from print and into the digital age, and who is enthusiastic about social media, I was surprised to find myself using a plastic bag stuffed with brochures. But many of our country's state and city tourism offices were producing nice work, and it was free, so I used it. Out here on the road, travel brochures were my favorite app.

By the time we reached the Bay Area, after stopping at Napa to visit some wineries, our vacation had become a journey. A vacation is a break from a job, school, or other routine. You pack your bags for a week or two, recharge your batteries, and return. During our first few weeks on the road, our trip had felt like a vacation, even though we knew we weren't returning to our old lives.

By now, things felt different. Our old life had nearly faded from view. Every day we focused on how far we would drive, what we would see, and where we would eat and sleep. Back when I ran the campus news office, where I always needed to be on top of things, I read four newspapers daily and monitored other news sites and social media feeds throughout the day. Now I barely looked at the news. In our hotel rooms, I was more likely to flip the television to Sports Center. Champa followed the early stages of the presidential primaries, while I checked TripAdvisor for places to visit the next day.

Our days were overflowing. We lived every moment. We missed our family and friends, but we spoke with our kids and grandkids on the phone or by Skype every few days. We traded updates and jokes with our friends on Facebook.

As we reached the halfway turn, our journey around the United States had carried us both geographically and emotionally to a new point in our lives. Before we'd left, I'd wondered whether I would be able to disengage from the work that had consumed so much of my time and played such a large role in defining my identity. If I just became myself again, rather than my job title, how would others regard me, and how would I regard myself? Champa was changing her life, too. How would she feel? Now we were learning the answer. We saw lots of sights, to be sure; but even more, we were shaking up our lives, like one of those snow globes at Mount Rushmore.

It was too soon to see how the landscape would resettle for us. But so far, the trip felt like it was working. We couldn't wait to wake up every morning, and we were already looking ahead to our planned trip to Nepal, and whatever followed. We talked with growing confidence about applying for the Peace Corps before leaving for Nepal, making real the dream we'd had for many years. That decision still awaited us down the road. But as we continued driving south, the horizon in front of us kept getting bigger.

CHAPTER 2

BACK ACROSS THE COUNTRY

We spent several days in Berkeley at the home of my aunt and uncle and had dinner nearby with my old college roommate and his wife and daughter. Bruce also invited their daughter's friend, who would depart soon for her freshman year at Duke. She wanted me to suggest some classes and activities, which I was happy to do even though I no longer worked there.

We left Berkeley to continue south, stopping in Castroville, the self-proclaimed artichoke capital of the world, where a giant sign advertising fried artichokes lured us off the highway. The restaurant also offered artichoke bread, artichoke cupcakes, and cream of artichoke soup. When Champa saw the menu, she started imitating Bubba from *Forrest Gump*, reciting the many dishes that one can make with shrimp. Throughout our trip, we sought out places like this, restaurants and vendors selling foods we couldn't buy back home. Two days later, at Avila Beach along the Central Coast, we stopped at a food cart selling a "California hot dog" and shaved ice. In the weeks to come, we'd enjoy Tex-Mex in Texas, jambalaya in New Orleans, and grits in Mississippi.

The architecture was changing, most obviously in places like Santa Barbara, with its Spanish Colonial structures, and around

Los Angeles, with its bungalows and mansions. The streets changed, too, such as along the palm-lined roads near the beach in La Jolla. More surprising were the changes we saw in fast food joints and other businesses whose design features we'd thought were universal. When we stopped for coffee at a Starbucks in Southern California, the interior looked like a Starbucks back home, but the exterior had a distinctly California feel, as did the Domino's next door. Red roofs were plentiful here. In North Carolina, I'd only seen them on an older Taco Bell or atop a Red Roof or La Quinta hotel.

Most spectacular were the changes unfolding in the natural environment.

Cornfields in Iowa gave way to vast ranges in the Dakotas and white peaks in the Rockies. Along the West Coast, redwood forests were followed by scrublands and crashing coastlines. In the coming days, they would be replaced by Arizona deserts, Louisiana bayous, and Mississippi cotton fields. As we headed into San Luis Obispo, along California's Central Coast, we would come face to face with the most stunning environmental sight of our trip.

That's where we saw a lake with no water. For many years, Lake Laguna — yes, that translates as Lake Lake — had provided an urban oasis for local residents. People brought boats from throughout the area. Families walked along the shore. Homeowners by the lake constructed docks next to their backyards. Now those docks rested above a lakebed parched from California's ongoing drought. Children played not only beside the lake but upon it. Fish were gone. Signs warning swimmers to take care without a lifeguard remained affixed to docks that rose high above barren ground.

Champa and I had spent the morning visiting San Luis Obispo's mission and other sights. We saw the park listed on a website and decided to visit it for a few hours before returning to our friend's house for dinner. However, the website hadn't disclosed that Lake Lake no longer looked like a lake.

As we discovered this, we struck up a conversation with a young woman playing with her dog. She told us she'd lived in the area her entire life and had never seen the lake become dry. She described fish stinking as they rotted a year earlier and wondered aloud whether the lake would ever return. Before this, the two of us had been familiar with California's drought, but it had seemed abstract. Now its impact was as apparent as the weeds growing on the lake bottom. Seeing this made me disgusted with politicians who denied in the face of overwhelming evidence that climate change was real. Perhaps, I thought, they should hold their next public forum here at Lake Laguna, the lake with no water.

Our friend worked in San Luis Obispo as a consultant and made time to travel regularly, often to exotic locations around the world. When we visited, he was preparing for a bicycle trip in Ethiopia. As we ate dinner on his deck, Joel was keenly interested in what we were planning, both in Nepal and thereafter. We also talked about his daughter, a graduate student at Duke whose research on mining pollution in Peru had been publicized by my office. Unlike our two sons, she had inherited her dad's wanderlust.

Years earlier, Joel had broken up with his wife, who later married another woman. Our host at our next stop, an old friend from Washington who had moved to Pasadena, was living with her girlfriend while raising two adopted girls from Vietnam. In San Diego, we visited another friend who had married and later divorced a guy from Sudan. These visits came after we'd visited our friends in Portland who are Jewish and Japanese. In Seattle, we'd stayed with a white Protestant guy married to a Jewish woman. Taken together, all of them illustrated how much America had changed since my aunt and uncle were married — indeed, since Champa and I married in 1979. Not that we were spending much time thinking about this. These were just our friends, doing wonderfully for the most part, and we treasured all of them.

Moreover, we knew from driving so recently through the heartland that social change was unevenly distributed across the country. Our sample here along the West Coast was further skewed by our choice of friends whose values reflected our own. Still, things were a lot different now from when I'd grown up in Long Island, or from what Champa had known in Nepal. The road provided a new vantage point to see everything.

From San Luis Obispo, we drove southeast to Pasadena, then to San Diego, where we ate brunch along South Beach with our friend and her son, a surfer who described the local scene for us. Then it was on to the Mojave Desert and Las Vegas, where we visited the Strip and only lost about twenty bucks during brief visits to several casinos. We ate dinner one night at an older casino just outside of town. As I walked through its sad lobby to where a country band played, a middle-aged woman grabbed me and asked whether I'd like to dance. Who knows what she had in mind, but I was momentarily flustered and pointed to Champa, who was wandering in behind me. "I'm waiting for my wife," I told her, much to the woman's surprise and Champa's amusement when I explained to her later what had happened.

We didn't like Las Vegas, although we'd been curious to see it. The glitz and revelry were not for us. We found it creepy to see so many desperate-looking people and we felt trapped in giant rooms without windows or clocks. We were relieved to see the sun the next morning as we headed to Arizona, stopping along the way to visit the Hoover Dam. We then drove straight through to Tucson, where we ate dinner on the patio of the Frog and Firkin, a college hangout recommended by a former Duke colleague who'd attended the University of Arizona.

Next, it was on to the tourist town of Tombstone, where we visited the O.K. Corral and the Boothill Graveyard, and to Bisbee and Douglas. The latter, adjacent to the Mexican border, was home to the historic Gadsden Hotel, whose spacious main lobby and white marble staircase entertained miners, ranchers, and cattlemen. We stopped there to take a peek and use the bathrooms. Shortly after noon, we left for a close-up view of one of America's most contentious issues.

As we turned east from Douglas toward Texas, we hadn't given much thought to our route. We still had a ways to go in Arizona, then across New Mexico, before we began our biggest drive of all, nearly 900 miles from one end of Texas to the other, with stops in San Antonio and Austin. It wasn't until we approached Rodeo, a small town northeast of Douglas, that I realized we had an interesting choice. We could either keep driving north to the main highway, I-10, then zip across to Las Cruces and White Sands, which my former colleague from Arizona had urged us to check out. Or we could take our chances before that with Route 9, a road so small it didn't even appear on one of our maps. The latter would reach El Paso more directly, although presumably at a slower speed. It also held the prospect of being more interesting.

We found Route 9 barely marked by a sign as we turned onto it. Even though it was in good condition, with a speed limit of 65 miles per hour in most places, its traffic was sparse. We saw far more cactus plants and sheep than passenger cars. What we did see was the Border Patrol, driving on the road, parked along the shoulder, and otherwise making its presence felt. Route 9 straddles the

U.S. border with Mexico, running east to west across the southern edge of New Mexico. Champa and I began keeping count: along the 227 miles between Douglas and El Paso, we saw the Border Patrol eleven times.

After we entered El Paso, where Mexico's Ciudad Juarez was so close we could almost look inside people's homes, we continued to see the Border Patrol, such as at a checkpoint in Sierra Blanca, 87 miles to the east. I did the math and calculated we passed a Border Patrol vehicle once every twenty miles or so. Of course, that's only what we saw from the road. Presumably, there were many more patrols closer to the border, not to mention aerial surveillance and who knows what else.

Was that a big presence, given the fierce debate that had broken out over illegal immigration, stoked by Donald Trump calling on the campaign trail for the construction of a wall near where we were driving? Champa and I had no way to evaluate what we saw, much less to offer a solution for the complicated politics of immigration. All we knew is that for us, two Americans from North Carolina, this was fascinating, something we hadn't seen before. It was just a glimpse of a bigger picture, but it made us ponder all of the lives, resources, and controversy represented by what we were seeing.

As we'd experienced earlier with the Western wildfires and drought, we'd come face to face with an important issue that had been something we just read about. Our road map didn't list it, but we'd stumbled across it just the same. In the months that followed, as the campaign heated up and candidates tried to outdo each other about how aggressively they'd protect the border, I found myself wondering how many of them had ever driven along Route 9. There were plentiful surveillance cameras along the route but no television cameras to show politicians looking concerned in a staged appearance, so I assumed the answer was: not many.

As we continued into Texas, we came across still another timely topic: wind energy. I'd always associated Texas with drilling and fossil fuels, as the home of Big Oil, and big personalities ranging from J.R. Ewing to George W. Bush. Yet, as we began our long drive across the state, we were surprised to see lots of wind turbines. By the end of our second day, as we relaxed after dinner, I went online and discovered that Texas produced the most wind power of any state in the country.

Texas is huge, of course, and it has bountiful winds blowing across its mountain passes and ridge tops. But still, Texas? I never would have gotten past my own preconceptions if I hadn't driven so far to discover this for myself. We saw evidence of wind power's growing importance elsewhere in the country as well: amid farms in the Midwest, on the range in Montana, and at a giant wind farm along the Altamont Pass of Northern California's Diablo Range.

This isn't to say the United States has shifted quickly enough from fossil fuels to wind power and other renewables; obviously, more action is needed, especially as climate change accelerates. San Luis Obispo's Lake Laguna was a reminder of that, and yes, the two of us were guilty of contributing to climate change by driving our car around the country. Still, it was encouraging to see so many windmills in Texas and elsewhere.

When we stopped in La Grange, the city immortalized by the band ZZ Top, we took a photo of our gnome posing in front of one. We didn't tell him it was designed to pump water rather than to generate electricity. After all, like Texas and other states we visited, it was turning in the right direction.

Driving across West Texas to San Antonio was endless. The thing I remember best was staying in a cheap motel in Van Horn whose breakfast buffet had waffles shaped like Texas. Apart from that, we just drove and drove through Balmorhea, Fort Stockton, Ozona, Junction, and Kerrville. Walmarts and shopping plazas dotted the landscape. Convenience stores had names like Rattlers, one of which displayed cowboy hats near the cash register, Hunt Brothers' pizza on its window, and a sign over the door promising "Friendly. Clean. Texan."

We finally reached San Antonio, visited the Alamo, and had dinner at River Walk, the charming network of restaurants, shops, walkways, and bridges along the San Antonio River. A block away, we discovered the Briscoe Western Art Museum. It was offering free admission that night, enticing us to take a look at Pancho Villa's saddle, Santa Anna's sword, and a full-size replica of a stagecoach, along with paintings and statues.

We were eager to see Austin, especially its evening music scene along Sixth Street, which was even livelier than we'd expected. The signs outside several of the bars there were amusing — a place called Sailor Jerry promised "Drink Here. Get Laid." We were more than relieved to see we weren't the only visitors our age.

During the day, we visited the presidential library and exhibit center for Lyndon Johnson and drove around the University of Texas. We also toured Austin's beautiful state capitol building, just as we'd visited the state capitols in Washington and Iowa earlier. We'd done the same in other states on previous trips. Capitol buildings provide insights into how a state regards itself, and they are free. They are typically filled with exhibits, portraits, and a sense of place that compensate for the self-important young legislative aides scurrying across polished floors. Here in Austin, for example, it was interesting to see portraits of former governors Ann Richards and George W. Bush hanging near each other but separated by a doorway. Our guide kept saying "we" when referring to David

Crockett, James Bowie, and the other Texans who fought the Mexican forces at the Alamo, making me wonder what the Chicanos in our group were thinking. On the grounds outside, monuments honored the Alamo heroes, cowboys, pioneer women, Confederate soldiers, and others.

A few days later, we visited two capitol buildings in Jackson, Mississippi. One was the old capitol that served as the statehouse for seventy years. Now a museum, it was recently restored after being damaged by Hurricanes Katrina and Rita. We were impressed by its discussion of slavery, the civil rights struggle, and other difficult aspects of the state's history. A few blocks away was Mississippi's current capitol, adjacent to an elegant governor's mansion and a short walk from the Eudora Welty library. It was covered with scaffolding and closed when we visited, which was a shame, because we'd learned to expect the unexpected when we visited these places.

When we toured the capitol in Madison, Wisconsin, a few years earlier, our guide did her best to avoid mentioning the battle then under way to recall Gov. Scott Walker, despite repeated inquiries from people in the group. The capitol's rotunda had recently been filled with shouting demonstrators, but our guide kept shifting the conversation to the nearby paintings, busts, and architectural details. I felt sorry for her.

In Augusta, Maine, one of the top Democratic Party leaders noticed us wandering in the hall and ended up showing us around while describing her battles with Paul LePage, the state's colorful Tea Party governor. It was an insightful — and hilarious — experience we never anticipated. State capitols also tend to have good bathrooms and water fountains. Since we were visiting Texas in August, we were happy to fill up our water bottles for free.

As we drove from Austin to New Orleans, the intense heat was eased intermittently by rain showers. We made the drive in a single day — our longest leg of the trip — and collapsed when we arrived at a motel I'd called from a gas station near the bayou.

We spent several days in New Orleans, which had topped Champa's "must go" list, and loved it. We sampled the culinary pleasures of Bourbon Street and other neighborhoods — beignets along Jackson Square, a seafood platter at Seithers, po' boys at the Parkway Bakery — and visited parks, cemeteries, and shops. Curious about how the city was recovering from Hurricane Katrina, we drove off the tourist path to the Lower Ninth Ward, where we saw some damaged homes but even more that had been repaired, as well as new homes like those built by the Make It Right Foundation, Brad Pitt's organization. A few weeks later, after we'd returned home, our airwaves were filled with retrospective stories about "New Orleans, Ten Years Later," showing some of the same streets.

By the time we reached Louisiana, we'd whittled our list of unvisited continental states to Mississippi, Alabama, Arkansas, Oklahoma, Kansas, Missouri, and Kentucky. So, instead of driving directly home from New Orleans, we diverged to check them all off.

We drove initially along the coast to Orange Beach, Alabama, whose sand was too hot to walk on except in the evening. We then headed northwest through Mississippi, visiting the state art museum in Jackson and the impressive Civil War battlefield in Vicksburg. In a town called Belzoni, we found a tiny museum dedicated to catfish, where a catfish farmer told us about the economic competition he and others were battling from Vietnam and China. They don't get many visitors at the Catfish Museum and Welcome Center, despite the gaily decorated catfish statues lining the town's sidewalks.

We then drove past miles of cotton fields before reaching the B.B. King Museum and Delta Interpretive Center in Indianola, with the legendary blues singer's bus parked out front. It was a terrific find, filled with interactive exhibits and musical selections that helped us understand how he emerged from the racism and economic hardships of Mississippi's cotton fields to achieve worldwide acclaim. We followed Riley B. King's path from tractor driver to the Chitlin' Circuit and beyond, and took photos of ourselves in front of his guitar, Lucille. A few months earlier, he had died in Las Vegas, and his gravesite beside the museum was now marked with only a wreath and a chain-link fence. Before the year's end, these would be replaced by a black granite slab engraved with King's signature.

Then it was on to Little Rock, where we visited Central High School, where an early battle of the civil rights movement was fought before a shocked national audience watching on television. A guide took us and another couple into the school, where the diverse current students had recently returned from summer vacation. We paused at several of the historic spots where screaming white mobs, federal troops, and brave black students changed history. An exhibit hall across the street described the events, some of whose participants still lived nearby.

Our last stop in Arkansas was Bentonville, in the state's northwest corner, where Walmart is headquartered. We visited a museum that told the company's story. It was filled that morning with Walmart managers being tutored by a tour guide about company founder Sam Walton. She described how Mr. Sam expanded a small Ben Franklin variety store into what became an international empire.

Across town, we were astonished by the Crystal Bridges Museum of American Art, a world-class structure that would bring pride to New York or Paris but had instead opened in this small Ozarks city. Founded by Sam's daughter Alice and designed by Moshe Safdie, the museum offered free admission to exhibits that read like a who's who of American art, from Charles Wilson Peale to Norman

Rockwell, Jackson Pollock to Andy Warhol. Its restaurant served gourmet salads and pinot noir, and the museum shop offered fine-art prints, hand-crafted jewelry, and books about famous artists.

There wasn't a Walmart smiley face to be seen anywhere.

While we were in Little Rock, we spent several hours visiting Bill Clinton's presidential library, which was featuring a temporary exhibit of animated dinosaurs. That sounded like a Republican prank but was actually interesting. Champa and I loved the museum's permanent displays about how the Clinton administration dealt with the economy, foreign affairs, the environment, and other issues. There were replicas of the Oval Office and the Cabinet Room, a glittering table set with White House china, and a powerful video recounting Clinton's first presidential campaign. However, the biggest battle of his presidency, his impeachment, was limited to a single alcove that emphasized Republican partisanship. There were no photos of Monica Lewinsky, no "it depends on what the meaning of 'is' is," and no real acknowledgment that Clinton did anything wrong that might have brought on the Republican attacks. Our tour guide pointed out the exhibit quickly and then glided us past it.

I voted for Bill Clinton twice and admired most aspects of his presidency and subsequent career. I opposed his impeachment at the time and am glad he remained in office. Nonetheless, I was disappointed by how his library dealt with this episode, presumably at his direction. It felt evasive and self-serving to me. The LBJ library in Austin had included a substantial exhibit about that president's biggest controversy, namely Vietnam. As might be expected, it emphasized the uncertainties and political pressures Johnson faced in the conflict, as well as the toll it took on him and his family.

But it also acknowledged Johnson's responsibility for at least some of what occurred.

Similarly, we'd just seen museums in Mississippi and Alabama that addressed the painful legacies of slavery and Jim Crow in those states. Having worked in communications for many years, dealing with everything from campus scandals to National Academy of Sciences studies that provoked Congress or the White House, I knew how challenging it could be for people and institutions to deal forthrightly with controversial topics. I certainly didn't expect the Clinton Library to display Monica's blue dress or beret. However, I was hoping for a bit more self-reflection and humility, especially after so many years had passed, and thought such a presentation would have made the "Republican partisanship!" spin more believable. Apparently not.

By the time we left Bentonville, after more than six weeks on the road, we were thinking only of returning to Durham. We still enjoyed every day but were weary of the constant travel, motel rooms, and search for interesting places. We missed our kids. We missed our grandkids. We missed our dog. We missed sitting at the kitchen table with dinner and a glass of wine. We missed waking up in our own bed. We missed home.

Bentonville is near the Arkansas border with Oklahoma, which is near Kansas, which bordered on Missouri, and we passed through them all within a few hours so we could check them off our list. We knew we were fulfilling our self-imposed challenge in the most perfunctory way at this point, but we didn't care.

On we drove through Missouri — Rogersville, Seymour, Mansfield, and Mountain Grove before we finally stopped in the wonderfully named Cabool. The next morning we expected to drive easily through western Kentucky to Tennessee, our last stop before North Carolina. About an hour after we left, however, the "low tire pressure" light flashed on my dashboard, and I barely made it to the next exit and the small town of Van Buren before the tire went flat. Fortunately, Champa spotted an auto repair shop, which fixed the tire for twelve dollars in just a few minutes.

An hour after we got back onto the highway, we turned onto a small road that led to a bridge across the Mississippi River. We drove along it for twelve miles, nearly to the bank of the river, when we saw signs blocking the road for bridge repairs. We had to drive all the way back and find an alternate route, which took us out of our way but still through Kentucky, the last state remaining on our list. When we crossed that border, I veered onto the road shoulder so we could get out and take a selfie of ourselves in front of the "Welcome to Kentucky" sign as cars whizzed past us. We'd now visited every state except Alaska and Hawaii.

Still, we weren't home.

We drove through Kentucky into Tennessee, forgoing Dollywood and other places we'd thought about visiting just so we could keep driving. We spent our last night at a motel in Harriman, west of Knoxville, and dined at the Cracker Barrel down the street. The next morning after breakfast, we steered east onto Interstate 40 towards the North Carolina border and home, which we reached that afternoon.

When we arrived, nothing had changed. Our house was still there. Our dog, Bailey, was happy to see us. A neighbor waved from down the block. When our house-sitter came home in the evening, he confirmed what he'd texted us during the trip, that everything was fine. We unloaded our bags from the car. I drove to the grocery store while Champa dumped clothes into the washing machine. We looked through a pile of mail to find the usual assortment of bills, magazines, and advertisements. Life had continued without us.

Over the next few weeks, we savored what we had accomplished. When we'd left two months earlier, I'd been consumed with my decision to walk away from the conventional working world, from a nice job title and paycheck, to wander with Champa around America. We'd hoped to find adventure and a new sense of ourselves, but we weren't sure what to expect. So many things could have gone wrong — a car accident, a medical emergency, a crisis with one of our kids or grandkids. The stock market could have crashed, as it had a few years earlier, putting our finances at risk. We might have gotten on each other's nerves in ways we never had before. Most of all, the realities of the road might have proven less appealing than we'd dreamed. Once the exhilaration passed of no longer working 9 to 5, we might have had a panic attack and thought, "What the hell did we just do?"

Nothing like that happened. We were exhausted but content. Already Durham felt like the place where we lived, not the place where my employer was located. My job, which had so dominated my time and perspective, seemed far behind me. I was back in Durham again, but not in the same place emotionally. Champa and I felt energized by what we had just done, overflowing with fresh memories.

I'd bought souvenir magnets at stops along the way for my collection. As I unwrapped them and placed them on our refrigerator, I thought, "Wow, we went there, and there, and there."

I put on an overpriced T-shirt I'd bought at the Briscoe Museum in San Antonio as a way to offset the free admission, looked in the mirror, and thought, "We went there, too."

That evening, I turned on my desktop computer for the first time in two months and added Durham to a Google map I'd created online to visually display our journey. It was the first and last dot in a circle stretching from Durham to Philadelphia, west to Seattle, down to San Diego, across to New Orleans, back up to Missouri, and finally home again. We'd gone to all of those places, across thirty-one states.

Over the next several weeks, we loafed around the house and avoided driving anywhere. Instead, we spent time with our son and his family. We put away our suitcases. I found a website where I created a poster showing G, our traveling gnome, in settings across the country, which I framed and hung near our dining room. I posted a final entry for this phase of our blog and went nearly silent on Facebook. I spent hours sorting hundreds of photos and uploaded some of them to Shutterfly for the family picture book I produced every year. I cooked and baked special meals, just for the fun of it. We took Bailey for walks.

As we began to catch our breath and the trip evolved from reality to memory, we had less than a month before we'd embark on our second adventure, one that promised to be even more impactful than the first, although not necessarily for the better. We'd pursued this first trip in our own country, with modern roads, clean drinking water, reliable electricity, and easy internet access.

Now we were about to travel to one of the poorest countries in the world, where we'd spend part of our time in remote areas rarely visited by Westerners. The recent earthquake there had caused devastation in places we'd be staying. The Himalayas were where I'd developed serious bronchial problems, two bouts of pneumonia, and a slew of parasitic infections. But they were also where Champa and I had fallen in love, where half of our family lived, and where part of our American family would soon come to meet them for the first time.

Nepal would confront us with dangers we didn't even imagine yet, from jeeps veering to the edge of sheer mountain roads to having to be rescued on a mountain highway amid political chaos.

We'd thought we knew what to expect as we continued to venture away from our conventional lives, but we were about to be surprised. An even bigger challenge awaited us.

CHAPTER 3

A RETURN TO NEPAL

I'd first visited Nepal with Mitch in 1975, staying in a cheap lodge in a Kathmandu neighborhood known as Freak Street. Long-haired visitors traveled there from across Asia, often beginning at Istanbul's Pudding Shop, where brightly painted hippie buses posted signs and waited for passengers.

Soon after we arrived in Kathmandu, we hired a porter to guide us to Mount Everest. We bought thick sleeping bags, goggles, gloves, and cooking equipment, as well as maps, tetracycline, and iodine to purify our water. We sent letters home to tell our parents our plans, then set off one morning for a village called Perku. Our three-week trek culminated when we gasped our way to Kala Patthar, an overlook of Mount Everest and the base camp beneath it.

Mitch took a photo of me in front of the great mountain holding the Army wings my father wore during World War II, including at D-Day, where he was nearly killed. He'd given these to me for good luck and told me to leave them on Mount Everest if I ever made it that far. I had carried them around the world and now was overcome with emotion as I dropped them into the rocks. I told my father I loved him and that I hoped he was proud of me. A photo of that moment is on the wall behind me as I write this.

Thus began my love affair with Nepal, where I later met the love of my life. From my first day there, I was entranced by its beauty and serenity, and by the warmth of its people. When we met the Peace Corps director on the mountain airstrip a week later, also waiting for a flight back to Kathmandu, I figured the local gods were trying to tell me something.

I'd always been interested in the Peace Corps, inspired by the vision of President Kennedy. When I was a senior in high school, I organized a fund-raiser to support a project for one of the school's recent graduates who was serving with the Peace Corps in West Africa.

As Mitch and I made our trip, I was already pondering how I might return to the developing world, preferably in a single country where I might serve in some way. The Peace Corps was an obvious possibility, and Mitch and I talked about joining it shortly before we ran into the country director at the Lukla airstrip. Meeting him settled for both of us where we wanted to apply.

When I returned to Nepal in the Peace Corps just a year after returning to the United States, another volunteer and I were put in charge of shepherding everyone on the Pan Am flight from New York to New Delhi and then on to Kathmandu. He and I were the only ones who had been to Nepal previously. When our group arrived a day later, Dwight and I roomed together. The first morning we woke up before dawn because of the jet lag and laughed out loud from our beds when we heard a rooster crowing. Dwight shared my love of the country. We were both so happy to be back.

Peace Corps called itself the "toughest job you'll ever love," which was surely true for most volunteers. For me, though, it was easier than traveling on my own with Mitch. Peace Corps taught me the local language, provided job training, paid my living expenses, and stood ready to back me up if I got sick or ran into trouble. By contrast, Mitch and I had traveled without a net, and our run-in with Idi Amin's goons in Uganda was merely the most dramatic incident that could have ended badly. As Champa and I rediscovered years later, every adventure has its own boundaries.

I loved being a volunteer in Nepal, teaching English my first year in Champa's town, Ilam, and my second at a school near the capital. I was transferred there after getting pneumonia and being sent to Washington for evaluation, a trip that proved to be an adventure itself.

I flew from Kathmandu to New Delhi, where I picked up a Pan Am flight to Washington. That flight had a refueling stop in Tehran, where the shah was still in power, and the Iranian Revolution was a few years away. Shortly after we took off from Tehran, the plane's left wing caught fire. The pilot came on the intercom to say in a Texas drawl that we needed to return to Tehran as soon as we dumped some fuel ... from a plane on fire.

As we landed, I could see red lights flashing atop ambulances and fire trucks at the end of the runway. People throughout the cabin were saying prayers and holding hands as the plane descended. It was a relief to touch down safely, especially for a poor Peace Corps volunteer who then got to enjoy two days of free meals and a nice hotel room while Pan Am scrambled to bring in another plane. Most of the other Americans on the flight were oil-field workers who complained about having to spend more time in Iran. I gladly ate extra desserts at Pan Am's expense.

Having lost a lot of weight in Ilam, I ate at every opportunity on my way home because I wanted to look as healthy as possible for the doctor I'd be seeing in Washington. He would decide whether I could return to Nepal. I wanted desperately to return to Champa, so I didn't go out of my way to correct him when he suggested my bronchial problems might be due to high altitude. Instead, I just agreed to his suggestion that I relocate to a school near Kathmandu, which is actually a bit higher than Ilam, yet lower than Denver. I knew this was the best outcome I could hope for. I didn't want to leave Champa but recognized it was better for me to be closer to the Peace Corps doctor in Kathmandu. Sure enough, a year later, I got an even worse case of pneumonia, and this time the Peace Corps terminated my service.

Champa eventually followed me to Long Island, and we were married in my parents' living room. They smiled bravely, and my grandparents were probably muttering "oy vey" as they watched from the first row of seats, but our life together had begun.

Over the years that followed, Champa and I retained close ties with both Nepal and the Peace Corps. While in Washington, where the number of Nepalis was much smaller than it is today, we were active in the America Nepal Society and occasionally invited to receptions at Nepal's embassy. We returned to Nepal a year after we were married, arriving a few days before Champa's mother died in her early fifties, already older than the average local life expectancy then. Champa reached her just in time to say goodbye.

Three years later, we visited again, this time with our newborn son and my parents, who made the journey to Ilam to meet Champa's family. We were welcomed with a feast and served *thumba*, a traditional beer made with fermented millet and served in bamboo mugs trimmed with brass. The next day, we posed for a joint family photo, which would receive a place of honor in our home, my parents' home, and Champa's family home for decades to come. My parents also toured Nepal, highlighted by a visit to the resort town of Pokhara, which we would soon be visiting again.

Champa returned to Nepal every few years after that, even though the trip was long and expensive, and we could barely afford it. Usually, I remained home with the boys, but sometimes we traveled together. We also stayed connected to her family through our two nephews who came to live with us — first Pukar, who attended the University of the District of Columbia, and then Shankar, who had been my fourth-grade student.

Shankar lived with us for a year, studying English and learning about American customs, an experience he later credited with opening his eyes to a different way of living. He grew up to become one of Nepal's most prominent human rights attorneys and a leader of the international movement to protect indigenous peoples, speaking at the United Nations and other venues. Especially after his parents died, we came to regard him almost as our third son, and we would stay with him during much of our upcoming trip.

During these years, Champa and I remained active in the Peace Corps community. Once I was invited to speak with other volunteers at an event in the rotunda of the U.S. Capitol, where I read from an op-ed article about my service I'd written for *The New York Times*. Years later, after I moved to Duke, two other former volunteers and I advised students who were considering volunteering, and I helped lead a year-long campus celebration for the Peace Corps' fiftieth anniversary. I also created a program with the National Peace Corps Association to encourage former volunteers to share their stories through local newspapers. Even though decades had passed, I retained a deep affection for the organization and the country where I had served. Both were about to become an even bigger part of my life.

At the end of September, less than a month after we'd returned from our U.S. road trip, Champa and I flew to Kathmandu from

Philadelphia, where we'd spent several days with our son Paul and his family. The entire trip, with a single stop in Qatar, took just over nineteen hours, much faster than usual. At the very end, our plane descended into the Kathmandu Valley, rugged green hills unfolded below us, and Himalayan peaks towered over the horizon. Ornate temples and brick houses came into view as we landed.

An hour later, as we emerged from the airport, Shankar and his wife were waiting for us with two old friends of ours. They placed colorful prayer shawls around our necks and placed their hands together to say "namaste." Champa and I couldn't stop smiling as we loaded our bags into a van provided by our travel agency and drove to the house where Shankar and Bindu lived with their son and daughter on the outskirts of town. Fourteen years after I had helped to arrange their marriage, it was wonderful to see them so happy together.

I'd come to Kathmandu then on my way home from reporting a magazine story in Bangladesh about a scientist funded by the philanthropy where I worked. I'd spent several days with him at his lab, where he studied parasitic diseases, and in the Dhaka slums where the diseases were prevalent. On our last evening together, I took him and his colleague to dinner, then returned to my hotel room, flipped on the television to CNN, and saw the World Trade Center tumbling into dust.

The next day, September 12, 2001, I stood in the Dhaka departure hall, a ticket to Kathmandu in my hand, surrounded by people staring at two television monitors. Almost all of them were Muslim and their horror was obvious. When I landed in Kathmandu, my sister-in-law greeted me with a hug, knowing my sister and her family lived in New York. As soon as we got to her house, I called home and learned they were fine, unlike a friend of mine whose wife was on the plane that flew into the Pentagon.

It was a tough time to be away from home but also fascinating, especially when we had dinner with a family friend and her husband, a top Nepali military official. He told me the CIA had already sought their help in identifying anyone who might have a connection to al Qaeda. That was unlikely, given the small number of Muslims in Nepal and the lack of fundamentalist extremism, but anything seemed possible then.

Over the next few days, it was a relief to focus instead on Shankar, who confided to me he loved a woman in his office and wished he could marry her. "So why don't you just ask her to marry you?" I asked in my blunt American fashion. Alas, she was a Newari, the main ethnic group in the Kathmandu Valley, and Shankar was from the Limbu tribal group, like Champa. Not only did he want a "love marriage," but it would be across castes.

That evening, I shared his dilemma with Champa's brother and sister, Raju and Sangita, and asked whether there was anything we could do to help Shankar. They laughed and told me they knew all about Shankar's "secret" and wished he would propose to Bindu already. I said I had only a few days left, so we should arrange their marriage right now. With Shankar's nervous agreement, we called Bindu and met her the next day.

"Yes," she said, she would love to marry Shankar.

We went to her parents' house. Like us, they already knew about the romance and were impatient to see things proceed. Raju, Sangita, and I then raced around the Kathmandu valley, buying a wedding sari, wedding bangles, and a traditional golden necklace for Shankar to present to his bride. Two days later, we assembled at a hilltop temple. A Limbu priest performed the wedding while Raju and I beat ceremonial drums. Shankar and Bindu were married.

Two days after, I flew to New Delhi, only to discover that United Airlines had canceled all of its flights to Washington. With my business class ticket and some discreet *baksheesh* to the desk agent, I was able to transfer my ticket to the last seat on the final British Airways flight to Washington. I was never so happy to fly in a middle seat in coach.

Shankar and Bindu had built a home in Changathali, not far from the airport. A decade earlier, their neighborhood was mainly farmland, but now it was filling up with houses and shops. As we walked around, we saw abundant evidence of the April 25, 2015, earthquake, which claimed nearly 9,000 lives across Nepal. Five months had already passed, but many houses still had damaged roofs and walls or were destroyed.

"Someone died here," Shankar said several times as we walked through an adjacent neighborhood called Lubhu.

Older brick homes suffered more than newer structures like Shankar's, but we also saw apartment buildings and other structures with big cracks. One building next to my sister-in-law's house in neighboring Patan was now empty after someone died in the quake. Across the valley, in the historic city of Bhaktapur, famous for its Newari brick homes and carved windows, the damage was even worse, with rubble still strewn and tent camps filled with families. Later in our trip, as we drove west, closer to the epicenter, the devastation would be even more visible.

Simultaneously and unrelated to the earthquake, new homes were springing up throughout the valley. Even though many carpenters and other construction workers had returned to their villages after the disaster, and repair jobs competed for skilled labor, Kathmandu continued to expand.

Another local neighborhood, Sanepa, had been a sleepy suburb when I lived there during my second year as a volunteer. I could ride my bicycle and encounter little traffic even along the nearby Ring Road that encircled the city. Now Sanepa was crammed with homes and businesses, and the Ring Road resembled Washington's Beltway at rush hour, although with more packed buses and fewer lobbyists in BMWs. Champa's sister Sangita had lived in a neighborhood called Kalanki, which was even more crowded. Everywhere I looked, Kathmandu was no longer the charming fairyland I remembered. It had become a sprawling Asian city.

The traffic and smog seemed intense to me, but everyone kept saying they were better than usual. Fewer vehicles were on the road due to petrol shortages caused by political unrest along Nepal's southern border with India, from where it imported almost all of its fuel. India's government was unofficially encouraging the protests, leading to long lines for gasoline, diesel, and kerosene across the country. On the black market, the price for a gallon of gas soared above $20 a gallon — this in one of the world's poorest countries.

Businesses closed. People stopped traveling. Mothers cooked with firewood if they could find it. Restaurants altered their menus. It was a mess, and it worsened throughout our trip. By the time we left, it would affect my American family as well as those in Nepal.

Although Champa and I paid attention to the earthquake's aftermath and the petrol crisis, these were diversions from Nepal's simple pleasures. As we walked in the morning or evening near Shankar's house, we saw children playing next to temples, women working in lush wheat fields, ducks waddling across the street, and students with uniforms and backpacks returning home from school. Shops still posted signs using English in amusing ways; "fooding and lodging" was one of my favorites. Swastikas adorned people's homes, a symbol of Hindu faith. Temples were everywhere, mainly

Hindu, but also Buddhist and a few mosques and churches, even a Jewish center in the Thamel tourist neighborhood. Nepal and Israel enjoyed close ties, and many young Israelis, including relatives of mine, visited the Himalayas after completing their military service.

Each neighborhood had at least one shop resembling a general store or bodega. Along with cloth, flour, and vegetables, they sold recharge cards for cell phones, as well as Mountain Dew, which everyone called Dew. Larger shops, especially downtown, specialized in bicycles, appliances, or something else. They were bunched on different blocks, with spice shops here, shoes there, and books around the corner. Merchants displayed goods not only in the shops, but outside of temples and on corners. Narrow streets led to even narrower alleys lined with bangles, televisions, office supplies, and beads. Motorcycles and rickshaws squeezed by. Horns blared. Fumes filled the air.

Some shops had curious specialties, like nose rings or unlocking iPhones. Champa and I joined Bindu one day on a shopping trip that began on New Road, a main thoroughfare, and wound through the Indra Chowk bazaar. We stopped at a jewelry store to repair a ring, a kitchen store to buy metal plates, and a hat store for a Nike cap. We climbed up two flights of a ridiculously narrow staircase to an attic stuffed with fabric.

I kept thinking to myself, "Please, don't let there be another earthquake now."

Along the way, we visited a temple and snacked on *momos*, traditional dumplings filled with meat. Then we drove to one of the city's few department stores, Bhatbhateni, where Bindu bought a rice cooker, and I bought decorative shopping bags made from rice paper, which I'd later pack with goodies to welcome my family. The store's escalator took me past a sign for luxury condominiums. I couldn't decide which amazed me more, the escalator or the luxury condominiums. Finally, we drove to visit Kumar, a tailor who worked near Shankar's office, to pick up a custom-made shirt I'd ordered.

By the time we reached home, after 7 p.m., the electricity at Shankar's house was already cut off, as happened almost daily, rotating across neighborhoods to reduce the overall load. We turned on a battery lamp and collapsed on sofas. Our purchases strewn around us, we waited to unpack the next morning.

The next day we hiked to Kirat Manghim. A traditional temple on a remote hill, it honored Falgunanda, a religious leader born in 1885, whose name was all but unknown to foreigners, even those who had lived in Nepal. Many Nepalis had never heard of him either. But if you were a member of one of the traditional Kirati ethnic groups of eastern Nepal — the Limbus, Rais, and others — there's a good chance you worshipped in front of his photo.

Champa is a Limbu, from the Dewan clan, so we'd known for years of the growing interest among Kiratis in Falgunanda, who revived traditional cultural practices and challenged Nepal's dominant Hinduism. Many Limbus and others now embraced him for both religious reasons and to assert their ethnic identity. It was part of a movement among Nepal's indigenous peoples to reclaim their history and demand a fairer share of the country's resources. Shankar was a leader of this effort and had tied its struggle to those of Native Americans, African tribal groups, and others around the world.

We walked for nearly two hours in late-summer heat to reach the temple's two modest structures. Outside were bells and a drum; inside was an altar adorned with faded photos of Falgunanda. We removed our hiking shoes before entering, made an offering, and received tikas on our foreheads from the temple's caretakers, who served us lemongrass tea. We signed their guest registry, which I filled out in English even though I know how to write my name in Nepali. Mine was the only Western name there, so I figured I was going to stand out anyway.

A few days later, I accompanied Shankar downtown to chat with friends who were encouraging indigenous Nepalis to make their own films. They sponsored an annual festival that had attracted 20,000 people the previous year, showing films about indigenous people in Nepal and around the world. The group's leader explained to me how they provided training, rented equipment, and organized events where young indigenous filmmakers could interact. They'd reached out especially to women, whose recent short films explored topics such as divorce in the Gurung ethnic community or how Limbu girls learn weaving.

As in our own country, most Nepalis preferred big-budget films with lots of action and melodrama. Working on a shoestring budget with a less popular format among marginalized groups in one of the world's poorest countries, this group struggled to recruit new filmmakers while still producing their own original work. Their modest office had a couple of editing computers, a film library, and old furniture. It was up four flights of stairs, with erratic electricity. They hoped a new project might show how indigenous groups suffered the most casualties in the earthquake yet received little international aid.

After our meeting, we walked down the block for dinner at a cafe with some of Shankar's other friends. One was a young man who appeared on television every night on a popular newscast. He told me how he had previously served in the Maoist army, fighting to overthrow the government. When the Maoist political party briefly assumed power after an election victory, he and others came out of the shadows to pursue traditional jobs. Now here we were, an

American and a Maoist, ordering rounds of momos and beer for each other, joking in Nepali. We toasted each other several times.

As we finished, I quietly went to the front desk to pay for the meal, but the others wouldn't hear of it. At their insistence, the waiter brought back my rupees, more than two thousand of them. Since the exchange rate was about 105 rupees for one dollar, that was less impressive than it sounded. Back when I was a Peace Corps volunteer, the exchange rate had been about 12 rupees per dollar. Now, exchanging dollars could mean receiving a thick stack of currency. Nepal's money looked different now, too. No longer did it feature the king's portrait. After the royal family was kicked out of power, the money was updated to highlight yaks, rhinos, elephants, tigers, and other animals, as well as Mount Everest. The coins were new, too.

My wallet also held a bank debit card, which I used to obtain rupees at an ATM, a transaction that would have been unimaginable a few years earlier. In addition, I had a Visa card that enabled me to make foreign purchases without an extra fee. Credit cards, though, remained less common here than back home.

My pants pockets contained other insights into Nepal, such as the tissues I carried in case I needed to wipe my nose or use in a bathroom, where toilet paper was scarce. I had a small medicine bottle that contained diarrhea medicine along with Tylenol and vitamins. There was also a small flashlight, for when the electricity went out. And in an effort to stave off a throat infection from the air pollution, as happened during my previous visit, I always carried a mask, as well as my asthma inhaler. Many Nepalis now wore masks, as well.

Before we left North Carolina, I'd bought baggier jeans to hold everything. Given the huge meals Champa and I were being served by our family and friends, and at gatherings like this one, I was glad to have them. My days as a skinny Peace Corps volunteer were behind me.

I relaxed at Shankar's house in a way I never could on previous trips. Back then, I always needed to race home to my job or, if the kids were with us, to get them back to school. This time we were also stranded because of the petrol crisis. We didn't want to waste the fuel in Shankar's car and buses were largely unavailable. Instead, I spent long hours taking walks or sitting around the house, reading books, and surfing on the Internet.

When Champa asked whether I was bored, I told her "nope." It was the truth, and it surprised me. As someone who had thrived in the fast-paced news business and raced from one crisis to another, I kept waiting to feel restless or guilty about relaxing so easily. I never did.

After more than a week, we flew to Ilam, Champa's home town in eastern Nepal. It was where I was initially posted as a Peace Corps volunteer at the school where Champa was among the other teachers. Shankar and Bindu joined us on the flight and gave me a seat on the left so I could watch Mount Everest and other peaks appear in the window.

When we landed in the southeastern town of Bhadrapur, Champa ran to hug her brother, who was waiting outside the gate. He placed prayer scarves around our necks, helped us with our bags, and guided us to an SUV and the driver he'd hired to take us on the four-hour drive to Ilam. He spent less for this round trip than I would have for a half-hour taxi ride from my house in Durham to our local airport. I had not made the trip in twenty years, so I was excited as we rose from the plains into the hills, winding our way across mountain vistas and switchbacks, stopping only for a toilet break and a late lunch of momos. When we finally arrived at Raju's new house, which he'd built only a few years earlier, his wife Sanjaya greeted us. We stayed in a room on the top floor with our own bathroom and an American style toilet installed for us just a week earlier.

Ilam's layout hadn't changed since I lived there, but the town had grown from a quiet district center into a bustling hub with shops, restaurants, cell phone stores, computer centers, bakeries, travel agencies, and schools. There were two newspapers, a radio station, and countless satellite television dishes offering everything from local soap operas to American movies.

Located across the border from India's Darjeeling, Ilam was Nepal's tea-growing center. Its tea gardens were now much larger than before but as lush and picturesque as I remembered them. The day after we arrived, we took a stroll with Shankar and Bindu through the main gardens to a new observation tower where we got a view of the whole town. Next door was a coffee shop where we sat in an outdoor room with bamboo walls, enjoying spicy snacks and free Wi-Fi.

When I first moved to Ilam in 1977, I lived in two rooms on the first floor of a house next to a field where young men were now playing cricket, something I'd never seen there before. A new family owned the house. After overcoming their surprise about an American wandering up and talking in Nepali, they invited me to take a peek inside, where I met a lodger and his two sons. I'd stayed in this house for several months before my school's headmaster moved me to a building in the bazaar, for reasons that remain a mystery to me. That place was miserable and made me sick. I lived on the second floor, above a tenant who cooked on an indoor wood stove every night, sending smoke up through the floorboards into my room. The situation exacerbated the asthma I'd developed during training, but the headmaster did nothing to help me, even after I pleaded to move somewhere else. Before long, I got pneumonia and was medically evacuated, taking me on my trip to Washington. Now, just seeing the building brought back those bad memories.

These were far outweighed, though, by Ilam's charms, which deserve more attention from foreign visitors. Ilam is especially photogenic on Thursdays and Sundays when farmers assemble at a big open-air market, but its tea gardens, temples, and other attractions are also waiting to be discovered. Whereas Kathmandu depressed me with its crowds and pollution, Ilam seemed like a place I could live happily for weeks or months. When I was in the bazaar this time, I saw a T-shirt saying, "I ❤ Ilam," which I bought for Champa. If I'd seen one in my size, I would have bought that, too.

CHAPTER 4

PRAYERS BY THE STREAM

O ur Nepali family embraced us in Ilam. Cousins, neighbors, and old friends invited us to their homes for tea or dinner. I reunited with some former students who now had families of their own, just like Shankar. The most fun was watching Champa walk through town. People would recognize her, call out with delight, and ask how she was doing. When they saw me, you could almost see their brains thinking: So that's her American husband. They'd smile even more when I joined the conversation in Nepali.

Raju owned several small plots of land where he grew rice, millet, beans, and vegetables. He'd rented one plot to a group that erected a modest church, which we visited for longer than expected on an afternoon when it started raining. Churches barely existed when I'd lived in Nepal, and proselytizing remained illegal, but a growing number of people here and across Nepal had converted to Christianity. This church illustrated why. Almost all of its members belonged to tribal groups or lower Hindu castes. More than one hundred names filled the church roster, and I saw only one that appeared to be from a higher-caste Brahmin or Chhetri group, both of which are plentiful in Ilam. The church members were sincere in their devotion to Christianity, but almost all had been socially and economically marginalized for generations. They had embraced something new, just as some Kiratis had turned to Falgunanda. The young wife of the church's minister asked about my own faith. She had never heard of Judaism and was surprised to meet an American who didn't accept Jesus as the messiah.

Nonetheless, she and the others proudly showed us the church's prayer books, podium, and satellite system, which they used to download Nepali-language religious broadcasts from South Korea. Champa and I wondered whether the videos came from the Unification Church of Rev. Sun Myung Moon, but never found out. That didn't stop us from teasing Raju about being a secret supporter of the Moonies, whom he had never heard of before.

Near the church was Ilam's open-air animal market, which was busy with the approach of Dashain, Nepal's biggest holiday. Families were buying goats for their feasts, much as Americans buy turkeys for Thanksgiving, although our turkeys are already slaughtered and sold in plastic bags.

On the Thursday morning we went to look, farmers displayed hundreds of goats from the surrounding area. Families came to buy one or two, and wholesalers bought truckloads to sell in Jhapa, three hours to the south, near the airport. Early in the morning, we'd heard goats bleating as they passed Raju's gate on their way to the marketplace. Now they were meeting their fates. Buyers looked over the choices and haggled with the farmers. Most would hire a butcher to slaughter and prepare the goat. So, too, if they bought a pig or buffalo, although they'd probably slaughter chickens themselves. All of this could be grim to watch, especially for an American. However, I found it more honest than going to the supermarket and tossing a package of steak or chicken wings into a cart without thinking about its origin. Here in Nepal, there was no mistaking where your dinner came from if you chose to eat meat.

We also learned about the local cheese supply, hiring a driver one day to take us ten miles along a winding road to Bakhor, a tiny village with a growing cheese industry. When we arrived more than an hour later, I looked around for the promised "cheese factories." They turned out to be little more than huts, each producing small batches of a product resembling Gruyère. Everyone just called it cheese, which is still a novelty for many Nepalis but is beginning to catch on in Kathmandu. Here it was produced with milk from cows, not yaks, as in some other parts of Nepal. The factories used simple equipment and were decidedly less pristine than facilities in, say, Switzerland or Wisconsin. Still, the cheese was tasty, and we didn't get sick from it. We bought a package of a hard variety called churpi to bring home to our dog. We'd seen three Nepali entrepreneurs on the television show *Shark Tank* selling churpi dog treats. The churpi here was a lot cheaper, and we knew our Bailey wouldn't care about the factory being filthy.

Ilam receives few Western visitors but was a bustling metropolis compared to our next destination, a small village called Samalbung, just above the Mechi River on Nepal's eastern border with India. That's where Champa's older sister, Sumitra, had lived before her death a few months earlier. We wanted to pay our respects at her grave and spend a few days with her children, our nieces and nephews, of whom Shankar was the oldest. He and Bindu had already left Ilam for Samalbung, where the family was finishing the construction of a new house. Now Champa and I would join them.

We hired a driver to take us as far as his car could make it down a road that started out paved but gradually deteriorated. When the potholes turned into small chasms, our driver said he could drive no further, so we got out to walk the rest of the way. We carried only day packs filled with water and snacks, having sent our suitcases ahead on one of the customized four-wheel drive vehicles that ply the rutted road, carrying goods, mail, and passengers brave enough to climb aboard. We'd end up riding one of these vehicles a few days later in hair-raising trips we would never forget, but for now, we were happy to walk beside fragrant tea plantations, cardamom fields, orchids, and wildflowers, pausing only to buy a plastic bottle of Sprite at a roadside shop. There were no street names, but it didn't matter. We told people whom we were visiting, and they pointed us in the right direction, asking us where we had come from and what we were doing there.

About three hours later, we reached a shop where we saw our suitcases near the entrance. The owner told us the vehicle had dropped them off a short time earlier. He took out his cell phone and called our nephew Santosh to come to help us. Santosh arrived from the house five minutes later, hoisted our heaviest suitcase on his back, grabbed the next heaviest with his hand, and led us down a tiny trail through the forest. As we approached his house, we saw Bindu and the rest of the family waiting with flower garlands. We all exchanged namastes and hugs, then came inside for tea.

When she entered, Champa started weeping, feeling the absence of her sister. Our nieces wept with her. All of us wished Sumitra was there to share in this reunion, which we had begun planning while she was still alive. Instead, after we'd finished our snacks and taken some photos, the two of us walked behind the house to see the grave where she was buried beside her late husband. Champa and I placed flowers and incense on top of both graves and spoke quietly. Then I left her to be alone with her sister while I headed back inside.

❖

After we ate breakfast the next morning, we walked down to a stream to join our family and neighbors in a ritual to replace evil spirits with prosperity, health, and good luck. This was the *maanghope* ceremony, which our family and their Kirati neighbors perform every harvest season. Jai Kumar, a second cousin who lived in the house next door, led the prayers. He wore a ceremonial white hat and chanted from a handwritten book. A farmer by day, Jai Kumar also served as the local *sikhsamba*, or religious leader, for Kiratis in Samalbung. Together, they had revived animist traditions and were following the teachings of Falgunanda, whose temple we'd visited in Kathmandu. In the spring, they'd hold a similar ceremony for the planting season.

Few Westerners have seen either ceremony, so I felt honored to be included as part of the family. People stood beside the stream, recited prayers, held candles, beat drums, and tossed flower petals and grain into the flowing water. Their chants blended with the bubbling stream and clashing cymbals. Even children held their hands together, eyes closed, heads gently moving, pausing only to toss flowers into the water when Jai Kumar nodded. One boy wore a yellow Qatar Airways shirt, which his uncle had probably bought while working in the Gulf, one of the many Nepalis who went there to earn money. Another child prayed but then wandered away to play with a plastic toy. A little girl smiled at me to show how many teeth she had recently lost. Jai Kumar expected no payment for leading the ceremony, which called on everyone to pray not only for themselves and their families but for the entire community.

On the previous evening, a few hours after we arrived, he'd come over to lead a ceremony to welcome us and bless the new house. We'd sat together on the floor of the front room, lit only with candles, and spoke softly as he chanted prayers. On top of a nearby dresser was an elaborate collage of Sumitra's life that Champa had spent months making in North Carolina. We'd had it framed in Kathmandu, and it survived the bumpy trip here. We could now feel Sumitra's presence as we dedicated her family's new home. Champa and I knew we were participating in something special with these ceremonies, a gift we had received only by making this journey. Together, we were about as far from the United States as it was possible to be, worshipping by candlelight with tribal mountain people in a tiny village in the Himalayas. These people were our family, and we were deeply content to be with them, surrounded by love, our previous lives far behind us.

A few days later, we took a trip with Shankar and Bindu to Antudanda, a village offering a spectacular vantage point to watch the sun rise over the eastern Himalayas and Mount Kanchenjunga, the world's third-highest mountain after Everest and K2.

We stayed in a modest lodge that one of Shankar's college friends had opened. It cost us less than twenty dollars for two rooms, four dinners, four breakfasts, drinks, and a guide to escort us by flashlight in the morning to the observation tower. We watched the mountains glow as the sun rose over a series of ridges, revealing Kanchenjunga in the distance while a rooster crowed and a bell rang nearby. We were so entranced that we stopped taking photos and just stared.

Even more memorable was the trip we took to reach the lodge. Champa and I had reluctantly agreed to drive instead of walk, using one of the four-wheelers we'd avoided previously. Anyone in the United States who complains about potholes should take a ride on one of these taxis. They climb and swerve along the unpaved roads of Samalbung, bouncing over cobblestones along the better stretches and struggling across longer stretches where pockmarked dirt turns to mud. During the monsoon season, the mud resembles a swamp. Even when rain is intermittent, as when we visited, water collects into pools. Drivers have to aim their tires on either side of a pool and avoid slipping into the middle or else charge through and try to reach the other side before losing traction.

Sometimes the driver doesn't make it. That's what happened when our driver, Arpan, was a moment late in down-shifting over a depression in the road. Since his four-wheel-drive equipment was temporarily broken, he swerved into a ditch, and then nearly burned off his left rear tire trying to regain contact. We all had to get out as he and his assistant gathered stones and gravel to provide traction. Eventually we got back on the road. The tires of these taxis puncture regularly, as happened to us a few days later as we left Samalbung to return to Kathmandu. Once again, we disembarked as Arpan and his assistant made a roadside repair.

The taxi routinely steered near the edge of precarious roads lacking side barriers. If it had gone over the edge, it would have fallen hundreds of feet before crashing amid the world's biggest mountains. There were no helicopters to provide rescue service in this remote part of Nepal; there were hardly any doctors. If you went over the side, you died. Just to make the experience more interesting, the vehicles might be piled high with luggage, grain, and other goods, all of which raised the center of gravity and reduced stability. This was balanced a bit by the passengers crammed inside, providing a counterweight. Many of the drivers were young men, who remained cheerful despite working long hours and earning little money. They regularly stopped to pick up passengers and cargo, and also ran errands such as delivering a cell phone or money for people along the route.

Champa and I took two trips and found both of them to be simultaneously terrifying and hilarious. As happened so often in Nepal, we eventually got used to the situation and began joking with the other passengers at each unexpected turn. We embraced a sticker on the driver's door that said "No Tension" in English. On the second trip, the fare for the four of us to travel three hours to our destination was eleven dollars, luggage included. That was nearly double the usual fare but ensured I had the front passenger seat while Champa, Bindu, and Shankar had the second row. Although sad about leaving, we were glad to have the seats to ourselves. We had a long trip ahead of us. It was nice to splurge on business class.

Our road trip from Samalbung to Kathmandu, just halfway across a small country, took nearly thirty hours, much longer than our trip from Philadelphia to Kathmandu. First, we drove three hours in our death-defying taxi to Fikkal, a junction on the main road from Ilam. After stopping for lunch, the four of us transferred to another driver, whom we hired to take us in his four-wheel-drive vehicle down to the plains and past the airport to a town where one of Champa's relatives lived. We took another break there, then transferred to a vehicle Shankar had booked through his friend, a newer SUV that would drive overnight to Kathmandu.

With each leg of the journey, the big question was whether the driver had enough gas. By now, Nepal's fuel shortage had become a crisis. Many gas stations were closed. The black market was thriving. Gas was still available near Samalbung since traders could smuggle it over the Indian border. Shankar bought some there to bring home, filling my Sprite bottle and other containers. The driver who took us down to the hills had a full tank, although he was vague when we asked where he'd filled up. On our last leg, we were delayed because the driver had to wait until dark to sneak into the backyard of a gas station on the main road, closing the fence behind him. That's where he bought fuel from a special pump, paying the owner several times the official rate to fill up the tank and two large containers, which he tied onto the roof. That was enough gas for him to avoid filling up again in Kathmandu, where gas was more expensive, if available at all. By the time we got there, the driver determined he had more gas than he needed, so he would sell a few small bottles.

Like most drivers, he earned little money, depending on tips and opportunities like this to increase his profit. As the four of us dozed, he drove through the night, stopping only at a checkpoint where the army was gathering vehicles to travel together. They provided an escort to take us through a section of the highway where protesters had recently thrown rocks at vehicles in an effort to prolong the fuel blockade and exert pressure on the government to negotiate with them. Back in Ilam, we'd seen a bus whose front windshield was smashed in this area, so we were glad to have the protection.

As we passed the trouble spot and the hours passed, we continued towards Kathmandu on a road built by the Japanese government, one of many projects in Nepal made possible by international support. We finally stopped at a town where Shankar was helping indigenous groups fight for compensation from an electrification project that had taken their land. We took a break there as the sun rose, ordering coffee at a shop while our driver took a nap. It was only then he admitted he had not slept for nearly a day. After he dropped us off, he said, he'd have a few hours to see his family and would then need to drive all the way back with new customers. He was a nice guy, but we watched him closely after that, ready to nudge him if we saw him nodding off.

Since his vehicle was not registered as a taxi within Kathmandu, he had to drop us off on the outskirts of town. There we hired another vehicle, which charged us three times the usual rate to take us to Shankar's house. The driver refused to negotiate, saying we were lucky to find anyone with enough gas and willing to drive to Shankar's neighborhood, where he had no guarantee of a return fare. Did we want to go with him or not? It wasn't a difficult decision.

We arrived just in time for the week-long Dashain holiday. Like Christmas in the West, it's a time when schools and businesses close, and people living away from home travel back to see their families. This year, with bus schedules and other transport disrupted by the fuel crisis, many people were skipping the trip.

Shankar had decided a few years earlier to stop celebrating Dashain because of its Hindu origins. Champa and I were less scrupulous. We figured it was a good time to move across town for a few days to stay with her sister, whom we'd meant to visit anyway. Meena was actually a cousin, but the two of them considered each other sisters since they grew up together. Meena's late husband was a famous singer who also had successful businesses. Their three children were now spread around the world: Pukar in Chicago, Poonam in Singapore, and only Pooja still in Nepal. Among prosperous Nepali families, this was common.

The highlight of Dashain was giving and receiving tikas, a ceremonial red mark on the forehead. Tikas are a mixture of a red powder, rice, and yogurt mixed with a little sugar. The person who bestows a tika is usually an older relative to whom one shows respect.

I received five tikas over the next few days. Each time I'd sit at a table with my hands raised in front of me like I was praying. The tika-giver used his or her thumb and finger to apply a dab to my forehead and then placed some shoots from rice plants, called *jamara*, behind my ear. While doing this, they chanted blessings for my happiness and prosperity.

Next, they gave me a piece of fruit and an envelope containing some lucky money. Three of the envelopes I received were adorned with swastikas, a Hindu symbol of prosperity. People gave them to me with love and generosity, so I let pass what the symbolism might mean to someone whose mother had fled Nazi Germany. After all, my late mom had traveled to Nepal twice and adored Meena's family, so I knew she would have understood. In any case, after receiving each tika, I bowed and thanked the person for their blessing. I wore the tika for at least the rest of the day before washing it off. I gave someone else a Dashain tika for the first time on this visit, fortunately after I'd received mine and understood the technique. I was relieved to do everything correctly.

Two of my tikas came from a Brahmin couple we'd met in New York when we were married. Gopinath had worked in Nepal's embassy at the United Nations there. He'd read my op-ed article in *The New York Times* about serving in the Peace Corps in Nepal and invited me to visit him. We became friends along with Champa and his wife, Roopa, and we invited them and their young son to our wedding. They were the only Nepalis there besides Champa. We had not seen them since that day, but Roopa had recently tracked me down on Facebook, and she insisted we come visit when we were in Nepal. We spent a wonderful afternoon at their home, where they showed us souvenirs and photos from their diplomatic travels. A highlight was their meeting with Nelson Mandela in South Africa, where Gopinath served as Nepal's first ambassador. Now, after so many years, they were giving me a tika for Dashain.

Just as in the other places, the ceremony was followed by delicious snacks and then by a feast. Even though I was with high-caste Brahmins, the experience reminded me of Passover meals at my grandmother's house where we'd recite the prayers and traditional stories until my grandmother got restless and said "let's eat," encouraging us to start dining on matzoh ball soup, gefilte fish, and other traditional dishes she had prepared. Her homemade horseradish was good training for some of the foods we ate now.

CHAPTER 5

OUR TWO FAMILIES UNITE

With our trips to Ilam and Samalbung behind us and Dashain winding down, Champa and I turned our attention to the arrival of our American family. My two sisters and their husbands were flying in from New York with two of our adult nieces, and my cousin and her husband were coming from California. None had been to Nepal before. Most had never been to a poor country. All would depend on us.

Ever since we'd gotten married, Champa and I had wanted them to see where she came from and why Nepal was so special to us, just as my parents had done. They loved Champa, but children, jobs, vacation schedules, and budgets prevented them from even considering such a trip. Now things had changed. All of our children had grown up. Everyone was able to get away from their jobs and was healthy enough to travel. Most of us were nearing or past retirement age. It was time to go.

More than a year earlier, I'd confidentially shared with everyone my plans to leave Duke, and asked them to consider making a two-week trip to Nepal, which we'd organize. I promised it would cost less than a trip of equal length to parts of the world where hotels, restaurants, and attractions cost far more than Nepal's. The savings would more than offset the airfare, which was only a few hundred dollars higher than a flight to Europe. We'd rent our own vehicle and forego guides in most places since Champa and I could show everyone around. Most importantly, our Nepal family would be waiting to welcome them, which would be unforgettable.

My sisters and the others said yes, which surprised and pleased us. They're decidedly more traditional than us in their tastes, and Nepal is not known for comfortable resorts and fine dining, although it does have those. My older sister and her family are also observant Jews, so they would be restricted in their diet and want to attend Friday evening services. We also had vegetarians in the group, a person with back problems, and other concerns — just another modern American family.

Over the next several months, I worked with an excellent Kathmandu travel agency, Sports Travel, to arrange an itinerary and make hotel reservations. When the earthquake rocked Nepal, we watched the situation carefully before deciding to move ahead. Since many tourists had canceled their trips, we knew the country would be hungry for our dollars. One of my brothers-in-law asked whether we should change our plans to assist the relief efforts for part of the trip. I told him the best thing he could do was spend money in the souvenir shops and elsewhere to help revive the economy. None of us anticipated that our biggest problem would be not the earthquake but the fuel shortages.

My older sister's family arrived first on one of the airlines operating out of the Persian Gulf, which everyone else would use as well. Shankar and Bindu joined us at the airport to welcome them with garlands of flowers we'd picked from their garden that morning. It was amazing to watch them emerge from the airport arrivals door with big smiles on their weary faces. After more than 35 years, our two worlds were coming together.

My younger sister and her husband came the next day, as did our California relatives. We greeted them with flower garlands, too. Our driver snapped photos of us, loaded their bags into a minivan, and then took everyone down the street from the palace where the king had ruled to the Yak and Yeti Hotel. Champa and I moved there, too, leaving Shankar's house to begin our full-time service as travel guides.

The Yak and Yeti is one of Kathmandu's best hotels. Back when I was a volunteer, living on seventy dollars a month, it seemed unapproachable. I went inside only once to examine the menu of its famous restaurant, which a Russian émigré named Boris had opened. It featured borscht and Nepali food. I felt little in common with the guests there, smug in my assumption that I was experiencing the real Nepal while they were in an overpriced Western bubble. As I'd gotten older and traveled in countries where I did not speak the language or know people, my views had softened. Champa and I still didn't often stay in places as nice as this — we couldn't afford to — but we had reached a point in life where we did want a comfortable bed, a hot shower, and a nice breakfast. One night at the Yak and Yeti cost more than we'd spent in a week in Samalbung, but we'd budgeted for it, and the next two weeks would still be a bargain compared to, say, Tokyo or London.

We gathered in the hotel bar on our first evening together, drinking bottles of Everest and Gorkha beer while toasting at finally being in Kathmandu after so many months of planning and years of dreaming. The final member of our group, our niece Rachel, would join us soon, and we were ready to start our tour. For now, everyone's exhilaration exceeded their jet lag, and we ordered a final round.

The next morning, we allowed them a chance to decompress after their long journeys by introducing them to everyday life in Nepal. We drove outside the city to Shankar and Bindu's house. Along the way, they passed entire families riding on a single motorcycle, street vendors, cows, and earthquake rubble. They saw military facilities and a children's amusement park, men herding goats, and dogs sleeping in gutters. The paved road gave way to a dirt road which then became little more than a rutted path. Dust rose into the windows. Fields replaced buildings. The landscape softened.

When we arrived, Shankar and Bindu were waiting at their gate with their daughter, who placed a scarf around each person's neck as they entered. We went to their roof patio, where Bindu had laid out oranges, bananas, curries, and *rotis* (a kind of Nepali donut) along with mineral water, beer, and Dew. To the north were the mountains; to the west, planes landing at the airport. Next door were neighbors threshing rice. Several members of our group walked there and, to the amusement of the farmers, assisted for a few minutes, undoubtedly the first time a software consultant, healthcare analyst, and chief financial officer had helped thresh rice in this neighborhood. Most of the group then took a walk with Shankar, exploring their new surroundings and getting a feel for Nepal. They loved it. We left later than planned. Our driver navigated giant potholes along the way, and then everyone slept at the hotel. We ended the night with a rooftop dinner at a restaurant overlooking the palace. It was a good first day.

The official tour, which we'd organized with the travel agency, began the next morning with a visit to the Swayambhu Monastery, the famous temple on a hill whose four pairs of giant golden eyes overlook the city and adorn many of Nepal's travel posters. Swayambhu is also renowned for its wild monkeys, which scamper everywhere. Vendors around the central *stupa* sold handicrafts as the Tibetan mantra *om mani padme hum* played from speakers behind colorful prayer flags. Incense filled the air. Worshippers and tourists twirled brass prayer wheels sending prayers into the heavens. Monks passed in robes. Dogs snoozed. Piles of bricks lay below walls destroyed in the earthquake.

Next was Durbar Square, the site of Kathmandu's old royal palace. I used to ride my bicycle there regularly, just because it was so beautiful. Its earthquake damage was even worse than we'd seen at the monastery. Several of the square's most glorious buildings were gone. I'd seen videos of the destruction on YouTube, so I wasn't shocked, but I nearly wept nonetheless. It was such a terrible loss. My family was awed by the structures that remained, including one with erotic carvings on its wooden roof supports. At the square's southern end was a temple housing the *kumari*, the living goddess who lived there with her family until she reached puberty.

After stopping at Sports Travel to settle everyone's bill and eat lunch, we ended with a visit to Pashupatinath, Nepal's most sacred Hindu temple. Dedicated to the god Shiva, it's where thousands of bodies are cremated every year in pyres beside the Bagmati River. Champa was the only one allowed inside since she is nominally Hindu. The rest of us waited while she paid her respects. A police officer came to shoo us away from the gate but relented and even smiled when I told her in Nepali that we were waiting for my wife. That seemed to please her.

The next morning we headed to Nagarkot, a mountain resort east of Kathmandu. We drove past farms and small towns before climbing a ridge to about 7,000 feet above sea level. There, we turned into the parking lot of Club Himalaya, a lovely hotel that greeted us with tea and snacks in a glass-walled dining room with a magnificent view.

The hotel had built a new wing since Champa and I stayed there several years earlier. Each room had a balcony facing north towards some of Nepal's most famous mountains: Annapurna, Manaslu, Ganesh Himal, and, in the distance, Everest itself. It was now afternoon, so fog covered the landscape, but we hoped to see everything the next morning. In the meantime, we ate lunch on the veranda and hiked nearby. Everyone was relaxed and happy; Nepal already seemed less strange to them. In just three days, they'd gotten a taste of daily life, seen some of the main attractions, and ascended for a view of the famous mountains.

The manager apologized that he couldn't offer the regular menu for dinner. The hotel had run out of cooking fuel and now had to cook by firewood. Its kitchen staff could only offer a buffet for everyone. The buffet choices proved plentiful and tasty, however, and our meal was accompanied by three musicians singing Nepali folk songs. Champa and I joined them on one song, and the rest of our group began improvising English lyrics to the tune of another, *Resham Firiri,* which they'd continue singing for the rest of the trip. The musicians were puzzled but appreciative.

Despite some lingering jet lag, everyone awoke before dawn the next morning to watch the sun rise over the Himalayas. Signs on the roof showed the location of each mountain. We had our cameras ready. As the sky brightened, however, fog persisted over the landscape. We waited an hour, hoping it would lift, but the view remained covered. We wouldn't see the mountains we'd come so far to see.

Everyone was disappointed as we ate breakfast and then headed back down the ridge, but our spirits lifted as we entered Bhaktapur, one of the valley's three great cities along with Kathmandu and Patan. Once again, we were awed by the beauty and scale of the

temples and statues in the city center and saddened by the earthquake's impact. The giant Nyatapole Temple, a five-story pagoda,
was intact, but the Taleju Temple and others were badly hit. So were
homes across the city, which suffered many casualties.

We also saw heart-breaking damage at Kathmandu's second great
Buddhist monastery, Boudhanath, our last stop for the day. Its
central golden stupa, whose giant eyes resemble Swayambou's, was
gone. It was as if someone had decapitated the Statue of Liberty.

The prayer flags that usually fluttered from the stupa were missing, too. Knowing what everything was supposed to look like, I
couldn't believe what I was seeing. Nonetheless, as the home of the
city's Tibetan refugee community, Boudhanath retained its spirit.
Around the corner, we heard the deep chanting of monks. On a
rooftop, dozens of Tibetans prayed together on carpets. A giant
red prayer wheel spun below them. Smaller brass prayer wheels
still surrounded the stupa. It was all like a Buddhist lesson on the
unwavering impermanence of existence: Everything changes; everything continues.

For such a small country, Nepal has remarkably diverse ecosystems.
It's best known for the mountains along its northern border with
Tibet, where the famous Sherpas live, but most Nepalis live either
in the hills, like Champa's family in Ilam, or in the southern plains
bordering India. This latter area, the Terai, the center of the current
unrest, was where we headed next. We switched our van for a small
bus to give everyone more room. Our niece Rachel had joined us
the night before, just in time for our journey to Chitwan, where
we'd spend two nights.

I first visited Chitwan as a Peace Corps volunteer. Hiking to see
my Peace Corps friend Dwight, I walked then along a road being

constructed by hundreds of Chinese workers. This was in January 1979, a few days after China's leader had visited the White House, which I'd heard about on my shortwave radio.

"Jimmy Carter!" some of the workers shouted at me as I passed then.

"Deng Xiaoping!" I called back to them, all of us laughing.

Now the road was well established and heavily traveled, a main artery connecting the southern Terai with the central hills and Kathmandu valley. Chitwan was no longer a jungle outpost. It was filled with eco-resorts offering elephant rides and other attractions to Western travelers. We were staying at one of these, the Green Park, whose slogan was "Where culture meets class." Instead of sleeping on a mat on Dwight's floor, this time I was sharing with Champa a bungalow equipped with Wi-Fi, a flat-screen TV, air conditioning and a well-stocked dining room next door.

The elephant ride through Chitwan's national park was the highlight of our group's visit, as expected, but we also rode a canoe along a river with crocodiles on the bank, traveled by ox cart to a local village, and took an early-morning walk to observe wild parrots, kingfishers, egrets, and other birds. One evening we enjoyed a cultural program performed by men from the local Tharu community, who coaxed several members of our group to dance with them. All of this was designed for tourists, but it was well done, and we enjoyed it.

Likewise at Pokhara, where we headed next, traveling back north along the Chinese road but turning west instead of east when we reached the main road across the hills. Pokhara is Nepal's second-largest city. It has a lively downtown but is known among visitors for its lake nestled below the Himalayas. It's where Champa and I had gone on our first date together before we were married.

I'd also brought my parents here thirty-two years earlier. We'd stayed then in the Fish Tail Lodge, in rooms shaped like slices from a pie.

Just as we'd seen in Chitwan, there were enormous changes. No longer was Pokhara's beautiful lake bordered by a few modest restaurants, shops, and hotels. Now there were hundreds of establishments offering everything from chunky Tibetan jewelry to elegant cashmere sweaters and cuisines ranging from Mexican to traditional Nepali food. Numerous trekking companies advertised hikes to the Annapurna base camp and other destinations. Others offered paragliding, although these trips were closed for a few days because someone had just died in an accident. Many of the shops had no customers. When I chatted with some of the merchants, they said they were only beginning to recover from the earthquake when the fuel shortage hit them even harder. A woman who owned one shop thanked my sister repeatedly when she bought several pashmina scarves and souvenirs.

While in Pokhara, we also stopped at the Bindhyabasini Temple, where several local teenagers took their photos with our two nieces, making them feel like Kardashians. We visited a mountaineering museum, a small cave, and the rushing water at Devi's Falls. Some of our group hiked up to Shanti Stupa, known as the World Peace Pagoda, while others strolled along the lake. Together, we ate dinner at a restaurant near our hotel that had one of the highest ratings on TripAdvisor. It was delicious and inexpensive, just as the reviews promised, and we were the only ones there.

We awoke before dawn to watch the sun rise from a hilltop in nearby Sarankot, but our view of the mountains was once again obscured by fog. The mist finally lifted just before we left, revealing the famous peaks and reminding everyone that nature follows her own schedule.

Nepal's fuel crisis was a constant presence. While we were in Kathmandu, we passed lines of cars, motorcycles, or buses that stretched for blocks. Hundreds of drivers stood behind each other, waiting for days in the dark and cold to buy a few gallons of gas. On our way to Chitwan, we saw similarly long lines of mothers, many with children, waiting with metal cans to buy kerosene for their stoves.

Our travel agent bought gasoline on the black market for our bus and loaded two canisters on the roof for our return journey. However, as we approached Chitwan and then continued from there, the bus strained to go up hills. The driver checked the vehicle's fuel line and told us the fuel had been adulterated. The bus barely made it to Pokhara, much later than we planned.

As we removed our bags in the hotel parking lot, the driver and his assistant told us they would try to buy fresh fuel, and we reassured them we'd pay for it. However, they couldn't find anyone in Pokhara who would sell them gas, not even at a military base where we thought the guards might deal some of the official supplies for *baksheesh*, as was happening elsewhere. When it came time to leave Pokhara to return to Kathmandu, we had no choice but to keep using our adulterated fuel.

The bus did fine where the road was flat or downhill but wheezed on the plentiful uphill stretches. We were able to stop for a break halfway, turning off the highway to ride cable cars to a famous Hindu shrine, Manakamana, where devotees went to pray and have their wishes fulfilled. Imported from Austria and operating since 1998, the cable car system enabled Hindu pilgrims and others to reach the shrine in a few minutes instead of hiking uphill for several hours. Tourists paid more than Nepalis to ride it; children and goats traveled at an even bigger discount.

The ride was lovely. As we glided up the mountain, we passed dozens of houses whose roofs were painted purple, the color of a local cell phone company. At the top, Champa made an offering at the temple while the rest of us watched people praying, smelled the incense, listened to the ringing bells, and snapped photos. We ate samosas and other snacks at a small restaurant before heading down on the cable car.

After we climbed back on the bus, our fuel problem worsened, and before long, it looked like we might be stranded. Almost all of our original gas was now gone from the tank, leaving only the adulterated gas. When we stopped a short time later at a roadside stand, where Champa bought a stalk of bananas to bring back to Kathmandu as gifts for people we'd be visiting, the driver called the travel agency to request a rescue. We were lucky that one of the company's vans had just dropped off other customers nearby and still had enough fuel to get back to Kathmandu. We met it down the road, transferred all of our bags to it, and squeezed inside. Nobody minded the cramped space. When the van started driving uphill and accelerated instead of slowing down, we all cheered.

Not for long, though. As soon as we entered Kathmandu, we got stuck in two huge traffic jams, which delayed us yet again. By the time we finally reached the Yak and Yeti Hotel, everyone was frazzled. Still, no one complained. They knew the drivers had done the best they could under difficult circumstances.

Before the trip, Champa and I had taken pains to tell everyone they'd be traveling in a developing country, so they would need to adjust to whatever problems arose. They were going to Nepal, a place where people are poor, infrastructure is lacking, and the political system is often inept. It's mountainous but definitely not Switzerland. If you are a visiting American, you can either get angry about what you encounter or modify your expectations and embrace the unexpected. I'd had my doubts about whether some members of our family would be able to do this. Now, here they were, laughing together at the end of a trying day. I was proud of them.

My family was experiencing Nepal as tourists, staying in modern hotels, visiting famous sights, and buying souvenirs along the way. For me, on the other hand, even during this part of the trip, I was taking stock of Nepal and assessing whether we might want to return here more regularly in the years ahead.

That was an option as we looked beyond this trip, uncertain as we were about whether the Peace Corps would accept us for service. We knew we would never move to Nepal permanently, not with our children and grandchildren in the States, but perhaps there might be a way to spend more time in this part of the world. I might get a part-time job working here with an NGO or as a stringer for Western publications. Or perhaps I could assist one of Shankar's groups or another nephew who would soon be returning home from medical school in neighboring China. Nepal was a mess now, both politically and economically, but things might improve. I'd shown I could remain healthy here, unlike when I was in the Peace Corps years earlier. But still, I wondered whether we'd be able to pursue a lifestyle that combined the best of West and East — a gentler existence that also included things like decent internet access and a bit of Western culture.

Our remaining days in Nepal provided additional insights and examples for me to consider. On the evening of our arrival, our hotel hosted the final night of a week-long jazz festival called Jazz-mandu, featuring jazz musicians from Nepal and around the world. We pulled into the parking lot as the last concert was starting on the back lawn. Even though we were exhausted, we walked over to check it out. Yaite Ramos, a Cuban artist now living in Paris, was singing "Besame Mucho." Her bass player had a small Nepali flag attached to his fretboard. A vendor sold concert T-shirts. People cheered by holding up cell phones with digital candles flickering on screens. It felt like home.

So did our lunch the next day at the house of Champa's sister, Meena, whom we visited in Patan after touring the city's temple square, the third of the valley's great city centers. With advice from Champa, Meena prepared a wonderful meal that combined *rotis* and other Nepali treats with several Western dishes, ensuring everyone had something to enjoy.

As we strolled outside her gate, I ran into Raina, a former Peace Corps volunteer in Africa who now worked at Catholic Relief Services in Nepal. We'd met earlier in the trip, along with her American husband and son. She was pursuing a life that was also among the options I'd been thinking about, namely as an expatriate development worker.

That evening, we were all invited to dinner by Meena's daughter Pooja, who lived nearby with her husband's extended family. Her father-in-law had parlayed an engineering career into one of the country's most successful family businesses. His three sons, including Pooja's husband, had largely taken over by now, each with his own specialty such as manufacturing or management consulting. All were married with children. Each lived in a wing of a joint family compound. They spent most of their time with their own spouses and children but came together for big family meals and events. They were not constantly together, like many adult Nepali brothers, but neither were they living miles apart, like our sons. It was a compromise that blended local and Western traditions, and they and their wives were making it work.

The sons were sophisticated businessmen who enjoyed comparing experiences with their dinner guests, whose own expertise ranged from software development and consulting to finance and marketing. To be sure, their family's considerable wealth enabled them to hire servants and send their children abroad for college, but it was still interesting to see how they maintained their heritage while engaging with the larger world. They were incredibly generous to us, providing an elaborate meal to a family they barely knew, except for the two of us, and even we were only the aunt and uncle of their daughter-in-law. By the time we left, we all felt like close friends.

Our family's trip to Nepal that began two weeks earlier with a visit to Shankar and Bindu's home was now closing with lunch at Meena's house and a dinner feast with her daughter's family. As much as we had loved seeing the mountains and riding the elephants, these get-togethers would be the experiences we all remembered most. Our two families had come to know and care for each other. They were no longer connected just by Champa and my marriage but by their own experiences. Simultaneously, these gatherings were helping me envision possible paths for my own journey after this trip was behind us.

On our last night together in Kathmandu, our family ate dinner at an Indian vegetarian restaurant where we toasted each other with Everest beer, and my brother-in-law recited a silly poem thanking Champa and me for organizing everything. Our meal was interrupted by a group of girls who appeared in traditional costumes at the restaurant's entrance, singing and dancing. They were celebrating Tihar, one of Nepal's biggest holidays, when houses and businesses adorn their walls with lights and flowers. Tihar is similar to Halloween. Children dress up and walk from place to place performing songs to receive treats or money. The girls were adorable, and we gave them money when they finished, as did the other diners and staff. Their singing capped a memorable evening. We all felt bittersweet as we walked back to the hotel for the final time, happy the trip had gone so well but sad it was ending.

The next morning, Champa and I awoke early to say goodbye to most of the group, who were taking an early flight to India for a few days to see the Taj Mahal and other sights before heading home. The others would depart for America in the afternoon after making a final visit to Swayambhu and the central temple square.

Champa and I were moving back to Shankar's house to pick up our other luggage and spend one last night together. On our way there, we stopped at the Bhatbateni store, where I bought a television to give Shankar and Bindu as a thank-you present for all of their hospitality.

The next morning, we left as well. As I watched the Himalayas disappear from the right-side window of the plane, the visible Nepal was slowly replaced by the incredible memories Champa and I had made on our journey. We both knew we'd return one day; for now, these recent adventures would have to sustain us.

When we landed in Qatar, we spent several hours in Doha's modern airport before flying on to Philadelphia to see our son's family and pick up our car for the drive home.

We arrived in Philadelphia early on a Saturday morning. We didn't want to ask our son to make the long drive to the airport to pick us up on the one day of the week when he got to sleep late. Instead, we decided to take the train from the airport to a station near his house where he could easily meet us. We hauled our bags to the airport train platform only to discover that trains weren't running because of track maintenance. Having already bought tickets, we had to take a bus to Philadelphia's downtown 30th Street Station, then wait forty-five minutes for our train — this after having traveled halfway around the world with a six-hour layover in the Persian Gulf.

When the train finally delivered us to the station, Paul was waiting with our two older granddaughters, whose hugs we'd been dreaming about. Paul told us the older one had a soccer game in an hour and wanted us to come watch. We told her we would love to but were exhausted and needed to sleep. After we got to their house and embraced Stephanie and the baby twins, that's what we did.

We woke up in the afternoon and spent the rest of the weekend together, as we'd anticipated when we'd bought the tickets so many months earlier. We gave them presents and showed some of our photos while they told us about school, their jobs, and everything else we'd been missing. Inevitably, that's where the conversation soon focused.

Years ago, when I returned from my trip around the world, and then from the Peace Corps, I'd learned that even family and good friends generally listen for a few minutes and then say something like, "Hey, do you want to watch the game this afternoon?" It's not that they're rude or don't care about what we'd done; they just have their own lives, as we do. Personally, I am intensely curious about other parts of the world and happy to talk with someone for hours about a place they've just been. I am less willing to endure a long slide show and will disappear if they start babbling about something they did on their trip that doesn't interest me. I don't take it personally if others feel the same way about our travels, even if they're too polite to say so. Still, even though I'd gotten used to this reaction, it remained an odd feeling to bubble over with an experience and then be reminded that life continued pretty much the same for others while I was gone. Indeed, at least some of them probably listened to us and thought: "Oh, they're nuts" or "Oh, they're rich" or "Oh, how could they leave their family?"

In the end, our experiences belonged to us, and we couldn't expect them to mean much for anyone else. We'd shared our stories through my blog, whose audience was growing. Some readers wrote me to say our experience was leading them to rethink their own lives, something we'd also hear later while we were in the Peace Corps in Moldova. Most people, though, just heard what we did and regarded it as a curious thing with little or no relation to themselves.

"David and Champa went traveling? Good for them. What time does the game start?"

I'd stopped hoping for, much less expecting, anything more than that.

Just as after our U.S. road trip, we returned to North Carolina exhausted but happy. It was now a week before Thanksgiving when ordinarily we would be cleaning the house and preparing for guests and a big holiday feast. Paul, Stephanie, and the girls would not be coming this year since we'd just seen them, and the twins were too small to travel. Instead, we'd join Jonathan and his wife, Jamie, at the home of her parents, who also live in Durham and generously invited us to their Thanksgiving dinner, which was delicious.

Over the next few weeks, I taught myself how to use iMovie and produced a short video about our Nepal trip, which I posted on YouTube. It came to the attention of a guy who runs Ilam's main Facebook page, and he followed up by conducting a long-distance interview with us about the video and our trip, which he featured on the site. Champa's brother Raju, who doesn't use Facebook, called her a few days later to say he was getting stopped in the market by people who saw the article, which got hundreds of "likes."

We also got interesting feedback after the video was featured on the Facebook page for former Peace Corps volunteers in Nepal and worldwide. I heard from long-lost friends, such as a woman who had served in the Peace Corps group a year behind me, married a Nepali guy, and settled in both Boston and Kathmandu. We hadn't communicated since then.

Simultaneously, Champa and I were looking ahead. While we were at Shankar's house, we had been tentatively accepted for Peace Corps Moldova, contingent on an interview we arranged to conduct by Skype from Shankar's home. It was already evening there when we logged on to my laptop, hoping the electricity and internet connection would hold up while we spoke with the recruiter, who had just arrived at his office in Washington. Sure enough, we lost the connection as he began working his way through a list of questions, including one about whether we would be able to adjust to living in a country that lacked dependable electricity supplies. "Are you serious?" I asked when we reconnected, also reminding him that Champa grew up without electricity or running water. The recruiter laughed, and two days later, we received invitations to join Peace Corps Moldova, so long as we made it through their medical, legal, and other clearances.

Five months had passed since I'd left my job. Our first two trips were now behind us. My successor at Duke had settled into her job. I began to feel more comfortable about ending my self-imposed exile and reconnecting with friends from the university, making dates to meet for coffee or lunch so we could catch up about our lives. When several asked my advice about one thing or another, I realized how much I missed the mentoring part of my job, but I felt only relief when they described the latest controversies they were handling.

Life slowed down. Champa and I attended some holiday parties. We went to the gym. We played with our grandsons. She worked in her garden. I finished producing our annual photo book, which was bigger this year than usual. Mostly though, we let the two trips seep. We didn't talk about them every day, but they were constantly on our minds. We knew our lives had changed, but we were still sorting out how. The answer would ultimately depend on what we did next, which was uncertain as we worked our way through a Peace Corps clearance process that proved far more rigorous than we'd anticipated.

I had no doubt I'd done the right thing in leaving my job. I was sure of that. My old life was behind me. Yet our journey so far could not compare with what we were proposing to do next. Instead of taking two trips of less than two months each, we now planned to leave the United States for more than two years. This time it would mean saying goodbye to our children and grandchildren, renting our house, and living modestly in a strange country where we'd be surrounded by foreigners and by American colleagues who were mostly younger than our children. We were proposing to shake up our lives even more, and the potential for a disappointing outcome, or even for disaster, was far greater than before. For now, we would rest up and get our affairs in order. We had several months to unwind, declutter, and reorient.

Our third and biggest trip would come soon enough.

CHAPTER 6

HEADING TO MOLDOVA

W hen I first served as a Peace Corps volunteer in 1977 at the age of twenty-four, I completed the application, packed a suitcase and backpack, ate a farewell dinner with my family, and headed off for Nepal. This time, the process was a lot more complicated.

The application itself was straightforward, but the subsequent clearances took months. Champa and I submitted resumes with details about everywhere we'd ever lived and worked. We provided references. We went to a courthouse to be fingerprinted. Most important, even though we were in good shape for people our age, we spent months working our way through the medical process. We received thorough exams from our physicians and dentist, updated our vaccinations, and filled out more than 40 forms, some of them several pages long. I scanned and uploaded everything to the Peace Corps along with electronic copies of our dental X-rays, eyeglass prescriptions, and the like.

The medical office ended up approving us but restricting where we could serve, mainly because of the asthma I'd developed in Nepal. I hadn't had an asthma attack in more than thirty years, even during several subsequent trips to Nepal, but the Peace Corps wanted me in a country with better medical facilities. Champa and I also needed a Peace Corps country offering both of the programs we wanted — English teaching for her and community development for me. I'd enjoyed teaching English in Nepal, but now I wanted to apply the organizational skills I'd developed during my career.

Only a few countries matched both our medical and job needs. Several of them were in Eastern Europe, where the Peace Corps had expanded following the dissolution of the Soviet Union. We ended up designating Macedonia and Moldova as our top choices, although we also said we were willing to serve anywhere. When the Peace Corps eventually sent us invitations to serve in Moldova, we said yes, even though we knew almost nothing about the country.

We did so only after speaking with both of our sons and daughters-in-law, making sure we had their support to leave for more than two years. Like many Americans in their thirties, they were all busy with their careers, small children, and other demands. Now their kids would be losing two of their grandparents for an extended period. Our younger son and his family lived near us in Durham, so they would feel the impact the most. No longer would Champa and I be cheering at soccer games, making dinners, or taking care of the boys when they were sick. Nor would we see our older son's four daughters in Philadelphia. Once in Moldova, we would talk with all of them online, but we knew that would be a poor substitute for giving them real hugs. Indeed, throughout our service, we kept telling ourselves we were doing something they might appreciate when they got older, but the truth was we missed them and talked about them every day. For both of us, it would be the hardest thing about being away.

Champa and I debated what to do with our home in Durham. We'd paid off our mortgage a year earlier after accelerating our monthly payments for several years. With our two sons gone, the house was now too big for us. I wanted to sell it and be done with it before we left. Champa wanted to keep it to return home to after our service even if we ended up selling it later. That's what we did, hoping to earn some rental income and perhaps see the house appreciate in value while we were away. Neither of us thought much about what turned out to be another benefit of keeping it, which was that we were able to store possessions in a small upstairs room and in the attic instead of having to rent an expensive storage facility. We also stayed in the house, which was temporarily empty until a new tenant moved in, when we came home for a vacation after our first year as volunteers. Best of all, we had a place waiting for us when we completed our service two years later. Champa turned out to be right (hardly the first time).

During the weeks before our departure, we worked our way through a long "to do" list. I canceled our gym memberships, forwarded our mail, and arranged to shut off our electricity, gas, water, and cable service. I notified our bank and credit card companies about our travel plans and ordered an additional card from a company that offered free foreign ATM withdrawals. I added my sister to our checking account and notarized a form giving her our power of attorney. I reviewed our wills and made electronic copies of recent tax returns, so I would have them with me when I filed future returns from Moldova. I suspended our medical insurance, canceled the EZ-Pass for my car, and ended our subscription to Netflix. I scoured our credit card bills to make sure I wasn't overlooking any other recurring charges. Since North Carolina was likely to be a battleground state in the 2016 election, we also made sure to order absentee ballots.

We hired a small Durham company to manage our home for two years. With their assistance, we hired painters and a handyman to spruce up the house before the first tenants moved in. Parents of a friend offered to take care of our dog, Bailey, for which we were grateful. We bought Champa a laptop, adding to the laptop and two phones we'd bought before our U.S. driving trip. She got a Lenovo since we heard from Peace Corps that PCs were more common in Moldova, where she'd be sharing files with her fellow teachers.

We used a Peace Corps discount to buy suitcases and a solar-powered flashlight. We bought shoes to walk on Moldova's muddy roads, boots to survive its winters, and a winter coat for me, overlooking that we would first confront a hot Moldovan summer. I bought spare cables for our electronic gear, converter plugs to charge everything from Moldovan outlets, and a Kindle to load with books. Slowly but surely, we worked our way through the "suggested packing list" from the Peace Corps, wondering how we would fit everything into the two 50-pound suitcases and one carry-on bag we were each allowed to bring.

Simultaneously, we downsized and purged 36 years of possessions from our house. We donated most of our furniture to Habitat for Humanity, hundreds of books to the Durham library, and dozens of bags of clothing and household goods to local charities. I visited the local Goodwill donation center so often that I felt like asking for a personal parking space. We sold Champa's aging Toyota Corolla to a friend and gave my newer Ford Fusion to my son and daughter-in-law, whose car was dying. We kept the Fusion until the morning of our departure, handing over the keys to Jonathan after he drove with us to the airport.

Two days before we left, I attended a retirement party for a longtime Duke colleague. It was an outdoor event at the elegant Washington Duke Inn & Golf Club on campus. Wearing a suit for only the second time since I'd left the university, I saw old friends and nibbled on cucumber cheese triangles, shrimp cocktail martinis, and pan-roasted lump crab cakes with lemon caper dill sauce.

People asked me what I was doing these days, and when I said I was about to leave for the Peace Corps, I got responses that ranged from "that's cool!" to incredulous, especially when they glanced at my plate of fancy hors d'oeuvres. Several people then shared their own stories about how they'd wanted to join the Peace Corps but never got around to it, a response I would learn to anticipate.

The next night, Champa and I slept on an inflatable mattress in our empty house, deflating it in the morning and placing it with our coffee cups and two plates in one of the few empty spaces remaining in the storage room. As we locked the door, we knew we were saying farewell to life as we'd known it, perhaps forever.

We drove to Jonathan's house to pick him up and say goodbye to his family. Then we departed for the Raleigh-Durham Airport, waiting at the American Airlines gate before they finally called us for the first leg of a trip whose ultimate destination we could only imagine.

When the Peace Corps invited us to serve in Moldova, the only thing we knew about the country was it had been part of the Soviet Union and was located somewhere in Eastern Europe. Through the internet, we learned it was the poorest country in Europe by a large margin over places like Albania and Kosovo. Roughly the size of Maryland, Moldova is landlocked between Romania and Ukraine. As part of the Soviet Union, it had provided abundant wine and agricultural products to Russia and the rest of the nation.

Since the fall of the Soviet Union, its exports had sagged, a situation exacerbated by an unofficial Russian wine boycott designed to keep Moldova in line politically. The country's heavy industry was limited and concentrated in a region called Transnistria, where ethnic Russians broke away after independence to form a *de facto* state of their own. As in neighboring Ukraine, pro-Western and pro-Russian parties in Moldova battled for power in the years after independence. Political instability was common, as was corruption. Shortly before we arrived, a billion dollars disappeared from the national treasury — a huge sum by Moldovan standards — and a powerful oligarch and leading government officials were widely believed to be involved. Life expectancy was nearly a decade lower than in the United States; babies were more than twice as likely to die. Many people lived in poverty, especially in rural areas. Well-paying jobs were scarce, causing many adults to seek work elsewhere. As we would see for ourselves, many children across Moldova grew up without a father at home and often without a mother. They were being raised by their grandparents and neighbors.

Yet, Moldova was also beautiful, we learned, with gently rolling hills and vineyards, delicious food, colorful dances, and people ready to open their homes and hearts once they knew you. Almost everyone spoke Romanian, Russian, and often other languages as well, with many people eager to learn English.

While we were in Durham, Champa and I had lunch with a young woman who had served in Peace Corps Moldova. Samira shared happy memories of the country's people, beauty, and hospitality. She also told us it was considered to be part of "Posh Corps," a phrase within the Peace Corps community that describes places where the volunteer experience is less arduous than the traditional image of living in a mud hut and bathing with a bucket of water. Serving in Moldova, she and others told us, would be easier than my stint in Nepal, where I'd gotten sick with pneumonia, asthma, amoebic dysentery, giardiasis, hookworm, and roundworm, to name just my bronchial and digestive issues. Still, Moldova was poor by both American and European standards. If that meant we could occasionally shop in modern stores or enjoy an outdoor cafe, well, we wouldn't feel guilty about it.

Heading to Moldova

I already knew a bit about Eastern Europe, at least its more famous cities. Before I moved to North Carolina, I worked for the Howard Hughes Medical Institute, a large biomedical research philanthropy based in Chevy Chase, Maryland. One of its grants programs at the time supported researchers in the former Soviet bloc. Every year the institute held a scientific conference for these grantees, usually in one of their countries. I was the press person at the meetings, working with reporters in Prague, Warsaw, Budapest, and Moscow, as well as in the United States and Canada. I got to know many of the scientists. They were among the best in their countries, some among the best in the world, yet most were struggling to keep their labs open following the Soviet downfall. They smiled less than Americans and sometimes seemed dour, puffing on cigarettes even while discussing their research on cancer, but they also could be funny and warm. I shared roots with some of them since my grandmother had grown up in Odessa. For the most part, though, Eastern Europe was a mystery to me, especially Belarus, Ukraine, Georgia, Armenia, Moldova, and the other states that had been part of the Soviet Union.

Champa and I had traveled more than most people, but we knew little about this part of the world — and that was part of its attraction. We were eager to discover a place off the beaten track. Moldova qualified.

We flew to Philadelphia for a three-day Peace Corps "staging" prior to our departure. We checked our four 50-pound bags for our flight and boarded with stuffed carry-on bags — everything we'd finally decided to bring after weighing our bags repeatedly on our bathroom scale. We had to make difficult choices: Nepali spices or American snacks, extra shoes or another electronic gadget. We called our older son as we drove by taxi from the Philadelphia airport to our downtown conference hotel — a Sheraton, more upscale than we'd expected. Paul and his family joined us to spend the afternoon and eat dinner at a nearby restaurant, and then we hugged everyone tight, knowing we would not see them again for a long time.

That evening in the hotel lobby, we began meeting our fellow members of M31, the thirty-first group to serve in Moldova since the Peace Corps began operations there in 1993. There were fifty-nine of us in Philadelphia, five of whom would drop out during training and many more in the following months.

Together, we served in four Peace Corps programs: Champa's group for English education, mine for community and organizational development, a third to promote health education, and a fourth to assist small businesses. As in all of the sixty-three countries in which nearly 7,000 Peace Corps volunteers then served, our host country had requested the assistance and helped develop the programs.

Since President Kennedy and Sargent Shriver started the Peace Corps in 1961, more than 220,000 Americans had served in 140 countries. New countries joined the list from time to time, such as Vietnam when we were beginning our service, and others dropped off for political or budgetary reasons, or because they had economically "graduated," like Brazil, Hungary, South Korea, and Turkey.

Many volunteers still taught English, as they had since the beginning, but now they also worked to control HIV-AIDS, promote women entrepreneurs, combat global warming, and provide other assistance that reflected changing needs in the developing world. Volunteer selection had become more competitive. Although there were still plenty of liberal arts graduates in their early twenties, many volunteers now had considerable job skills and work experience, and they were more reflective of America's diversity. Our own group was white, black, Hispanic, and Asian, gay and straight, young and old, born in the United States or somewhere else.

Before we arrived in Philadelphia, all of us were required to study the agency's mission and protocols. During two busy days in hotel conference rooms, we reviewed this material and more, including a "Let Girls Learn" program championed by Michelle Obama, who spoke to us through a video. We had a long session on sexual assault, a topic we'd also cover repeatedly in Moldova — a response, no doubt, to widely publicized criticism a few years earlier from women volunteers who said the Peace Corps didn't stand behind them after they were raped. Our trainers in Philadelphia were Peace Corps employees who had served as volunteers in Ethiopia, Cape Verde, Romania, and Morocco. They mixed serious presentations with lighter activities to help us bond with each other, encouraging us to hang out together but also to avoid getting drunk or into trouble — a message we'd hear again and again in Moldova. Our last activity at staging was to form a circle with everyone facing out. The trainer told us to close our eyes and visualize ourselves in Moldova, working together and dedicating our lives to service for the next two years.

"We are now connected to each other," she said, "about to embark on a journey that will change our lives." She let the silence linger, then told us to open our eyes and get ready for our big day tomorrow.

The next morning we boarded two buses that took us from Philadelphia to Kennedy Airport in New York, passing the Statue of Liberty and the New York City skyline along the way. It took a long time for our group to check in for our Lufthansa flight to Munich and then on to Chişinău, Moldova's capital. As we waited with our bulging bags, almost everyone worried about the weight limit, and a few people had to pay excess baggage charges. However, we all made it through. After eating a final American meal of overpriced sandwiches from an airport kiosk, Champa and I boarded with our new friends, settling in to watch movies and doze along the way. In Munich, several people changed into better clothes for our arrival in Chişinău since we'd been told the local news media might be there to cover us.

When we landed at Chişinău and went inside to retrieve our luggage, we learned that Lufthansa had not loaded all of the bags onto the plane in Munich since there were so many of them, and they were all so heavy. Both of my bags showed up on the carousel, but Champa got only one of hers, and some trainees didn't get any, although we all had our carry-ons. The head of administration for Peace Corps Moldova was inside the terminal and told us not to worry. This happened regularly, he said, and the bags would come in a day or two. He turned out to be right. It was our "welcome to Moldova moment," and we hadn't even gotten our passports stamped yet.

As we emerged into the terminal, some of Moldova's current Peace Corps volunteers waved signs and cheered for us. They were our group mentors with whom we'd been communicating for weeks by e-mail and on an M31 Facebook page. Interacting like this reminded me of the incoming freshmen at Duke and other universities who check each other out online before coming to campus. I was doing the same thing at the age of sixty-three.

The mentors loaded us and our luggage onto buses, and we drove to our hotel in downtown Chişinău. Over the years, Champa and I had stayed in more than our share of cheap hotels around the world, so we weren't expecting luxury, but the Hotel Turist was an especially grim Soviet relic with tiny rooms, aging décor, and a receptionist who treated guests as an intrusion.

Fortunately, it had a nice patio connected to Andy's Pizza restaurant, a popular chain in Chişinău. Tired from our journey and excited to finally be "in country," we sat outside with our mentors and members of the Peace Corps staff, ate pizzas, and drank Cokes. We then went into a cramped room where the new Peace Corps country director for Moldova welcomed us and began an orientation that would continue through the next day. As heads began sagging around the room, she cut the meeting short and suggested we go to our rooms and crash.

Our orientation the next day was at ASEM, a relatively modern building where we would gather throughout our two-month training for weekly "hub site" sessions that brought together all four groups from the neighboring villages where they were dispersed. Still groggy from jet lag, we received our first language lessons: basic expressions in Romanian. The Peace Corps doctor spoke at the first of many sessions she would lead concerning the dangers posed by the local water supply, sexually transmitted diseases, and other topics.

We met the program officers who led our technical training and the security officer who spoke to us regularly about everything from avoiding bar fights to how the Peace Corps would evacuate us in an emergency. We were given some Moldovan money, local SIM cards for our cell phones, and wallet cards with emergency phone numbers.

We also got our first glimpse of Chişinău, a city all but unknown to Americans but still a European capital with about 650,000 people. Its Soviet-era architecture was utilitarian and drab, but Chişinău also had shops, restaurants, parks, and statues. I would come to know the city well over the next two years and to enjoy its laid-back charms; although, I never fell in love with it as I had with Kathmandu, which is far more picturesque.

On the third day, our groups left for their villages on the outskirts of Chişinău. Champa headed for a larger village called Costeşti while my group went to Bardar and Ruseştii Noi, two smaller villages a few miles away. I was assigned to Bardar along with five trainees with whom I would share my language class.

Our van dropped me off at the home of an older couple with several grandchildren, two of whom were staying with them during the summer. Their house was modest but was equipped with a television, Wi-Fi, and a washing machine. Most importantly, they had running water in the bathroom, so I wouldn't need to use an outhouse or take bucket showers in the backyard. I had my own bedroom with a fold-out couch, a few drawers in their dresser, and a desk for my laptop. My new host mother welcomed me with a meal, and I began to settle in.

She and the others treated me well, but I couldn't speak Romanian, and they knew no English. It was difficult to communicate, and the mother didn't seem very interested in trying. Her husband stayed in the house's garage all day and barely spoke to me, even after I wandered over several times to try to interact. Their two grandsons were friendlier. They rode their bicycles as they showed me around the neighborhood, but I felt lonely eating my meals alone, usually by myself at the kitchen table while I did my language homework. I was so exhausted from my classes that I didn't have a lot of energy anyway, but I wished the family, which was supposed to be a "host family," treated me like more than a tenant paying rent. The arrangement was OK for a couple of months, I figured, but I hoped it wasn't a harbinger of things to come.

A couple of weeks after we arrived, I finished dinner and was working in my room when I heard people weeping outside my door. The next afternoon the Peace Corps housing director called to tell me that my host mother was very sick and needed me to move out immediately. I left my class to walk back to the empty house, repack my bags, and leave an encouraging note for her before I was picked up by the Peace Corps van and driven to a new home, about which I knew nothing. I wished the best for my host mother but, unexpectedly, was about to benefit from her misfortune. The Peace Corps had upgraded me.

Until then, I had the longest walk to school of anyone in my group, along an uphill path that got very muddy when it rained. My new home, by contrast, was one minute from the school. It was much bigger than before with a spacious garden, abundant fruit trees, and grapevines overhanging an outdoor dining table.

Vladimir and Maria were my new host parents, a phrase we used loosely since Maria was the same age as me and Vladimir only a few years older. Empty nesters with a half-empty house, just like Champa and me, they were curious to have an American stay with them. When Maria showed me three vacant rooms at the end of the house and asked which ones I liked, Vladimir suggested I use all three. One was a bedroom with a beautiful dresser and a computer with Wi-Fi. The second was a study with an exercise bike and a private porch. The third was the family's ceremonial room, common in Moldova, with a dining table and chairs, a large bookcase, elegant glassware, family photos, and a beautiful carpet. I ended up using only the first two rooms, but even those were more spacious and luxurious than anything I'd expected for my Peace Corps service. The only thing missing was a neon sign flashing "Posh Corps."

Both of my hosts were much friendlier than the previous family, and the food they prepared for me was delicious. Maria was a superb cook, producing specialties such as *placenta* (savory stuffed pies), *mamaliga* (like polenta), borscht, barbecued pork, stuffed peppers, cabbage rolls, and homemade cheese. Summer fruits and vegetables were in season, so she picked tomatoes, beans, cucumbers, raspberries, and strawberries before dinner. We drank cool glasses of *compot* prepared with berries, peaches, apricots, or apples from the garden. Sometimes we drank wine from three large barrels in the cellar.

I spent many happy evenings sitting with Vladimir and Maria under the vines as we ate dinner, sipped wine, and tried our best to communicate even though they spoke no English, and I was terrible at Romanian. We shared photos of our grandchildren and, as my language slowly improved, compared our lives and countries. They had wanted to be among the original hosts, I later learned, but weren't sure their rooms would be available. Luckily for me, they ended up on top of the backup list.

Just outside their gate was a memorial honoring local heroes who died fighting for the Soviet Union in World War II. I often waved hello to the outstretched arm of the heroic soldier as I walked after breakfast to the school named in honor of a prominent local artist.

The school year was winding down when we arrived. Graduating students came for a few final days to take placement exams to determine whether they could attend a university. The Peace Corps rented three rooms in the school — one for a classroom, one for storage, and one for a lounge. Our teacher was a 33-year-old Moldovan woman, Diana, who taught English at a university and somehow found time to teach Romanian to Peace Corps trainees every year. We were lucky to be assigned to her. Diana was a gifted teacher — skillful, lively, and determined to help us succeed even though our training period was several weeks shorter than in years past.

Romanian, a romance language, is similar to Italian, French, and Spanish. It shares the same alphabet and many words with those languages as well as with English. I found it easy to understand the meaning of *discuta, studia, dansa, telefon*a, or *permite*. As a *voluntar*, I could describe myself as *activ, sociabil, inteligent,* or *optimist.*

All of this was far more familiar than when I first learned Nepali years earlier. Nepali is Sanskrit-based, with a different alphabet and syntax than English. Verbs usually come at the end of sentences. The literal translation of "What is your name?" is "Your name what is?" I initially struggled to get my head (and mouth) around such strange structures.

Once I got the hang of Nepali, though, it was predictable, without a lot of irregular verbs or other exceptions. Romanian was the opposite: easy enough for an American to grasp but much harder to master. The words fit together in sentences similar to English, and even more like French, which I once spoke fairly well. But the verbs fell into numerous groups, each conjugated differently. Almost every noun is masculine or feminine, and I had to memorize these, too, along with endless exceptions. Accent marks changed the pronunciation and meaning of *s, t, a,* and *i.*

I felt my age as I tried to memorize all of this. My brain couldn't hold the information as easily as it had before. I made flashcards, wrote worksheets, and tried everything except squeezing my notebook against my head. It was frustrating when my younger colleagues would hear something once and remember it. I had previously been able to do that, too. Now, like an aging pitcher trying to compensate for his slowing fastball, I focused intently during our four-hour language classes, woke up early to study, and then studied again in the evening. This schedule left me little time for anything else.

The six members of our group sat side by side, hour after hour, in the summer heat that sometimes topped one hundred degrees despite our oscillating fan. Tom was an attorney from Berkeley and a few years older than me. Shannon was in her thirties and from

New York's fashion industry. There were also three guys who just graduated from college: William from Kentucky, David from Connecticut, and Reggie from North Carolina.

We were like the soldiers in an old Hollywood war movie who were forced to live and work together despite their divergent backgrounds. For the most part, we got along, sharing laughs and helping each other out, but not always. One person regularly asked questions that threw our lessons off track. Another was entranced with obscure grammar points. Another provided running commentary in English while forming a sentence in Romanian: "*El este* — no, that's wrong — *fericit* — wait, that's "happy," right? — *El este* — how do you say that again? ..." Tom and I sometimes annoyed the others with dated cultural references, which they matched with rap lyrics and memorized dialogues from *South Park*.

More importantly, I had to take care, not always successfully, to avoid referring to my prior work experiences, which my younger colleagues could not match, and to appear engaged with discussions aimed mostly at people new to the workplace. If I talked about my experiences leading large projects and managing teams of people, the others might see me as arrogant. If I asked them what they had learned as a dorm advisor or in a class group, it could look like I was condescending. If I kept quiet and let others take the lead, I could appear indifferent. I liked my colleagues and admired what they were doing, but the interactions could be tricky for me and some of the other older volunteers.

For about a week, our group grew to seven people after we added a trainee who'd been unhappy in a neighboring village. However, she soon got sick and returned home. This left us with the original six, which was still more than the four or five in most other groups.

Following our daily lunch break, we'd usually travel by van to the village where the rest of our group lived. There we had "tech classes" where our program manager, current volunteers, and guest speakers prepared us to serve in our communities. On Thursdays, we'd wake early and travel on public minibuses and city trolleys to our hub site in Chişinău, where all of M31 gathered for full-day sessions packed with classes on everything from Moldovan history and traditions to health, security, Peace Corps policies, and, just in case we'd forgotten from the previous week, alcohol abuse, a message aimed mainly at the majority of our group in their twenties.

Before Champa and I joined the Peace Corps at the age of sixty-three, people often asked us how we'd feel to be surrounded by volunteers younger than our two sons. Many of our fellow volunteers were indeed young, and most of them were smart, enthusiastic, and fun to be around. Yet the two of us were hardly outliers. Fourteen of the fifty-eight people in our training group — nearly one in four — were fifty or older.

Regardless of their ages, the trainees of M31 were connected to the internet and aware of world events, notably the upcoming election between Hillary Clinton and Donald Trump. Since we were all so busy and focused on our training, the world often seemed far away except when something momentous happened, as with shootings at an Orlando gay nightclub that killed forty-nine people. All of us were outraged when we heard about the tragedy, and our country director discussed it at the beginning of our weekly hub site meeting, reminding us we were there to promote "peace, friendship, and understanding" — the very values challenged by what happened in Orlando. Even though we were far away, she said, "Know you are in the right place at the right time."

As we shared a moment of silence, I found myself thinking back to my volunteer days in Nepal when my only news sources were a shortwave radio and a weekly international edition of *Newsweek*. My village postmaster looked forward to the magazine's arrival as much as I did since we'd flip through it together before I went home. One week, the *Newsweek* cover showed bloated bodies strewn in the jungles of Guyana. It was the Jonestown massacre, where hundreds of American cult members drank poison and died. The postmaster looked at the photos and asked me to explain how this could happen. I didn't know what to say. Years later, when I was in Bangladesh on the day of the 9/11 attacks, I felt the same way. I stood in the Dhaka airport the next morning, one of the few Westerners there, staring at the television monitors and watching the footage from New York and Washington. Once again, I felt very American and very far from home.

So I should have known what to expect emotionally when I heard the news about Orlando and during other memorable moments that would follow while we were in Moldova. But familiarity was not a vaccination. It was still unsettling to watch from a distance as historical events changed my country. I could discuss them with Champa and the other trainees when we had a moment between language classes. Soon enough, though, we'd be back to memorizing the Romanian words for fruits and vegetables or learning how to conjugate the third-person plural form of a verb.

Even in Moldova, I was still an American, but, simultaneously, I was an American in Moldova. Conjugating *that* wasn't always easy.

Sometimes we left our classrooms to talk with people in the community. In Bardar, we went to speak with Ecaterina, the long-time librarian of the children's room in the modest library tucked into the back of the village cultural center. Ecaterina described how her annual budget included less than $500 to buy books and provide programs. This amount was enough for only a few Romanian-language books to supplement the aging Russian volumes on her shelves.

The same was true next door at Bardar's town hall, where we met with the mayor. He described his wish to expand the village's sewer system, install street lights, build a new daycare center, and improve the rutted roads. Yet, as in the library, he had almost no money to do this.

Likewise in the village of Dereneu where we met with the mayor and a Peace Corps volunteer who was posted there. The mayor greeted us with a traditional Moldovan welcome of bread and salt. Afterward, she and a colleague described their struggles to help the village grow and respond to community needs.

At the end of our training, our group organized events for the two villages where we'd been living, to thank our host families and communities. We started by cleaning up the main park in Ruseştii Noi. Local residents helped us to transform the park in less than three hours from an eyesore with overgrown grass into a place where families were strolling the next evening. In Bardar, we organized a cultural festival and introduced them to American baseball, football, hula hoops, and swing dancing. Both events went well, and we were pleased to contribute for a change instead of just discussing development in a classroom.

Champa was in Costeşti, a few miles away. Like me, she had a nice living situation with her own bedroom in a house with a modern kitchen, bathroom, Wi-Fi, and a dining room. Even though she was near me on a map, no public transportation connected us, so one of us had to travel into Chişinău and then back out again if we wanted to get together during the weekend. We'd known when we applied that we would probably be separated during training, and the arrangement undoubtedly facilitated our language learning since we had more time to study and couldn't speak English or Nepali together at night.

Nonetheless, we missed each other, especially as the weeks wore on. We'd been separated before when Champa traveled by herself to Nepal, or I had business trips, but never for so long. We didn't complain. We knew we were lucky compared to most of the other trainees and, especially, to the many Moldovans whose spouses lived abroad. Champa and I spoke by phone every morning and evening, and we remained in touch with our family back home. Nonetheless, we were counting the days until we reunited.

We soon learned where we would be living after we completed our training. On a sunny afternoon exactly one year after I'd walked away from my job at Duke, we gathered with the other trainees in a parking lot outside our training building in Chişinău. We were blindfolded and guided one by one to spots on a giant chalk map of Moldova. Then we were handed envelopes and told to remove our blindfolds. We looked at the name of the village or city on our envelope, which corresponded to where we stood on the map.

The name on the envelopes for Champa and me was Ialoveni (pronounced Yeh-lo-ven). It was a big town close to Chişinău through which we'd passed several times on the road to our villages. I would work with the district government there, and Champa would teach at a school one block away. We'd be living with a family that was currently hosting an older trainee in the health group, who had told us even before she knew we were moving there how much she loved the family. A few days later, Champa and I had a get-acquainted visit with them and briefly toured our future work sites with our partners.

After a few more weeks of intensive language training, we finally reached the finish line — or, more accurately, the starting line. Two of the four groups, including mine, wrapped up just before the official Peace Corps swearing-in ceremony. Champa's group of teachers and the health education group continued their training for two extra weeks, which gave them more time to practice teaching before they, too, departed for their posts. Everyone took the language exam, with our Bardar group scoring among the highest. My own score was better than I'd expected, confirming Diana's reassurances that I had been doing fine.

Our group celebrated with a visit to a zoo located incongruously on the outskirts of Bardar. It turned out to be more like a petting zoo, with lots of goats and chickens along with some ostriches and peacocks, but we were all so happy to be finished that we enjoyed it just the same. Well, all but one of our younger members enjoyed it. A few days before the swearing-in ceremony, he was kicked out for drinking and misbehaving.

Peace Corps countries make a big deal about these swearing-in ceremonies, which mark the culmination of a rigorous training process and the beginning of a volunteer's service for two years. One of my most painful memories of Nepal was of the ceremony I attended as a guest for the group that entered a year behind us. It was at the Yellow Pagoda, then one of Kathmandu's better hotels. Everyone was dressed up, including dignitaries from both countries. No sooner had the new volunteers repeated the Peace Corps oath and lowered their hands than an older guy from my group walked to the center of the room and started smashing drinking glasses on the floor. Before anyone knew what was happening, he lay down and rolled on the broken glass, freaking out in front of the new volunteers who'd just sworn to live in remote villages like him.

"Oh my God, what have I just done?" you could see them thinking.

The Nepali officials were stunned, and the Americans watched in horror as several people finally pulled him away from the broken glass. Several of us took turns staying with him around the clock, essentially a 24/7 suicide watch, until someone accompanied him back to the States. Needless to say, he never returned.

Nothing so dramatic happened at our ceremony in Chişinău, which was attended by a similar mix of dignitaries along with our host families and work partners. The Peace Corps director and the American ambassador took turns swearing us in, and we heard speeches from several Moldovan officials, as well as from five of the new volunteers, who spoke in either Romanian or Russian.

Local television crews covered the event, which included performances of Moldovan songs and dances by some of the new volunteers. There was a reception and a final business meeting where the volunteers and new host families signed agreements about their living arrangements. Most of the families would prepare three meals a day, but some volunteers chose to make breakfast or lunch on their own. Champa and I were exceptions in that our new host family preferred for us to do all of our own cooking, which was what we wanted, too. After the contracts were signed and the final photos snapped, the new volunteers loaded their suitcases into vehicles and headed with their host families for their new lives across Moldova.

I moved in with Champa for her final two weeks since our rooms in Ialoveni were still occupied by our friend in the health education group. While Champa worked, I studied Romanian, worked on my blog, and made a video of a series of student performances organized by the volunteers in Champa's group and their partner teachers. Their Moldovan students sang American songs, told jokes in English, danced, and played Twister — a fun way to learn the English words for colors and body parts. Champa and I also attended two birthday parties, one for the older son in her host family and the other for the son of their friends. Both were feasts with lots of wine which led to dancing and laughing long into the evening.

Champa and I always felt welcome in our villages and were embraced by both of our host families, even though they couldn't understand why an older American couple would leave their family for more than two years to serve in a country where they didn't know anyone.

Perhaps we were CIA agents?

Perhaps we had committed a crime and fled the country?

Volunteerism, civil society, and a belief in the value of diversity are much stronger ideals in the United States than in some other parts of the world.

Back home at this time, racial tensions were flaring, and Donald Trump was stoking the fears of white voters in his presidential campaign. Yet, despite these problems, most Americans still embraced the idea of diverse people living together and celebrating each other's differences.

Not so in Moldova, where one woman asked me during training why I married Champa instead of a white woman. When I responded it was because I love her, she said she could understand this, since she liked Champa herself, yet she still wondered why I wouldn't marry someone white, since that was obviously preferable. She went on to share her disdain for people of color, saying it would be a huge mistake for a white person to marry one. "Black no good," she said in English. Her racism was blunt and, to my ears, disgusting, but it reflected a culture more homogenous than our own.

Conversations like this made me feel immense admiration for my black Peace Corps colleagues who served with patience and grace in the face of this prejudice, providing a powerful example with their very presence. Similarly, most of our LGBTQ members chose to stay in the closet instead of confronting Moldova's rampant and occasionally violent homophobia.

I felt only a tiny measure of prejudice myself when people asked about my religion. Moldova had an ugly history during World War II of helping Nazis exterminate Jews across the country. There had been a small revival of Jewish culture in Moldova in recent years, and I never felt any personal danger about coming from a Jewish family. Yet, I did learn to expect an awkward moment of surprise whenever I shared my background. People would pause and look at each other around the table before nodding and smiling as if to say: *We think you're OK even though this is weird.* On the other hand, when Champa responded, "Hindu," her response was so far beyond their understanding that the conversation barely stalled.

We came face to face with all of this during our training, right up until a Peace Corps van came early in the morning to pick us up at Champa's home in Costeşti and drop off our luggage at our new house in Ialoveni. She and I then continued on to Chişinău for a conference, returning that afternoon to begin unpacking. Now, after more than two months of studying a new language, learning a new culture, enduring high temperatures and, until recently, living apart, the preliminaries were over. We could begin what we'd come so far to attempt.

Our trip to Nepal and our drive across the United States were far behind us. My job at Duke was a fading memory. Our families in America and Nepal remained close in our hearts but were far away. Finally, we would begin serving for two years as Peace Corps volunteers. Still, we had no idea whether this would actually work out.

CHAPTER 7

BEGINNING OUR SERVICE

I aloveni was bigger than the villages where most of the other volunteers were posted. It had supermarkets, banks, shops, an active cultural center, and several modest restaurants. Our host family, the Bordeis, lived near the city's largest employer, an ice cream factory. We moved into their second floor, where we had a small bedroom, a workroom, and a storage room along with a private bathroom with a washing machine. There was a dishwasher in the kitchen downstairs adjacent to a dining room, a living room with leather couches, and three bedrooms. Downstairs, a cellar was stocked with homemade wine and glass jars stuffed with peppers, pickled cucumbers, and other bounties from the garden, which included a small greenhouse. We didn't have a television or air conditioning, and a family dog barked too often in his outdoor pen below our window, but the house was grander than we'd expected. It was "Posh Corps."

Two people lived there with us. Alisa, in her late twenties, spoke excellent English and worked as an accountant for her uncle's company. She kept an eye on our other housemate, her grandmother, or *Bunica*, who was 85 years old when we arrived. Alisa's parents Mihai and Nina lived in an apartment nearby with their son, Andrei. Mihai worked as a commercial driver, and Nina was the chief accountant for the district government, where I was working. Andrei bought and sold building supplies. All of them toiled for little pay but remained in Moldova, unlike their third child, Tatiana, who studied and worked in Paris like so many other Moldovans seeking a better life abroad. We paid the Bordeis a bit more than $100 per month in rent, plus utilities, but our relationship blossomed over the next two years into something much richer than landlord and tenant.

I was assigned to work with Igor, a young economist at the district government office, or Consiliul Raional, a Soviet-style cement structure about a kilometer from our house. His small team wrote grants and oversaw projects involving roads, water systems, and the like. I shared his office on the fourth floor. Igor and others along his dark corridor usually kept their doors closed, seemingly to discourage any citizen who might approach for help.

The council's president invited me to join his weekly staff meetings with his department heads for the police, education, social services, cultural events, and other units. They gathered in a room with a large map showing Moldova connected to Romania, as it was before the Soviet Union took it over in 1940. The map signaled this was a pro-Western part of Moldova, where people favored reunification with Romania. During the next two years, Champa and I would visit other regions where people opposed this idea and mainly spoke Russian, which most people in Ialoveni used only as a second language. The map included Transnistria along Moldova's eastern border. The pro-Russian region across the Nistru River had been operating autonomously since 1992, with its own government, flag, army, and currency. As we were learning, Moldova was complex despite its small size. Even within Ialoveni, political parties jostled for power, as did the district government and the primăria, or mayor's office for the city.

My job was to help Igor and his colleagues with new projects. However, there was little money available since Moldova's banking scandal had wiped out about 15 percent of its GDP. The international community had responded by cutting off much of its assistance until the culprits were identified, which never happened over the next two years. Igor's team, like its counterparts in district and village offices across Moldova, ended up competing for tiny grants from various sources, spending weeks preparing detailed proposals to build, say, a section of a water system in a single village rather than the district-wide system they needed.

Everyone on the team was educated and experienced. Since my written Romanian at this point was even more limited than my speaking, I didn't see how I could contribute much to their proposals unless they needed English translations. Instead, I looked for other ways to help, such as by drawing on my communications background to produce a promotional video and an English-language presentation for the president to use when describing Ialoveni to potential foreign investors and partners.

I also assisted the president when he had English-speaking guests, such as when the British ambassador visited. I spent several weeks working with Maria, the head of the family services division, to develop a proposal to bring together social workers and the police to work more cooperatively on cases of domestic abuse. Just as we were about to finalize the proposal, which we developed collaboratively with the country's leading center on domestic abuse, Maria lost interest and backed out for reasons I never fully understood.

I asked Igor for guidance on what to do next, but the only thing that interested him was me tutoring him for free to improve his English and find a better job or leave the country. I organized an English class for him and others on his team and led discussions on themes I assigned; however, Igor wanted me to teach him personally since he was my official partner, and we shared an office. As he pestered me to review vocabulary lists or practice dialogues, I wondered whether this was the real reason he had requested a volunteer. In any case, it wasn't why the Peace Corps had sent me there or why I had become a volunteer. Before long, I began looking around the city for another place where I might be more useful.

I found it at the public library, which I'd visited with Champa shortly after arriving in town. It was named for Petre Ştefănucă, a folklorist and local hero who died in a Soviet gulag. Since several members of my Peace Corps group had been posted to village libraries, I'd made a point to visit ours with Champa. The director, Valentina, greeted us and invited me to return to teach a class. A few weeks later, she followed up and asked me to take the lead with Hour of Code, an international initiative to teach young people basic coding skills, which Moldovan libraries were being encouraged to join.

Even though I had no coding experience, I told Valentina I'd give it a try, figuring I could use online videos and websites to teach myself the material before the class. Valentina organized an afternoon meeting for local kids where I showed some of the site's inspirational videos and got them started writing mock code for the computer game Minecraft, one of several programs offered in Romanian. The students were soon clicking away, instructing their characters to move in different directions, shear sheep, and search for treasure. Several finished the 14 tasks in less than an hour. All were engrossed, giving me high fives as I walked around to help them. Even before we finished, the librarians were excited and asked me to create an ongoing Hour of Code club, which we scheduled for Wednesday afternoons.

The next week we wrote code for a *Star Wars* game, then a module based on the movie *Frozen*. As the class continued over the next weeks and months, I sought out other free online resources. My kids logged onto Khan Academy to learn the basics of the popular programming language JavaScript. They mastered the simple commands to create ellipses and rectangles, which they then resized and moved around their screens to form snowmen and robots. A few weeks later, we moved on to WordPress, which they used to create simple websites, such as Mihai's introduction to his family and Victor's humorous salute to the local wine industry. ("I am 13 years old. And I love wine. Relax I just joking.")

Coding is a valuable skill in today's world, and, especially in poorer countries like Moldova, it can open the door to the global economy. As someone who spent many years writing about technology and overseeing website projects, I wasn't afraid of coding, but my knowledge was shallow, and the kids eventually overtook me. My own role evolved into identifying free resources and encouraging them while training the library's program manager, Lidia, to run the class without me.

My biggest disappointment was my inability to attract more girls to the class. The librarians helped me reach out to a nearby school, but we had little success, even when I offered to teach a separate coding class for girls. A few came to some of the first classes, but they often clicked to dance sites on Facebook or YouTube. Similarly, some boys proved more interested in shooting aliens and playing video games than in coding. All of the librarians were women, so I expected them to be enthusiastic about recruiting girls to coding and, later, to robotics, but I was the only one who kept pushing. One of our missions as Peace Corps volunteers, especially while Michelle Obama was First Lady, was to encourage girls to pursue STEM fields — science, technology, engineering, and math. I agreed with the importance of this and even ordered science kits online for my own granddaughters back home while we were away.

As our coding class moved into its second and third month, I ended up with a small group of seventh- and eighth-grade boys. They were great kids, although they could become rambunctious, occasionally tackling and punching each other when they weren't working at the library's computer stations. They also liked to blast YouTube videos while they were typing. "Thunder," the Imagine Dragons song, is now etched permanently into my brain. ("Thunder, feel the thunder, lightning and the thunder. Thunder, feel the thunder.") Almost all of them hoped to pursue programming as a career, which they and their parents perceived as one of the few ways they could latch onto the international economy. I'd have more luck later attracting girls to robotics.

The coding class was part of a larger effort by the library to redefine itself in a world where local residents downloaded books and searched for information online. Like many libraries elsewhere, including in our country, it had begun emphasizing its role in providing expertise and bringing people together. Its transition was even more challenging since library budgets and salaries were tiny in Moldova. Buildings were old, and collections dated back to Soviet times. Moldova's libraries had almost no resources to buy books, much less comfy sofas or cappuccino machines. However, under Valentina's leadership, Ialoveni's had recently launched a film animation class, an art club that produced crafts from recycled materials, and a workshop to teach modern advocacy techniques. It was adding programs for people with special needs, such as with a Braille collection, and reaching out to its community through an active Facebook site.

Novateca, a program supported by the Bill and Melinda Gates Foundation in partnership with USAID, was the driving force behind this modernization push for Moldova's libraries, building on similar programs in neighboring Romania and Ukraine. During the previous five years, it had provided thousands of computers and other resources, trained librarians across the country, increased public support, and promoted a more expansive vision of their role. I became a fan of its work and befriended its director, Evan, himself a former Peace Corps volunteer in Turkmenistan. I also came to admire Valentina and her team, who were doing so much with so little, each earning less money in a year than what many American librarians make in a couple of weeks.

As I spent more time there, my program director at the Peace Corps suggested I leave my unproductive post at the district government and join the library full-time, which I did after meeting with Igor, the president, and others to reassure them I was still available to help with grant proposals or other needs that might arise.

In addition to Valentina, my main partner was Lidia, whose dedication was exceeded only by her energy and eagerness to try new things. Lidia was a few years younger than me, with grandchildren of her own. She probably would have been a successful engineer or entrepreneur if she'd been born twenty years later in America. After some limited training from Novateca, she'd become an enthusiastic producer of simple animated films, teaching students and librarians from other villages how to use "stop motion" to move images around a screen and accompany the action with narration and music. She organized community programs, such as one that taught Ialoveni's parents how to protect their children from predators and other potential threats online. As my Hour of Code classes wound down, Lidia was the one who urged me to join her in launching a robotics program, which she'd heard had been a hit at other libraries. I agreed, figuring that if I could handle a computer coding class with no experience in my sixties, I could probably teach robotics, too. It would turn out to be a highlight of my Peace Corps experience.

We applied for and won a small grant from Novateca to purchase several Lego Mindstorms EV3 robotics kits, which students could use to program small robots to roam around the room, pick up objects, avoid collisions, and roar like dinosaurs. Students in the United States and around the world use the same kits, which combine familiar Lego components with a brick-shaped computer. The user programs the brick and snaps it together with the other pieces to create a vehicle that performs different functions. The software is colorful and easy to learn.

Lidia and I started with two weekly robotics classes. We gave our students a brief introduction, and then set them loose on the first program, which told a robot to drive forward, back, and forward again. Before long, they were also making the robots rotate, speed up, or make funny sounds. Word about the program spread, more kids came, and we added a third class and then a fourth, including one for girls. The kids kept coming, with their parents often lingering to watch.

We selected some of the best students to represent the library in a national "sumo bot" competition in Chişinău, where their robot would fight others and try to push them out of a circle, like a sumo wrestler. Our team didn't win, but the kids had fun.

We enrolled them in another competition, this time the "First Lego League" where they'd design and program a robot to carry out a series of tasks within two and a half minutes. That year's theme was hydrodynamics, so the students needed to program their robot to turn a faucet, fix a broken pipe, water a garden, and do other tasks involving water. There weren't real faucets or pipes, of course, just Lego structures representing them. Previous themes had included animals, food, trash, and climate. Our team joined students aged nine to sixteen from eighty countries in the event, which challenged them to think like scientists and engineers. They also had to give a presentation sharing an original solution for a problem involving water. Their overall score assessed their research, presentation, and teamwork skills along with their programming prowess. Novateca gathered teams from across Moldova at the two-day competition at the National Children's Library in Chişinău, treating them to free meals and a hotel stay overnight — the first time many of them had ever stayed in a hotel or without their parents. Music blared, and an electronic scoreboard tracked the action as each team's robot raced to carry out the tasks. Ialoveni's team scored in the middle of the pack but got more points than the boys had expected, so they were proud of their performance.

When they joined the organizers on stage to receive medals, Lidia and I cheered, and Valentina featured them on the library's Facebook site even before they returned home. I doubt any of them will become robotics engineers, but they gained hands-on experience with new technology and related skills such as giving public presentations. They'd selected "Bookworms" as their team name, complete with a logo featuring a wiggling worm, and younger students now hoped to be selected as future Bookworms. Thanks mainly to Lidia's leadership and with some help from me, robotics had become a significant activity at the library, an important victory in its effort to modernize its portfolio and identity.

I made several videos about the robotics team, which we featured on the library's Facebook page and on a community Facebook page read widely within Ialoveni. Thousands of viewers around the city saw how the library was changing. Some came for the first time to enroll their children in the robotics classes or other activities. I also produced a video to entice people to visit the library's collection of English-language books, ranging from Dr. Seuss to Harry Potter, many of which had been donated by former Peace Corps volunteers in the area. I made another video to highlight the library's collection of books that people could download for free onto their smartphones using QR codes, and one in the dramatic style of a Hollywood trailer that summarized its new services.

One of my favorite activities was an English conversation class I organized for advanced students. I'd taught a similar weekly class at the Consiliul Raional but wanted to shift the focus here away from grammar and formal lessons to something more fun. I planned initially to host a weekly book club, but a Moldovan friend who ran an English school downtown suggested I'd be better off using shorter selections that students could download for free and read comfortably within a week.

He was right. Our club ended up reading articles from *The New Yorker* and other sources, all of which I previewed and selected. One week we discussed "You May Want to Marry My Husband," a heart-breaking essay by Amy Krouse Rosenthal that *The New York Times'* "Modern Love" column published ten days before her death from cancer. We listened to the actress Debra Winger reading the essay, which described the devotion of the author's husband and her desire for him to find new happiness after her impending death. The previous week we read "The School," a chilling 2007 article in which C.J. Chivers described a Chechen terrorist attack in the Russian town of Beslan. Before that, we read three essays by humorist David Sedaris, a Walter Isaacson article describing the science behind Mona Lisa's smile, and Atul Gawande's article about how he and other physicians needed to do more to help dying patients. We also discussed travel destinations, teenage anxiety, and even the linguistic implications of emojis.

My students ranged from a Moldovan online journalist to an art student. All spoke English well enough to understand and discuss the articles, and they generally came ready to share their reactions, which fascinated me. Our discussion about the Gawande article, for instance, led to a great exchange about how our two cultures handle death, not only in medical settings but in everyday lives. For our discussion about a Cincinnati Enquirer series on "Seven Days of Heroin," which went on to win a Pulitzer Prize, we were joined online by a friend of mine back in America who lost his son to heroin, leading to a discussion about how different countries handle addiction.

When I wasn't teaching or making videos, I often worked with Lidia on enhancing the library's outreach and communications with the community, which both she and Valentina recognized as essential to attracting more visitors. I'd only been there a few days when Valentina spotted a new Novateca competition, this one for libraries that used infographics. Americans see infographics everywhere — on television and websites, in magazines, even with academic articles or corporate sales reports. In Moldova, institutions are still learning to share information with their stakeholders and to present it attractively to engage their interest.

Lidia and I played around with Piktochart, a free site I'd used during our training. It resembled PowToon, which she'd used for video animations, so she picked it up quickly even though she barely speaks English. We produced a colorful promotional poster for the library, which ended up winning one of Novateca's prizes. When Novateca asked us to organize an infographics training session for librarians from neighboring communities, we were happy to help, teaching them how to create a free account with Piktochart, adapt its templates, use icons, insert data, and transfer their work to websites, blogs, or posters. Novateca sent one of its trainers to help, and a representative from the National Library came as well.

My objective as a Peace Corps volunteer wasn't to do the work myself so much as to train and encourage my Moldovan counterparts to embrace new ideas and take ownership of them. During my last several weeks of service, I scaled back my day-to-day involvement with the robotics classes, putting the reins firmly in Lidia's hands. I also encouraged Valentina to find someone else from the community to take over the coding classes, which she did before I left. I preferred to work with them as partners from the beginning of any new project, but sometimes it made more sense for me to do most of the work myself at the beginning, and then turn it over.

That's what happened with the library's website and blog, which I helped my colleagues replace with a new version that was more attractive, informative for users, less expensive, and easier for the library to manage. Having worked on several web redesign projects back home, I knew how to guide them through the process of organizing their data into categories that put user needs ahead of internal organizational lines. I then crafted everything into a site that featured the library's many new services and activities. The website also highlighted the library's popular Facebook site and its blog, which was well-written but rarely visited. We added an automated calendar to feature upcoming events, a snappy new map with directions, a video section, and an online exhibit about the library's namesake. We did all of this on a free Romanian-language template offered by WordPress, so Lidia and the others could easily maintain it.

I followed the same philosophy with writing grant proposals, which have become as important in Moldova as they are for public institutions and nonprofit organizations in the United States. With official budgets so tight, Ialoveni's library and others were looking increasingly to external funding sources, especially for projects.

Lidia received training from Novateca on modern forms of fund-raising and advocacy, mastering it so well that Novateca recruited her to train librarians elsewhere. When our robotics program needed several hundred dollars to buy new equipment, she worked with several boys on the Bookworms team to write a proposal for a local competition giving small amounts to youth groups. She asked me to write part of the grant, but I limited my role to discussing the idea, talking through the budget, and proofreading their draft language. She and the boys needed to do the work themselves. Sure enough, they prepared an excellent proposal, got the money, and kept the robotics program moving forward.

One of my favorite moments at the library was creating an exhibit about North Carolina with one of the other librarians, Stela. It featured brochures about the Wright Brothers Monument in Kitty Hawk, the Biltmore mansion in Asheville, the NASCAR museum in Charlotte, and attractions across the Triangle region where we live. It also offered information about where to taste wine, go fishing, or ride in a hot-air balloon. Before we came to Moldova, we gathered the brochures at the North Carolina tourism office on Interstate 85, just south of the Virginia border. I'd brought them with me and had finally found a way to put them to good use. I didn't expect many of the library's visitors to actually visit North Carolina, but I knew they would be interested to see where Champa and I came from.

It was also fun to watch my colleagues interact, as I had during our weekly staff meetings at the district government. As someone who attended thousands of meetings while in the United States, I was a connoisseur of how people behave in professional gatherings. Here in Moldova, I found similar behavior, such as the woman who pretended to participate but kept checking her smartphone, or the two people who whispered to each other, or the curmudgeon who rolled his eyes when someone made a comment. Even though I couldn't understand everything people said in Romanian, their body language was familiar, although more formal and polite than back home. In both countries, a meeting could include someone bemused (or irritated) by everything. One person might speak with a rhetorical flourish, while another mumbled in a monotone from a notebook. Some people addressed the entire room while others spoke only to the person leading the meeting. Similarly, if a meeting dragged on too long, people might start staring ahead, flipping through papers, or glancing at their watches regardless of whether the conversation was in English or Romanian. One big difference in Moldova was that everyone was called *Domnul* or *Doamnă* — Sir or Madam. When it came time to schedule their next meeting, they were more likely to check paper daybooks than a calendar on their smartphone.

One of the best things about meetings in Moldova was that they had fewer PowerPoint presentations, although I did see lots of people sneaking peeks at Facebook. In turn, they probably noticed the older guy from North Carolina glancing frequently at the Google Translate app on his iPhone.

CHAPTER 8

PROJECTS BELOW THE RADAR

I was doing more than working at Ialoveni's district government and library, which were my official Peace Corps posts. During my two years as a volunteer, I also encouraged young people to become entrepreneurs, assisted the country's tourist industry, taught journalism, provided media training for scientists, produced a music video, and wrote more than 150 posts for my blog. I knew our time in Moldova was limited and tried to make the most of every day, although my schedule was less packed than when I'd run a news office.

Champa and I usually got home in the late afternoon and were able to cook and enjoy dinner together while we sipped some Moldovan house wine and watched YouTube videos of Stephen Colbert and other comedians from the previous night. Our situation differed from that of some of our Peace Corps colleagues, especially those in smaller villages, who complained they had little to do. On our group's private Facebook site, some said they were binge-watching *Game of Thrones* or traveling to the capital on weekends to hang out together. Almost all of them were doing good work at their posts and contributing more than they may have realized, but Champa and I knew how fortunate we were to be posted in a place where we could feel so productively busy.

During our training, one of the previous volunteers told us about Diamond Challenge, an international competition based in Delaware that encourages high school students to become entrepreneurs and develop business plans for a profit-making or socially worthwhile venture. Nearly 2,000 students worldwide had participated in Diamond Challenge since 2012. Moldovan students had done well, recently sending two teams to the international finals. One Moldovan team won the grand prize in the social venture competition with its project to connect expatriate Moldovan workers with teenagers back home who could help care for their aging parents. Another Moldovan team won the social impact prize a year earlier with its plan to produce clothing with reflective thread that could be seen at night by drivers traveling on dark rural roads.

I'd worked with entrepreneurship programs back in Durham, so I volunteered to mentor one of the new teams. I ended up with three wonderful young people from Chişinâu — Elizabet, Lucia, and Victor. The group already had an idea to produce personalized comic books to help children learn about science. Lucia was a gifted graphic artist, Victor was a computer whiz, and Elizabet was interested in business and marketing, so they made a great team.

We met weekly to refine their plan, guided by Diamond Challenge modules on market analysis, customer needs, pricing, and other topics. Lucia considered dozens of fonts and color schemes before settling on a design for their company logo. Victor created a computer demo showing how the comic books could be personalized. Elizabet took the lead in drafting a business plan and proposal. The Diamond Challenge judges chose Team BUK as one of the finalists for the pitch competition to determine the winner.

I led a workshop for all of Moldova's finalist teams, helping them sharpen their public speaking skills and presentations. Together we watched videos from sources ranging from the television show *Shark Tank* to Guy Kawasaki, the renowned Silicon Valley entrepreneur. Since they would have to give their pitches in English, I also showed the students a hilarious video excerpt from *The Pink Panther* in which Steve Martin plays a Frenchman struggling to pronounce "hamburger." I loved interacting with the students, who were overflowing with ideas and brave enough to present them in a foreign language on a stage in front of a group of judges. All hoped to win the $1,000 local prize and, even more, to travel to Delaware for the international competition in one of the two categories: for-profit business or social venture.

A few weeks later, they gathered at the Dreamups entrepreneurship center in the capital, a high-tech space adorned with inspirational posters from the likes of Mark Zuckerberg and Steve Jobs, and with television reporters joining parents and supporters in the audience. When the judges narrowed the list of teams in the business category to just two, we hoped to hear Team BUK announced as the winner, but that honor went instead to a team whose idea was to install speed bumps in parking lots to slow down drivers. My three students were gracious in applauding for the winners but fought back tears. I was disappointed, too. Still, it had been a great experience for them and taught them not only how to be an entrepreneur but also to create a business plan, work together, and meet deadlines. I was inspired by their creativity and dedication. Later, I would help Lucia land a job as a graphic artist for a web firm in Moldova.

The following year, when I gave a similar presentation to another group of finalists, I opened with a moving speech Oprah Winfrey had just delivered at the Golden Globe awards, describing her memories of growing up in Milwaukee and watching Sidney Poitier receive an Oscar for best actor at the Academy Awards. "I remember his tie was white, and of course, his skin was black, and I had never seen a black man being celebrated like that," Oprah said. "I tried many, many times to explain what a moment like that means to a little girl, a kid watching from the cheap seats as my mom came through the door bone-tired from cleaning other people's houses." Oprah went on to celebrate the power of our voices more generally, tying her experience to the burgeoning Times Up movement. The Moldovan students knew her — doesn't everyone?

I told them they had their own stories, too, which they should share when telling the judges how they identified a problem and devised a product or service to overcome it. Just as I used to urge scientists and professors to come down from Mt. Olympus and share their own voices and experiences instead of just trying to dazzle with their intellects, I told the students to speak to both the heads and hearts of their audience.

Once again, the finalists this second year included a group I mentored. This time it was a team of three girls from Ialoveni — Adriana, Alina, and Alisa, whom I nicknamed Triple A. Their proposal was to create a website and business to help Moldovan teenagers make better decisions about their educations and career plans. They were responding to a problem they'd identified in their own lives, namely a lack of guidance and career counseling. Adriana hoped to become a journalist or an accountant. Alina was interested in clinical psychology. Alisa dreamed of becoming a doctor. Yet, none knew what steps to take or what challenges they might encounter.

They demonstrated in their presentation how they could create a free site filled with useful information from existing sources and make money by arranging for students or parents to meet for a fee with experts in different fields. It was a clever idea, which they did a great job of presenting with graphics, examples, and a sample video interview. They also created a persuasive pitch for the finals, which they repeatedly practiced while I timed them. They won second place behind a team whose idea was to find employment for people with autism. Much like the previous year, I was proud of the students on my team and grateful for having had the opportunity to work with them. All six of my Diamond Challenge students gave me hope for Moldova's future. They were gems.

Diamond Challenge was among several efforts to promote entrepreneurship in this poor former Soviet state whose risk-averse people often despaired about making a change in the world. I was already familiar with the Dreamups center where the competition was held, having reached out to one of its founders, Sergiu. He had spent several years in Silicon Valley and then returned to work on his own projects while joining several friends in creating the Dreamups Innovation Campus, which hosted networking events, pitch sessions, and discussions with mentors.

About 3,000 people had participated in Dreamups activities, Sergiu told me. The ones I saw reminded me of people I'd met in Durham, with their laptops adorned with stickers, endless coffee, sneakers, and regular use of "cool" and "awesome" when describing things.

"No one will mistake [Chişinău] yet for Silicon Valley, much less Boston, Paris, or Shanghai," Sergiu said in an article I helped him prepare for a popular European website. "Yet its entrepreneurial scene has quietly begun to emerge over the past couple of years, and it's been exciting to watch."

Across town, I visited Tekwill, a modern center near Moldova's technical university where engineers and entrepreneurs were filling up "co-working spaces" and taking advantage of a "pre-acceleration program," startup competitions, business events, and resources ranging from 3D printers to international guest speakers. Champa joined me at a mini "Maker Faire" there, a mashup of science fairs, craft festivals, and tech enthusiasts. We had a fun afternoon watching a virtual reality demonstration, listening to talks on starting a business, speaking with inventors, and checking out gifts ranging from educational games to jewelry made from computer chips. Spending time there was a booster shot of optimism, a reminder that change might be possible in Moldova.

Moldova has much to offer to foreign visitors: delicious food and wine, magnificent monasteries, beautiful countryside, an interesting history, and travel options ranging from eco-tourism to adventure travel. Its hotels, restaurants, and travel destinations are a bargain, and some offer warm and attentive service. Its people can be gracious and generous. Yet, with the exceptions of tiny San Marino and Liechtenstein, it was the least-visited country in Europe when we lived there.

When several of us discussed this at a Peace Corps meeting, we wanted to help but weren't sure what we had to offer. We knew we had no money to address big problems like Moldova's poor roads. As Americans who had made lots of travel decisions ourselves and were familiar with Moldova, though, we realized we could contribute by helping the owners of hotels, restaurants, and tourist destinations understand what foreign guests expect in terms of customer service and how they use the internet when making travel decisions. Many Moldovans knew little about sites like TripAdvisor, and their staffs generally had little training in how to interact with foreign guests.

In coordination with the Moldova Competitiveness Project of USAID and the leadership of ANTRIM, Moldova's national inbound tourism association, we spent several months creating a Romanian-language brochure for Moldovan businesses seeking to attract foreign tourists. Its message was that customer service is critically important, as are a strong online presence and favorable reviews. Several of my volunteer colleagues wrote drafts for the different sections, which I edited and pulled together with the head of ANTRIM to create a colorful final product filled with examples and photos from across the country. As soon as we finished it, she posted it online and shared it for free with their hundreds of members.

I initiated the tourism project with Shannon, a member of my group who worked in a small city about an hour north of Ialoveni. Among her projects was a journalism club she started with her partner, which she invited me to teach one Friday afternoon.

After being introduced, I challenged her teenaged students to write stories and headlines in just a few minutes, like real reporters. One described an imaginary murder. Another imagined a fight in a local store. Others chose more peaceful or funny scenarios. All did a great job of answering the 5 W's — who, what, where, when, and why, or *care, ce, unde, cand* and *de ce* in Romanian, plus *cum* for "how."

I traveled to Călărași by minibus, toured it with Shannon, taught the class, and then returned home that afternoon by rail, my first time on a Moldovan train. The train had several sleeper cars since it originated in Moscow. It was nearing the end of its journey, and the conductor didn't even bother to come by my berth to sell me a ticket.

Haley, another member of our group, also had a journalism club, which I visited one weekend with Champa when we traveled south to Comrat, a small city that is the capital of Moldova's autonomous region of Gagauzia. Comrat has notable red wines and a lovely church, but it is best known as the home of the Gagauz people, an Orthodox Christian ethnic minority with ties to Turkey and Bulgaria. Almost all Gagauz people now speak Russian instead of Romanian, and they have little interest in Moldova reuniting with Romania, as many people did in Ialoveni. Their memories of Romanian rule are far less happy.

Haley and another volunteer, Danny, showed us around town. She took us to her post at Miras Moldova, an NGO that advanced Gagauz culture. I told her students there about some of my experiences as a journalist and communicator, and we then began reviewing the projects they were developing on topics such as Gagauz cuisine and traditional medical practices. The highlight for me was when they asked Champa to teach them some phrases from Nepal. Everyone laughed as they went around in a circle, raised their hands together in *Namaste,* and introduced themselves in Nepali, a moment President Kennedy probably didn't anticipate when he launched the Peace Corps.

Shannon, Haley, and I had all gone through training together as members of the "community and organizational development" group. Our program director led our training, selected our posts, coordinated with our host families, and oversaw programmatic matters after we swore in as volunteers. I spent much more time, however, with another member of the staff, Liuba, who managed communications for Peace Corps Moldova. Soon after Champa and I started our service, the country director asked me whether I might assist Liuba a day or two each week, mentoring her about communications planning and how to use social media. It was unusual for an active volunteer to work so closely with someone on the staff, but I lived nearby and could tend to my primary assignment while also taking this on.

I coached Liuba as she expanded the post's Facebook presence and launched several feature campaigns on it. She created an Instagram account, posted new videos, produced a brochure, and added communications issues to the training curriculum for new volunteers. She expanded the number of Moldova volunteers sharing their experiences on a popular international site called Peace Corps Stories, for which I provided editing support.

During our last several months together, Liuba also helped to organize a big event to commemorate the twenty-fifth anniversary of Peace Corps Moldova. She hired a professional video team to chronicle the experiences of seven diverse volunteers and got others to add their own photos and videos for the ceremony, which we supplemented with material from former volunteers, Moldovan hosts, the Peace Corps director in Washington, and others. As the deadline approached, she and I compiled everything into a tightly choreographed program at Tekwill, which went off smoothly.

Unfortunately, some volunteers stayed away from the event, either being too busy at their jobs or wanting to have nothing to do with the country director, who had alienated many of them by then and would soon announce her own departure. The unclear process by which Moldovan job partners and host families were invited — or not — also caused some hard feelings. Champa's school director, for one, complained loudly to her after she didn't receive an invitation, even though Champa had nothing to do with it. Still, it was a great event, and I was happy to see Liuba and the other organizers shine. Her success came on the heels of an award she received from the Peace Corps for her many innovations. As I was getting ready to leave, the senior staff organized a surprise party to thank Liuba and me for the work we'd done together. By the time she and her husband, Andrei, invited Champa and me to their apartment for a farewell dinner with their kids, we had become dear friends.

My program manager considered all of this a waste of my time. Even though I was in the Peace Corps office regularly to work with Liuba, she never asked me what we were doing or how it was going. When I listed my communications activities in the volunteer reporting form we had to submit every four months, she didn't acknowledge them in her feedback. My program director also had little to say about my activities with entrepreneurship, tourism, journalism, and the like. I mentioned these in my first few reporting forms, including the requested data about how many local people we'd touched, but she ignored them, as she did my reporting about my blog and videos, which attracted more than 100,000 views during my time in Moldova and were used by Peace Corps headquarters in its advertising and recruitment efforts with older Americans. On the other hand, my program director responded positively to almost everything I submitted about my work at the Ialoveni library. As an experiment during my second year, I limited my reporting only to my work there, omitting any reference to other activities. As I expected, my program director responded enthusiastically, telling me what a great job I was doing.

My program director didn't have a close relationship with Liuba, who worked on a different floor of the Peace Corps building. She was also busy with her many responsibilities. During my second year, she stepped down from her job after nearly a decade, so she may have been preoccupied.

She was otherwise a kind and thoughtful person who worked long hours and cared deeply about her volunteers and our work in Moldova. Her single-minded focus on my primary assignment reflected a campaign by the country director for volunteers to stay away from the capital and devote themselves entirely to their communities. This was the Peace Corps philosophy, after all, the thing that differentiated it from USAID and other development efforts.

Since its founding, the Peace Corps had embraced the ideal of volunteers serving in the world's poorest communities, learning the local language, eating the local food, and making a change at the local level. We'd all signed up for this approach, and I could understand the director's concern that some volunteers were spending too much time in Chişinău. However, I wasn't among them, and neither was Champa. Nor was I neglecting my job at the library. On the contrary, I was productive and enjoyed good relations with the library staff, my host family, and the Ialoveni community. If I was willing to use my own free time to advance Peace Corps goals in other ways and to use the special expertise I'd brought as an older volunteer, why was Peace Corps Moldova trying to make me feel guilty about it? What was the problem with my taking a quick bus ride from Ialoveni to the capital to, say, meet the head of Dreamups and help him raise Moldova's profile with other European entrepreneurs? Because he was in the capital and the capital was bad for us? If I'd abandoned these other activities and spent every minute in Ialoveni, where I already had a full schedule, I probably would have started watching *Game of Thrones* myself. But especially since I'd served in the Peace Corps previously and understood its history and mission, I knew the "official policy" we were presented in Moldova was being implemented with more flexibility and finesse elsewhere.

My own bottom line was that I'd come to Moldova to serve the people there as best I could. My experience in the communications world and the workplace was an asset to share, not to hide because it didn't fit neatly into a one-size-fits-all dogma designed mainly for recent college graduates. Some of the other older volunteers shared my frustration about policies that made little sense for experienced adults who'd proven throughout their lives they could be counted on to behave responsibly. For that matter, so did many of the younger ones, who felt like an elementary school class being punished because a few of their classmates misbehaved.

As I approached my final months, I avoided Peace Corps' scrutiny as I pursued projects I'd hoped to undertake before I even came to Moldova. One was to teach interested students about news writing and opinion writing, as I'd done at workshops back home. Early in my second year, the head of the American Language Center in the Buiucani neighborhood of Chişinău reached out to me to guest-teach a few such classes. I told him I'd love to, but it would be difficult, if not impossible, to get approval from my program director.

"You mean you can't come here on a Saturday, when your library is closed, and teach a class?" he asked me.

"That's about the size of it," I responded.

Who knows? Perhaps my program director would have agreed. At that point, I was so worn out from her lack of support that I didn't even want to ask. After I received the surprising news that she was stepping down, I waited a few weeks and sent a message to the acting program director. She agreed, and several weeks later, I was teaching my first class with nearly twenty adult students, showing them how to craft a news article.

I opened the lesson with a surprise mock fight with one of the other teachers, who "shoved" me and caused me to have a fake heart attack. After slumping over for several seconds in front of the shocked room, I jumped up and told them they were reporters who had just witnessed a news story, which they now needed to write up in the next fifteen minutes. The center's program director, who was chuckling the entire time, filmed and posted the encounter, which went viral on their site. It turned out to be a great class, followed by one where I trained the students on how to write op-ed articles.

I also reached out to the head of research at Moldova State University, the country's flagship academic institution, to organize a media-training workshop for some of his top faculty members. I was humbled by the challenges they faced. The university didn't even have a news office, much less someone to focus on research news. The participants in our workshop were experts in renewable energy, decision-making models, biomedical systems, and more, and they were on their own.

By contrast, the news office I'd led at Duke had three research communicators, videographers, photographers, social media experts, and others. Other research communicators at Duke focused on medicine, engineering, and the environment. The same was true at other top U.S. universities, as well as at national labs, corporations, and other research institutions. The National Association of Science Writers had nearly 2,000 members, with active regional groups, and there were U.S. groups for professional communicators in medicine, health care, environment, and other fields.

In Moldova, I found nothing like any of this, mainly because of a lack of resources. The professors themselves earned less than a U.S. teenager working at McDonald's. Knowing they wouldn't get support from the university anytime soon, I encouraged them to use social media, which they could do themselves for free. I showed them how researchers were doing this in the West, along with examples from Moldova and Romania. The workshop was supposed to be in English, but most of the participants had such limited comprehension that I ended up teaching it mainly in Romanian as best I could, making sure to leave time at the end for everyone to break into small groups and practice explaining their work to someone in a different field.

Just like back home, this exercise led to laughter and applause as the experts struggled to speak without jargon. Several months later, after I'd completed my service in Moldova, I returned to the region to teach a similar workshop, this time at a Sabin Vaccine

Institute workshop in Romania, where health experts learned how to communicate about vaccines more effectively with journalists and the public.

My favorite project was a farewell gift I made for the people of Ialoveni to thank them for all of their kindness to Champa and me. Working with Laura, a young singer at the city's art and music school, I produced a music video extolling Ialoveni's charms. We called it Oraşul Meu, or "My City," basing it on the music and lyrics of "My Kind of Town," the song about Chicago made famous by Frank Sinatra. I adapted those lyrics to describe Ialoveni, which Laura polished into a final song. I then recorded her as she sang it to the soundtrack of "My Kind of Town" playing in the background. Laura needed to adjust to the American rhythm and phrasing for the song, not to mention the lush orchestration, but she has a beautiful voice, and her final version was amazing, especially as she stretched the final "Ialoveni" through the closing crescendo.

I shot a video to accompany the soundtrack — along the main street, at the schools, in front of the markets, near the playgrounds, and especially at two large "Ialoveni" signs that welcomed visitors along the main roads into town. I edited the video to track what Laura was describing in the lyrics, such as the Number 35 bus rolling through town and a crowd dancing the hora in a dramatic final shot.

After I finished the video and Laura approved it, I posted it on the city's community Facebook page, as well as on YouTube and my blog, where I added the lyrics in Romanian and English. Within minutes, people across Ialoveni began sharing it, and expatriates wrote from abroad that it made them miss their homes. As I left the supermarket a few days later, a woman I'd never met stopped me on the sidewalk and said, "Aren't you that American who made the video? I love it." One of Moldova's leading television stations, TVR Moldova, sent a reporter to interview Laura and me about it. The Peace Corps featured it as well.

Best of all, my new program officer saw the video online and told me she enjoyed it, too. That was a pleasant change. Perhaps I hadn't been wasting my time after all.

CHAPTER 9

CHAMPA'S SCHOOL

C hampa was busy, too, and she was among the few Peace Corps volunteers in Moldova, or anywhere, who could vouch from personal experience how volunteers can transform the destinies of people across the developing world. She especially remembered two volunteers, Susan and Janet, who taught at her school in Ilam. Another mentor was Dorothee, a Peace Corps volunteer who befriended Champa at a training workshop after Champa became a teacher herself. Susan, Janet, and Dorothee all taught Champa new skills and encouraged her to keep moving forward, helping her become the excellent teacher I encountered when I was posted there a few years later.

After Champa and I got married and moved to the Washington, D.C. area to start our lives together, Dorothee reappeared in Champa's life. The two of us were invited to a reception at the Nepali embassy. We were dressed up and chatting politely with people when I noticed Champa staring at a young woman across the room. She went up to her and said, "Dorothee, what are you doing here?"

Dorothee replied, "What am I doing here? Champa, what are you doing here?" The two of them embraced, introductions followed, and Dorothee and her husband, Mel, who also served in Nepal, became our dear friends.

Now that she was a volunteer herself, Champa's identity as a Nepali-American made her service — and mine — much richer in Moldova. When we hosted a dinner party for some local friends, we served them Nepali curries and rice with an American chocolate chip cake and ice cream for dessert. We also made Nepali food several times for our host family, who came to love the spicier meals.

For almost everyone in Moldova, like the girls in Comrat she taught how to say "Namaste," Champa was the first person from Nepal they'd ever met. Only a handful of other people from Nepal lived in Moldova, one of whom married a Moldovan woman and ran a restaurant, Himalayan Kitchen, which was popular among Peace Corps volunteers looking for a change from the food served by their host families. For the most part, Moldovans knew nothing about Nepal but, then again, neither did most Americans. As people got to know Champa, they might ask her about how she grew up, how Nepal compared with Moldova, or whether she could see Mount Everest from her house. (Answer: No.)

Our unusual marriage made us stand out even more in Moldova, where "diversity" typically meant someone was from, say, Ukraine instead of Moldova or primarily spoke Russian instead of Romanian. There was a small Roma population but almost no people of African, Asian, or Hispanic heritage. Moldovans were familiar with American diversity, such as from our music videos, but Champa and I were the first interracial couple most had seen, much less gotten to know. We were aware from the beginning that our very presence would be as impactful in some ways as our teaching or projects.

Champa taught English at Liceul Teoretic "Andrei Vartic" in central Ialoveni, across the street from the city hall and next to the cultural center where school groups and others staged shows regularly.

She worked with the school's five English teachers, sharing classes rather than teaching solo. Like all the members of her group, she was expected to teach at least 18 hours per week, which she did with classes in grades three through eight.

School opened on September 1 with a colorful ceremony called First Bell at which local leaders and school officials gave speeches, students performed songs and dances, and the oldest students each escorted one newcomer. The event concluded with one of the new students ringing a bell while teachers, students, and parents cheered. It was such a lovely event, both in Ialoveni and across Moldova, and I wondered why we didn't do the same thing back home.

Champa had taught for many years previously, first as a Nepali literature teacher in Ilam and then teaching Nepali to Americans in the Washington, D.C. area. She knew her way around a classroom. Yet, now she was teaching English, which she speaks fluently but is not her native language. Sometimes when she was preparing a lesson, she'd check with me about a point of grammar or how to pronounce a word. She'd ask whether the textbook was correct about something, which it sometimes wasn't, or mutter about her students cheating on their tests or staring at their cell phones, which she wasn't allowed to confront as she would have on her own. Her Moldovan colleagues spoke English well and had years of experience, so Champa wondered why she'd been posted there instead of in a smaller village where the need for American teachers was greater. Ialoveni's school even had electronic whiteboards.

During our second winter, when she got sick for several weeks with a bad cold, she asked even more frequently why she'd left home to teach at a school like this. For a few days, she was so sick and discouraged that she barely got out of bed. Nina worried about her and whipped up a local remedy with warm red wine, black pepper, honey, and herbs. It smelled nasty but made Champa feel better. She also had bouts of plantar fasciitis, causing pain in her foot that caused her to hobble for several days, as she had a few times before we left for Moldova. Eventually, though, her cold got better, her foot improved, and she was happy to be teaching again, feeling useful and engaged.

When we walked together down Ialoveni's main street, one student after another would pass us and say, "Hi Miss Champa!" The other volunteers liked her, too, and even voted to post her photo atop the Facebook site where they exchanged the latest news and sought each other's help with projects. The photo showed Champa waving a small Moldovan flag in Philadelphia's Fourth of July parade when we marched with the Peace Corps group there while visiting home for three weeks after we completed our first year in Moldova.

A few months after we arrived, Champa surprised her school with a big box of English-language books, including everything from illustrated children's readers to short story collections. Champa had requested them from Darien Book Aid, a nonprofit organization in Connecticut that's been sending free books to developing communities since 1949. Its volunteers ship 20-30 boxes each week to 190 countries. A former Peace Corps volunteer in Colombia picked out and packed the books for Champa's box, along with a personal note. Darien Book Aid also sends free books to libraries, prisons, hospitals, and community groups in the United States. We were happy to discover them.

For International Children's Day festivities in June, Champa brought marker pens and large sheets of paper to the center of town, where she asked children and parents to write in Romanian or English what the day meant to them. Their answers included

"Love," "Happiness," "Fun," and "Health." My two favorites were "Best Friend Forever" and "iPhone 7." When the city's mayor saw the crowd gathering around Champa, he jumped in to help her.

I joined Champa whenever possible at her school's cultural events in their auditorium or at the cultural center. The school organized annual programs to commemorate Moldovan independence, celebrate Christmas, welcome back alumni, and mark other special occasions. After a while, I began to recognize faces among the students, who performed traditional Moldovan songs and dances accompanied by accordions and violins as well as classical music and ballroom dances and an occasional American pop song as well. Moldovans take the arts seriously. So does Champa, who bought a traditional Moldovan *nai*, or pan flute, and began taking lessons at the local music school.

Like me, she pursued several projects in addition to her primary assignment. She organized a weekly class at our library, where she taught English to younger students, engaging them in conversation instead of the grammar-based lessons that dominated their school lessons. She made weekly visits to a new home in the community for kids with special needs or whose families were too poor or abusive for them to remain at home. The kids were starved for attention and looked forward to Champa's visits, sometimes accompanied by snacks or small gifts she brought. J.K. Rowling, the author of the Harry Potter books, supported the center through her foundation.

Stella's House, which was just two blocks from where we lived, provided a refuge for young Moldovan women who had no safe homes of their own. They were prime candidates for trafficking, which is a serious problem in Moldova. An evangelical group back home created Stella's House to protect them. It was managed by a young couple from Alabama with whom we became friends. Champa helped them to start composting their food wastes and plant a vegetable garden. She also created a compost pile with our host family and spent many hours outside with our host mother weeding the garden, hoeing the soil, or picking fruits and vegetables. All of these activities, together with her main job at school, kept Champa busy in Ialoveni, but her biggest moment lay ahead.

CHAPTER 10

DAILY LIFE IN 'QUEENS'

B ack in America, we had lived in a large family house. We each had a car, credit cards, and clothes in our closets. We went to shows and restaurants, took vacations, volunteered in the community, and met often with friends. Our monthly expenses included bills for gas, electricity, cell phones, subscriptions, medical insurance, and more. We had lived American lives.

Now we were living on the second floor of a family's house in a country we'd barely heard of, with no car and many restrictions on our movement and activities. Ialoveni was bigger than the villages where many of our friends were posted, but it was still a long way from home. Since it was near the country's biggest city, I joked we were living in Queens, but all of Ialoveni's people could have fit into a few blocks along Queens Boulevard, and its overcrowded minibuses made New York's F train seem luxurious.

We had several food stores nearby, including two that resembled small American grocery stores. Their products included familiar items such as Heinz ketchup, Lay's potato chips, Tide detergent, Coca Cola, and Snickers. The American brands were expensive, though, so most of the products we bought were grown or produced in Moldova, Ukraine, Russia, or Romania. Local bread was cheap and tasty. So were the cheeses. Salami was a local favorite, and fresh meats were delicious. The markets often displayed their pork chops next to a pig's head. Sometimes, we splurged on cheeses from Holland, persimmons from Israel, or beer from Germany.

Champa and I especially loved the seasonal fruits and vegetables. I could buy a bag of apples from a street vendor for 75 cents, enough to make a big pie. There were pears, peaches, apricots, cherries, raspberries, and strawberries, which we often got for free from our host family or friends. We loved the cauliflower, eggplants, onions, potatoes, and especially the beets, which were an everyday commodity. Champa learned to make beet salads with buckwheat, carrots, tomatoes, and cucumbers, sprinkled with olive oil and balsamic vinegar.

The stores didn't make a big deal about their "locavore" products, which included cakes and candies from Ialoveni companies and produce from local farmers. Champa and I became regular customers at all of Ialoveni's stores and got a discount card for Market Victoria that we could scan when checking out. We often bought produce from vendors in the outdoor market and along the main street. We also had a convenience store up the street from us, just past the ice cream factory. At the other end of the spectrum were Moldova's two Metro stores, which resembled Costco. We visited those a couple of times with our host family and found a familiar mélange of oversized cereal boxes, giant bags of laundry detergent, blenders, and Barbie dolls.

The prices for most products and services in Moldova were far lower than back home. A bus ride from Ialoveni to the capital was about 30 cents. A city bus ride cost just over a dime. We could fill two daypacks with groceries for less than $20. It cost us two or three dollars for a bottle of local wine. On the other hand, a pair of Nike running shoes cost about the same as back home, and a pair of Levi's cost more, as did an iPhone. According to one website at the time, consumer prices in Moldova were 62 percent lower than in the United States. Rents were lower, too, with apartments in Ialoveni starting at just over $100 per month.

Before we came to Moldova, Champa and I had never gone to the opera. We couldn't afford it. Now we could buy orchestra seats for ten dollars each for a performance of *La Traviata* in Chişinău's national theater. Dinner for two at the outdoor restaurant next door to the theater that night was thirteen dollars. Transportation home was a dollar. We ended up attending performances of *Tosca* and *Madama Butterfly* as well. I've still never been to the Metropolitan Opera in New York, but it surely costs more than that.

These prices were great for us as Americans but not for Moldovans, whose average monthly after-tax disposable salary was $214.52, nearly ninety-three percent lower than ours, according to the same website. Even if those numbers were imprecise, monthly paychecks were minuscule by our standards. As Peace Corps volunteers, we received enough money to pay for rent, food, transportation, and miscellaneous expenses, and we also had some money set aside for a "readjustment allowance" after we completed our service. Our paychecks were far less than what we'd spent on basic living expenses back home, not to mention on college tuitions and other major outlays, but we could still live comfortably without having to worry about utility bills or medical insurance premiums. Our only recurring bills were a few bucks every month for online subscriptions to *The New York Times* and *The Washington Post* and iCloud storage to back up our photos and files. We left our retirement savings untouched, and, as we hoped, they grew while we were gone, although they could have moved in the other direction, too.

I shopped in stores and on the street. One time, I stopped while walking home from the library and bought peaches from a woman on the sidewalk, which she weighed with a hand-held scale. They cost about 20 cents per pound or $1.30 overall. I told her I planned to bake an American-style pie, which I showed her on my phone. The woman's husband came by, and since he spoke some English, he encouraged her to try saying "peach pie" in English, which made us all laugh. After I got home, I listened to a podcast of NPR's *Fresh Air* while I made the pie, which we shared that evening with the Bordeis. Nina reciprocated a few days later with one of her delicious walnut tortes.

Other times, I shopped in the central piaţa, or market, in Chişinău, where vendors filled several blocks with stalls selling everything from Turkish dried fruit to used German clothing. There was a big pavilion for meat, another for vegetables, and sections throughout the complex that specialized in housewares, electronics, shoes, toys, and almost anything else you might buy. Women stood along the street holding up dresses or bras. Farmers spread their produce on tables or blankets. A grim-looking woman sold batteries. Touts shouted the destinations of departing buses. Women raced to pick up food for dinner, holding children in one hand and plastic bags in the other. Teenagers laughed together with their headphones dangling from their heads. The colors and chaos reminded me of the bazaars in Kathmandu. I loved mingling in the madness and exploring the city there and elsewhere, always expecting to be surprised. I might stumble across a night club called Marilyn with giant pictures of Marilyn Monroe or a group of veterans selling medals and other paraphernalia from Soviet days.

I also attended activities in Ialoveni just to see what might happen. One Thursday evening, I stopped by city hall to observe nearly fifty citizens discussing a proposed high-rise building in the center of town that would add residential and commercial space but affect traffic, municipal services, and the environment, disrupting a park and church. Some residents were concerned about its impact on their property values. I didn't understand everything that was said and sometimes shouted, in Romanian, but the meeting fascinated me. Both men and women participated. Everyone was dressed comfortably for the late-summer heat, including the mayor, who presided at the end of a long table. They took turns standing to speak. Some held up documents. Some tended to children. Some listened quietly, sipped water, or played with their phones. A city expert pointed to one of several maps on the wall, explaining the project in detail. A local journalist recorded it all.

Another time I mailed two holiday cards home, learning how the post office worked. I waited in line behind two elderly customers collecting their monthly pensions. The man in front of me was at least 75 years old, probably older. Moldovans used post offices for much more than mail. It's where they paid utility bills, transferred money, and collected their pensions, and where brides and grooms came in their wedding finery to pick up their marriage licenses. In Bardar, where we had our training, there was even a hair salon.

I also loved to scan the outdoor bulletin boards beside Ialoveni's bus stops, their clutter reminding me of what I used to see in college dorms or coffee shops back home. Pieces of paper competed for space, many with phone numbers to rip off, drooping after a past storm. People advertised apartments and cars, job openings, or upcoming events, such as Ialoveni's annual circus. Most of the signs were printed simply in black and white, with no photos or graphics. Some were scrawled by hand. Moldovans had also begun using online sites similar to Craigslist, notably 999.com, which sold an array of products. New mobile shopping apps were popular with younger customers, just like in our country.

I paid more attention than I expected to all of this after our host mother surprised us near the end of our first year by saying we had to move out when the school year finished. She thought their son, Andrei, was going to get married and needed to move with his bride into our rooms. Champa and I scrambled to find an apartment, searching all of the bulletin boards along the main street. Fortunately, Nina told us a few days later that Andrei wasn't getting married after all, and we were welcome to remain on her family's second floor for the rest of our service.

One of the most moving events we witnessed was Paştele Blajinilor, or Memorial Easter, which occurred a week after Orthodox Easter. Families gathered at the graves of loved ones at churches across the country, placing flowers and food beside the tombstones, lighting candles, and enjoying meals together. At a church overlooking Ialoveni, we saw dozens of families spreading colored eggs, special bread, and other foods together with bottles of soda, wine, and cognac on tables or cloths near the graves. Families dribbled wine on the tombstones. A priest circulated to say prayers. The mood was relaxed but respectful. Paştele Blajinilor, which traces its origins back to pre-Christian times, reminded me of the Mexican holiday Día de los Muertos, although it correlated religiously with Easter instead of Halloween. We saw a family we knew, who insisted we have some food and accept a small gift bag with treats inside.

Paştele Blajinilor was among the many holidays Moldovans celebrated annually, a rhythm we began to master just as we were leaving. Ialoveni also organized a big Christmas party every year, culminating with a colorful parade from a holiday tree in the center of town to the cultural center a few blocks away. Groups from neighboring villages, all wearing traditional costumes, played accordions, violins, drums, and cymbals as they sang, danced, and marched down the street. They posed together for a photo on the steps of the cultural center and then headed inside to take turns performing.

Like most Moldovan villages and cities, Ialoveni also celebrated its own birthday. The first time we saw this, a few months after we arrived, the city marked its 580th anniversary with something special: the dedication of a bust in front of the district government building. It honored Ferdinand I, the king of Romania after World War I when Moldova was part of Romania. The Romanian ambassador and other dignitaries attended, with many calling for Moldova's reunification with Romania. They denounced the Soviet era, describing the suffering of Moldovans deported to Siberia and other remote regions under Stalin's rule. They recalled how their families couldn't practice their religion or speak Romanian in public settings. They criticized Russia's current meddling in Moldovan affairs. I filmed the event for a video I planned to share with the district government and became uneasy when I realized how political it had become. As a Peace Corps volunteer, I needed to stay away from politics. I did my best to produce a video my colleagues could use without including the most provocative material, which I left out of the footage I showed them for editing.

I also saw another special birthday celebration, this one for Spiridon Vangheli, one of Moldova's most famous writers, who turned eighty-five. Ialoveni had named its children's library after him, and it was fun to watch a group of local kids in traditional costumes present him with flowers and serenade him with songs and dances. Several stepped forward to recite short speeches they'd memorized with their parents and teachers, some of whom mouthed the words nervously as they watched.

Another time we watched the dedication of a local playground, which coincided with a "diaspora day" that welcomed home some of the city's many citizens living abroad. After the mayor and others cut a ceremonial ribbon, children raced to try out the new equipment, and an Orthodox priest lit candles, chanted prayers, and walked through the crowd to sprinkle blessings on people and playground equipment alike. The mayor carried the water beside him — an example of how government and religion mixed openly in Moldova. The same priest once walked into my office at the district government office and spritzed me with holy water, working his way throughout the building.

When we were eating dinner one evening on the outdoor patio of one of Ialoveni's restaurants, a guy walked up to us and said in Romanian, out of the blue, "Please, don't go to Albania!" I assured him we had no plans to visit Albania. He then leaned over our table, stared at us, and repeated, "Please, don't go to Albania!" before turning around and heading back to the street. We never did visit Albania, which I guess would have made him happy.

Then there was the time when we were home with our host family and opened the door to see an older woman with three children, who began chanting and singing after Nina invited them inside. They were celebrating St. Vasile, or Basil the Great, a religious figure born in the year 329 who established monasteries, served the poor, and was canonized by the Orthodox Church shortly after his death. On the evening of his special day, children across Moldova walked from house to house to sing carols and chants in his honor. Nina gave our visitors fruit, candy, money, and loaves of a traditional round braided bread. Champa and I gave them a gift, too. Events like this often surprised us since our host family usually didn't tell us about them in advance. Dinner invitations often came at the last moment, too. Sometimes, though, we knew to expect something special, especially during our second year, after we'd begun to figure out the cycle.

When we celebrated Orthodox Christmas with our host family the second year, our guest singer was a family friend, Viorica, who came for the traditional dinner with her husband. We shared steaming bowls of chicken noodle soup, followed by Nina's baked chicken, pickled vegetables, and salad. For dessert, I made an apricot cake, which I served with a plate of Oreos we'd spotted during a recent trip. As the meal wound down, Viorica sang several songs, her voice like an angel. At moments like this, we knew how lucky we were to be in Moldova, surrounded by a family that had become our own.

Mihai and Nina welcomed guests often. Most were from Ialoveni and other parts of Moldova, but they also included a group of priests from Romania, friends from Ukraine, and a Moldovan psychologist living in Paris, who came with her French boyfriend. She spoke French and English in addition to the usual Romanian and Russian. Her French boyfriend spoke neither Romanian nor English. I could converse a bit in French, although not well, so the conversation unfolded in four languages, plus the Nepali that Champa and I sometimes whispered to each other. However, the food and company were delightful, and we all laughed, toasted, and ate too much.

These dinners and parties always included rounds of wine or cognac, even in business settings. At an event to honor local farmers and food manufacturers, national officials joined our district's president in handing out awards before everyone moved to tables overflowing with traditional foods and beverages. I joined my friends as they began passing around glasses of local cognac and plum wine.

The toasts began: *Noroc!* (Good luck.) *La mulți ani!* (Long life.) *Sănătate!* (Good health.) *Succes!* Others at the event toasted each other, too. A DJ played old American songs such as "Feelings" and "I Just Called to Say I Loved You," mixed with Moldovan tunes and a sort of East European Muzak. As the party wound down, a Moldovan friend took over the sound system to replace the outdated music with "Ne Bucuram In Ciuda Lor," a song by the popular local band Carla's Dreams.

Alcohol was omnipresent in Moldova, whose citizens drank nearly three times the global average, second only to Belarus worldwide, according to the World Health Organization. Throughout our training, the Peace Corps medical and security officers urged everyone to exercise good judgment with alcohol. Champa and I followed that advice but did toast and drink many times with our Moldovan friends, who eventually learned I was serious when turning down their many offers of additional rounds.

We also shared their traditional foods, our favorite being the soft, savory, mouth-watering pastries called *plăcinte*, which were stuffed with cabbage, potatoes, apples, cherries, or other fillings. We especially enjoyed plăcinte made with *brinza*, a traditional cheese usually produced from sheep's milk similar to crumbled Greek feta cheese. Champa learned how to make plăcinte with our host family. The recipe combined the brinza cheese with eggs, dill, and salt, all wrapped in a flaky pastry dough. When the plăcinte emerged from the oven, they were fragrant and irresistible.

The best way to describe these meals and experiences was *frumos*. The word means "beautiful" in Romanian, as in a beautiful song or a person's beautiful soul. A well-behaved child could be *frumos*. Most of all, *frumos* meant beautiful as in *beautiful* — a bouquet of flowers, a majestic sunset, a gorgeous woman. We heard the word constantly, which was no surprise in a country where people were usually well-dressed in public. Many women wore makeup whenever they went outside. Men ironed their clothes and cleaned their shoes. Few people were rich, but almost everyone showed pride in their appearance. For Americans like us who never paid much attention to clothes, *frumos* posed a challenge. Champa and I had to take care to always dress neatly. Near my library, I could see a hair salon, a beauty salon, a cosmetics store, two flower shops, a shop displaying fancy foods, and another selling lacy lingerie. *Frumos* was in the eye of the beholder, but it was more than skin-deep in Moldova, a beautiful thing that helped me understand the country.

Similarly, people addressed each other more formally than I'd known most of my life. Just as it took me a while to get used to saying "Sir" and "Ma'am" after we moved to North Carolina, now I had to learn to say *Domnul* and *Doamnă*, which mean the same thing in Romanian. In Moldova, one says *Doamnă* to a woman who is married and *Domnişoară* to a younger woman who is not. There is no equivalent of Ms.

To complicate matters, there were two forms of "second person" in Romanian, with the less formal version commonly used with children, family members, and friends. As for greetings in the opposite direction, my colleagues and students called me *Domnul David*. Champa's colleagues called her *Doamnă Champa* or just Champa. Most of her students called her Miss Champa. As a whole, these salutations reminded me a lot of what I'd found in North Carolina, although there was no Moldovan equivalent of *y'all*.

CHAPTER 11

MAKING SENSE OF MOLDOVA

My father, Seymour Jarmul, was part of the "greatest generation" that fought in World War II and returned home to resume their lives and start families. He was a navigator in a bomber group, flew multiple missions over Germany, and was nearly killed on D-Day. On his last mission, his plane was shot up by antiaircraft fire. It limped back over the English Channel, escorted by RAF fighter planes on either wing, and barely touched down. My dad's description of that harrowing day was among the few stories he ever shared about the war. Like so many other men of his time, he didn't want to burden us with his bad memories. He never forgave Germany for what it did, especially to the Jews, and he wasn't a fan of the Russians even though they'd been our allies during the war.

In Moldova, there was no escaping the legacy of World War II. Moldova had been part of the Soviet Union, which suffered more than fifty times as many military and civilian deaths as we did, according to some estimates. Families and communities were devastated on a scale most Americans do not comprehend. When we think of World War II, we recall Normandy, Iwo Jima, and other battles where our soldiers bravely fought and died. Families in the former Soviet Union are more likely to recall Stalingrad, Berlin, Moscow, and Kharkov.

During my training in the village of Bardar, the first thing I saw when leaving my host family's home every morning was a Soviet memorial honoring local heroes who died in the conflict. Its base listed more than one hundred people, including several named Sava and several others named Tonu. I lived with a family named Sava and previously lived with the Tonus. Their extended families, like most in Moldova, experienced the war personally. When my training group visited a nearby village called Dereneu, it had a war memorial, too. So did Ialoveni, where there was also a memorial honoring a local soldier killed in Afghanistan, shortly before Moldova gained its independence. I knew almost none of this history before moving there.

During our first springtime in Moldova, Champa and I visited the country's most prominent war memorial, a complex in the heart of Chişinău built around a circle of five dramatic red pillars with an eternal flame in the center. Nearby were sculpted murals depicting the bloody struggle to defeat Nazi Germany. Smaller monuments honored the names of Soviet soldiers who gave their lives to liberate Moldova in August 1944. Rows of white grave markers in an adjacent cemetery resembled Arlington Cemetery, although with Russian inscriptions. The Soviet gravestones lacked any religious markings while those erected since Moldovan independence, just a few yards away, were adorned with crosses. The cemetery also honored Moldovans who died shortly after independence in the war in Transnistria, the pro-Russian region that broke away and remained largely autonomous. Champa and I visited with two Peace Corps friends shortly before Moldova's Victory Day on May 9. Soldiers were mowing the grass, pulling weeds, and sprucing up.

Many Moldovans still retained close ties to Russia and cherished its glorious triumph in World War II. Just outside the park, we saw a billboard promoting Victory Day, complete with a Soviet hammer and sickle. Thousands of Moldovans marched or gathered in Chişinău on Victory Day to celebrate their shared history with Russia, as they did around the country, especially in Russian-speaking areas.

Americans inevitably view our joint victory in the war through the lens of the subsequent Cold War. For Moldovans, the legacy was more complex since the German occupation was followed by decades of Russian rule. More than seventy years after the war ended, its impact on the history and psyche of this region remained profound. The legacy was intertwined with painful family memories of the many local people whom the Soviets deported during and after the war. In front of the Chişinău railroad station was a memorial depicting families being sent away on trains, many to never be seen again. In Ialoveni, the city's World War II memorial was flanked by two smaller memorials in white stone topped with crosses, showing they were built after the Soviet era. They honored the Moldovan victims of Soviet repression under Joseph Stalin. For a visitor like me, all of this was a reminder that history was never far away here. Like the flame inside Chişinău's monument, memories smoldered, flickered, and burned. Every day was Memorial Day.

Moldova's complicated relationship with Russia could also be seen in the annual celebration of its national language, the *Limba Noastră* holiday. The words mean "our language," and a poem of that name provided the lyrics for Moldova's national anthem, which proclaimed the Romanian language to be a "treasure" that is "more than holy." What the anthem didn't mention was that one in four Moldovans spoke a language other than Romanian as their native tongue, mainly Russian, Ukranian, or Gagauz, all of which had official status in certain regions. One of my fellow volunteers living in a Russian-speaking area said his host father called the holiday *limba voastră*, or *your* language. The relationship between Moldovan language and identity was complicated and not always easy for an American to understand. We wrestle with many of these same issues in our own country, though, so the story felt familiar despite the translation.

Champa and I came to Moldova only two years after Russia annexed the Crimean peninsula from Ukraine, and the conflict in that neighboring country simmered while we were there. Many of the same tensions were playing out in Moldova: Should the country align itself with the West or with Russia? What should happen to ethnic Russians whose families had settled in the region decades earlier? What could be done to reign in powerful oligarchs? Most important to Moldovans, when would honest leaders emerge to fight the country's pervasive corruption, with people forced to pay bribes to build a house, operate a business, or even pass a school exam?

One week before Americans went to the polls in the 2016 election between Donald Trump and Hillary Clinton, Moldova had its own spirited presidential contest. One of the two final candidates was a friend of Vladimir Putin, who championed conservative rural voters and promised to restore the country's greatness. The other was a progressive woman who appealed to more urban and educated voters, calling for Moldova to align with Western allies. The election reflected our own in many ways, and, just as in America, the conservative candidate won a close contest.

Our Moldovan friends paid little attention to the U.S. election, which most of us in the Peace Corps followed closely. They didn't care about it, just as they didn't care about the Super Bowl or the Oscars. I was humbled as an American to be reminded regularly that

Moldovans didn't consider our country the center of the universe. It was an insight I treasured as a Peace Corps volunteer, a gift of a new vantage point, and it reminded me of what I'd seen in Nepal and other countries. People around the world live their own lives. They have their own countries. They generally know more about the United States than we do about them, and some of them pay attention to our affairs. For the most part, though, they tuck their kids into bed at night without giving a thought to things that loom large for us. No matter how loudly people screamed on Fox News or MSNBC, most people around the globe never heard them. We shared the planet but lived in worlds defined by our families, neighbors, and countries.

I saw this again a couple of months after the election when Americans paused for our annual holiday honoring Martin Luther King, Jr., whom I count among my heroes. I mentioned the MLK holiday to one of my colleagues at the library, who told me she had never heard of him. Others at the library recognized his name but were more focused on Moldova's own holiday that day honoring the great Romanian poet Mihai Eminescu, whose name adorned local schools, street signs, and other landmarks. He was even more unknown to Americans than Dr. King was to Moldovans. A few months later, after President Trump called some developing countries "shitholes," a friend from home wrote to ask whether Moldovan newspapers were coming up with their own phrases for "shithole." I told him not a single Moldovan friend had mentioned the controversy — and I interacted every day with librarians and others who were well-educated.

Champa and I tried to learn as much as we could about Moldovan traditions. At a travel fair at Chişinău's convention center, she spotted a woman painting Easter eggs, a tradition that nearly disappeared during the decades of Soviet domination when religion was suppressed. Now it was making a comeback. The woman showed Champa how she drained the egg's contents through a small hole, marked it with hot wax lines, and painted it with exquisite designs that symbolized the sun, a leaf, wheat, or the cross.

Other traditions were newer, like an "Ethno Jazz Festival" we attended at Chişinău's philharmonic center. We enjoyed a flamenco band hailing from, of all places, Poland, and a jazz quartet whose members came from Portugal, Ireland, and Sweden. We also attended a high-tech fashion show at the city's convention center, where we cheered for Igor's wife, whose hand-painted outfits were among those shown. Models strutted, judges scribbled, and photographers clicked as Ludmila watched nervously from backstage. In the small city of Criuleni, I saw another aspect of the fashion industry when my training group visited a small jeans factory opened by a local entrepreneur. Even though his seamstresses were racing to fill an order, the owner agreed to sell jeans to several of the volunteers. They looked great and cost about thirteen dollars a pair.

Another new event was the Chişinău International Marathon. About 17,000 runners from Moldova and abroad, including several Peace Corps volunteers, filled the city's main square at one race I attended. It included racing bibs, water stations, a big stage, music, and colorful signs, with sponsors ranging from a local supermarket chain to familiar international names such as Lenovo, Hyundai, and Herbalife. Booths sold running gear, vitamins, and souvenirs. Food merchants offered everything from energy drinks to draft beer and barbecue. Just as in Boston and other cities, Moldova's marathon disrupted local traffic, as I discovered when my bus downtown was canceled.

Chişinău's dining scene was changing, too. Most restaurants still specialized in traditional favorites such as barbecued pork, polenta, and brinza cheese with sour cream. There were a few popular chain restaurants — La Plăcinte for traditional food, Star Kebab for kebabs, and Andy's Pizza for Western options — along with several McDonald's and a KFC. Tucano Coffee resembled Starbuck's. Restaurants offered cuisines from several nearby countries, including Italian, Czech, Turkish, and Georgian, and there were several new Asian restaurants, too, as well as an American barbecue joint opened by two former Peace Corps volunteers and a Moldovan friend.

Change was everywhere if you looked carefully. When I visited MedPark, a new private hospital where Peace Corps took volunteers for outpatient specialty care, I was struck by its colorful posters, brochures, and signs, which were startlingly different from the drab signage and dim lighting I'd seen in Ialoveni's public clinic. The lobby had an attractive coffee bar, a free charging station for cell phones, and bright play equipment for children. The hospital pharmacy sold fancy creams and lotions along with medical prescriptions, and its eyeglass frames were artfully arranged in a glass kiosk. For me, a visiting American patient, it all felt reassuring. I realized they were sending me a subliminal message: We're modern! You can trust us! Having worked in communications, I knew someone in the hospital had given this a lot of thought, right down to the aqua color palette and the lower-case logo in sans-serif type.

I enjoyed reading street signs while traveling to MedPark or other places around Chişinău. When I traveled to the Peace Corps office, I took a bus along a street named for a Moldovan writer and artist, turned at a street named for a poet, and continued past a street named for a lawyer. I got off at a street named for another writer. Finally, at a street named for a historian, I reached the Peace Corps, which was named for ... well, nobody. The Moldovans might have called it "Peace Corps John F. Kennedy" since they were passionate about naming streets and institutions after prominent people, especially writers and political figures. The central street in Chişinău was named for the beloved king Ştefan cel Mare şi Sfânt, or "Stephen the Great and Holy." (We sometimes called him "Big Steve.") Other large streets in the city honored everyone from Orthodox church leaders to Yuri Gagarin, the first man in space.

I grew up near New York City, which has a systematic grid of streets and avenues with numbers. Many other U.S. cities have numbered streets as well. For many years, Champa and I lived near Washington, D.C., where many of the streets are named after U.S. states. In Durham, our subdivision has streets named after trees. To be sure, New York also has the George Washington Bridge, the Lincoln Tunnel, and the FDR Drive, and many cities in America have streets named for Martin Luther King or others. My personal favorite is Champa Street in Denver. But we also have plentiful streets with simple names like "Main Street" or "Market Street." Well, they are simple if you are an American. For a Moldovan visitor, "Rock Creek Parkway" may sound as foreign as "Strada Mihail Kogălniceanu" did to me. It would be easier for foreign visitors if they handled him like Duke University's famous Mike and just called him Coach K.

Champa and I welcomed opportunities to tell others about the Peace Corps and share our American culture. We visited Criuleni, where I toured the blue jeans factory, to participate in a week-long celebration of Peace Corps Week organized by two volunteers. We gave presentations highlighting Peace Corps activities around the world, with a fun quiz that challenged students to guess the location of photos showing volunteers in China, Africa, and other parts of the world. We gave the winners souvenir postcards from Durham.

On the morning of our second Thanksgiving in Moldova, I awoke early to head downtown and join a television reporter in describing the holiday to viewers across Moldova and Romania. We chatted in Romanian and English while a chef from one of the city's leading restaurants prepared a turkey roll stuffed with herbs and butter. We discussed Thanksgiving foods and traditions, and I showed how American children trace their fingers to make turkey pictures for placemats. After our first segment, we took a break and ate the cooked turkey with pistachio-infused rice. After the second segment ended, I headed back to Ialoveni to finish preparing our own Thanksgiving dinner, which we'd share with our host family and a volunteer from Minnesota. I'd bought the turkey from a local farmer, sweet potatoes at a specialty store, and dried cranberries in the local market, which I cooked with juice and brandy to make a sauce. We served these with mashed potatoes, chocolate chip cookies, and more, including wines we'd bought during a recent trip to Armenia and Georgia. The feast brought back memories of Thanksgiving holidays I'd enjoyed at the home of my grandmother, who grew up in Germany but fled to America to escape the Nazis and find a better life.

All four of my grandparents immigrated to America for religious freedom. My other grandmother, Sarah, grew up in Odessa, Ukraine, not far from where I was now serving. Her family — my ancestors — fled to America to survive the violent anti-Semitism depicted in *Fiddler on the Roof*. At that time, more than 50,000 Jews lived in Chișinău, comprising forty-six percent of the city's population, according to an 1897 census. In 1903, forty-nine of them were killed in anti-Semitic riots. A survivor said: "Dead bodies were everywhere, many of them horribly mutilated, and in most cases with the clothes torn off. There were ears, fingers, noses lying on the pavements. Babies were tossed in the air to be caught on the points of spears and swords. Young girls were horribly mistreated before death came to end their torture. I saw these things with my own eyes."

It's hard to imagine anything more chilling than that, but things got worse for Moldova's Jews. A few decades later, they were nearly wiped out by Nazi death squads who rounded them up and executed them in every corner of the country, sometimes with local help. Shortly before Champa and I joined the Peace Corps, *60 Minutes* broadcast a chilling story about a French Catholic priest investigating "The Hidden Holocaust" in former Soviet states. "We traveled with Father Desbois to the former Soviet Republic of Moldova, where in one day he took us to four unmarked mass graves," reporter Lara Logan said in the story. "In this field, he told us, sixty Jews beneath this farm, one hundred above this city, under this hill, a thousand."

In a small village near Telenești, an eighty-five-year-old man told them what he witnessed as a boy: "The Jews were facing the ditch, so they were shooting them in the back of their heads or their backs to fall into the ditch. They were shooting them as if they were dogs." Moldova's Jews were murdered in their homes, in ravines, on death marches, in camps — everywhere. By the time the Soviet Army returned in August 1944, the Nazis had killed as many as 300,000 Jews across Moldova and neighboring areas of Bucovina, Bessarabia, and Transnistria. Few survived.

After we were accepted as Peace Corps volunteers, one of our sons saw the *60 Minutes* story and told us he was worried about our safety in Moldova, even though I am not an observant Jew, and Champa grew up with local religions in Nepal. He needn't have worried; we were both welcomed warmly. I encountered some surprise and hesitation when people learned I was Jewish but never sensed any open anti-Semitism, even though it still exists in Moldova and extremist groups can be found in much of Europe.

What I did see were promising, if modest, signs of a Jewish revival. According to one estimate, about 25,000 Jews lived in Moldova when we were there, many of them in Chișinău. Their numbers grew under Soviet rule until the 1970s and 1980s, when anti-Semitism led many of them to emigrate, mainly to Israel and North America. Many of Moldova's Jews were now elderly and living on small fixed incomes. Organizations such as the American Jewish Joint Distribution Committee were doing wonderful work to support the community.

Shortly after arriving in Chișinău, my friend Tom and I visited a local synagogue run by the Orthodox Chabad movement. They looked at us skeptically but welcomed us after I joined them in the prayer they were reciting, although I declined their energetic attempt to wrap me in *tefillin*. Tom and I also passed a shattered synagogue along one of the city's main streets, the sky showing through its smashed windows. A few blocks away, on Jerusalem Street, we found a red granite monument honoring victims of the Chișinău ghetto. At the Chișinău history museum, Champa and I saw a Torah, menorah, and other Jewish symbols. In an old Jewish cemetery on the outskirts of town, we wandered among aging tombstones where Hebrew letters were fading, and weeds filled tiny paths. The Jews buried there were luckier than those whose bodies were strewn in the forgotten ditches dotting Moldova's landscape. As I looked at the broken cemetery stones and the synagogue's bullet-pocked walls, I felt their spirits whispering to us.

My mother was one of the lucky ones. She emigrated from Berlin to New York in 1937 when she was twelve years old, shortly before Hitler began carrying out his Final Solution. She spoke only a few words of English but grew up to become the editor of her college newspaper, and, later in life, a college counselor and community journalist. She died several years before we left for the Peace Corps and remains my role model in life.

Several months after we'd settled into Moldova, one of my nieces back home reminded us our family still had my mom's German passport, with its photo snapped in Berlin. There were swastikas on the passport stamp, a chilling reminder that my mom would have been murdered if America had not welcomed her. You would not be reading this book because I would not exist. Nor would my children and grandchildren have been born. Instead, my mother grew up to become a proud American citizen who contributed to her society in countless ways. She gave birth to my sisters and me, and we were followed by our children, their cousins, and the next generation following them. We were always grateful to America and never forgot our family history. We were all appalled after Donald Trump took office and demonized immigrants, slashing the number of people who could seek refuge like our mother did.

Living in Moldova enabled me to see the immigration debate through the eyes of people much poorer than me who were desperate to find a better life. We met many families where one or both parents were working outside the country, sometimes in America but more often in other Western countries. Champa's host mother during training was raising two energetic boys while her husband worked construction in Tel Aviv. In another family, the adult daughter and her husband were working part-time in Germany, with two school-age girls at home. Our host family's youngest child was working in Paris. When Champa and I sipped coffee outside a cafe one day, a guy sat beside us, said he was on a break from his job in England, and asked whether we could help him get a green card to America. Many people wanted green cards. A work colleague told me he applied but didn't get one. Someone I knew through the Peace Corps told me he wanted one, too.

Good-paying jobs were scarce in Moldova. People who wanted to start their own businesses had few sources of capital, lots of red tape, and officials everywhere looking for bribes. Moldovans didn't trust the banks or politicians. They were tired and discouraged. So they went to Russia to drive trucks. They served meals in Italy, cleaned houses in Germany, and raised other people's children while their own grew up with grandparents or neighbors. According to the International Organization for Migration, one-quarter of Moldova's working-age population worked abroad. Many sent money home and returned for visits laden with televisions, laptops, and toys. Their earnings paid for some of the loveliest homes in the villages we saw.

Money exchange shops lined the streets of Chişinău, and we had several in Ialoveni as well, one of them next door to an office with a blue sign saying "Lucru legal în Europa!" — work legally in Europe! Across the street were signs for MoneyGram and Western Union. These shops and banks were so ubiquitous that I barely noticed them after a while. They weren't there primarily to assist foreign tourists looking to exchange currency or Moldovans traveling on foreign vacations; their main function was to process foreign remittances from husbands, wives, sons, and others. Workers sometimes brought money home when they returned for a visit or sent it in cash with a trusted friend. Generally, they relied on banks and money-transfer companies, selecting one after comparing the fees and exchange rates. Moldova was among the world's top "remittance-receiving" countries on a per capita basis, according to the World Bank.

Moldovans were hardly alone in wrestling with these problems.

Our country's toxic immigration battle was fueled by immigrants from many countries looking to improve their lives, sometimes leaving children behind in Honduras, Mexico, or somewhere else. During our time in Moldova, we watched Syrian families flee horrific conditions. When we visited Nepal, we met several families whose sons worked in the Persian Gulf. In North Carolina, we'd assisted a Rwandan refugee family. None of this was new to me, in other words, but I'd never been surrounded by it like I was in Moldova. As a father and grandfather, my heart went out to the many people we met who felt forced to move abroad. They needed to feed their families and hoped to provide them with a few simple pleasures, like a nicer home or a modern bathroom. They loved their children as much as we did and tried everything they could to help them.

Living among them broadened my perspective on our immigration debate even though Moldova itself didn't figure much into that debate. When I visited Champa's host family and watched the two boys race to the computer when they heard the Skype tone of their dad calling from Israel, I knew I wasn't watching that family alone. Theirs were the voices rarely heard in our debate, and they were the ones that spoke to my heart.

Moldovans sometimes asked me whether Champa and I liked Moldova. When I told them we'd come to love Moldova and would miss it when we returned home, which we did, they were often surprised. Their eyebrows went up. Their eyes widened. "Really?" they asked, in disbelief that an American might admire their country.

Yes, really.

Inevitably, they responded by reminding me how many people were leaving the country to find work. They told me about the low salaries, bad roads, and overcrowded buses. They bemoaned the daily corruption and feckless politicians. Near our house in Ialoveni, at least some of the fancy houses and cars were paid for with bribes and corruption, just like the pink Hummer we saw one day near Chişinău's downtown cathedral. A poll taken around this time showed seventy-three percent of Moldovans thought the country was going in the wrong direction; seventy-six percent said young people did not have a good future.

These and other problems were real, but so was the beauty of Moldova's countryside, its glorious churches, its delicious fruits, vegetables, and wine. I loved the laughter of the country's children, the grandmothers talking in the market, the mothers carrying babies, the dads holding their children's hands. I loved everyone's hospitality and generosity. I loved Bunica's smile. I loved so much about Moldova and considered it a privilege to serve there. Champa and I were grateful to have this opportunity.

We knew we would return to a country with profound problems of its own. Yet even though Trump's election and other events back home sometimes made me despair, I never wavered in my pride about my homeland. Yes, we had a messy democracy and corruption in our own politics; but, we also had backyard barbecues, Saturday Night Live, Fourth of July parades, and Little League. We had LeBron James and Beyonce, overstuffed shopping centers, and food trucks lined-up beside our farmer's market in Durham. Living abroad reminded me of how lucky I was to be an American.

Simultaneously, I wished more Moldovans could recognize and celebrate the wonderful things about *their* country. By the time I'd lived there for two years, I had come to regard its biggest problem as not politics or the economy, but the "glass half empty" view of its people. I'd lived and traveled in other countries much poorer than Moldova, with deep challenges of their own, but the people I met in Nepal, Peru, South Africa, and other places were generally proud of their homelands. In Moldova, there was a "cloud of pessimism," as Eric Weiner described in *The Geography of Bliss*. Not always, not with everyone, but often.

To my foreign eyes, Moldova's negative self-image was out of alignment with its reality. Even recognizing its many challenges, I came to know it as a beautiful place with dedicated, hard-working people who have the skills and hearts to make it prosper. First, though, they had to believe in themselves. When they asked someone from another country whether they liked Moldova, they had to expect the answer to be "yes." In any case, that was my answer, and I knew many other Peace Corps volunteers who felt the same way. I didn't just like Moldova; I loved Moldova. I wished more Moldovans felt the same way. Really.

CHAPTER 12

SHADES OF GREY

Before Champa and I joined the Peace Corps at the age of sixty-three, we knew most of the other volunteers would be younger than our two sons. We were surprised to discover that one in four of those in our M31 group were fifty or older. Worldwide, Americans over the age of fifty comprised about seven percent of Peace Corps volunteers then. With better medical facilities and programs in fields such as business development, Moldova attracted people with lots of real-world experience, particularly with our group.

Whatever their reasons for choosing Moldova, our fellow older volunteers were impressive. They'd worked as professors, attorneys, IT managers, nonprofit leaders, teachers, city administrators, and management consultants. Coming from Harlem to California, they were single, widowed, divorced, or married. Like the other volunteers, they were also diverse ethnically, reflecting the country we represented.

We differed from our younger counterparts in some ways. Champa and I weren't the only ones who found it challenging to learn Romanian. We ran slower at group soccer games if we played at all. When our younger friends went to get tattoos, they knew better than to invite the two of us, although some of the older volunteers joined in. Some of our younger peers also partied harder than us and made surprising cultural references. When I was in the Peace Corps office one day, a Carole King song started playing, and the young woman next to me said, "Hey, it's that song from the Gilmore Girls!" On the other hand, they were usually polite when we made our own references to people and events from before they were born, so it tended to even out.

There were advantages to being an older volunteer in Moldova, just as there were in other Peace Corps countries. People in our host communities generally showed respect towards people our age. Having children and grandchildren provided us with an instant bond with older members of those communities, including the folks running the schools and other institutions. Our experience enhanced our credibility in our workplaces. My future colleagues wasted little time in checking me out online, so they knew I'd held positions of responsibility back home. This led them to treat me more like a peer or mentor even before I'd proven myself. As older volunteers, we could also share our long-standing hobbies, which included art and gardening for Champa.

The medical clearance process was especially tedious for older applicants, with our own taking several months even though we were in good health. Given all of the medical problems that arose with some of our older friends, I understood why the Peace Corps reviewed its applicants so carefully. It did accept some who were considerably older than us. A woman who joined the group two years behind us, just before we were left, was well into her seventies and starting on her third Peace Corps tour.

Many older Americans have family obligations, medical problems, and other constraints that make the Peace Corps unrealistic. Nonetheless, it is a proven program through which many Americans of all ages have served their country and the world. It isn't as strange or exotic as some people back home suggest, and it can't just be dismissed with, "Oh, I could never do that at *my* age."

Our friends Brent and Dee walked away in their sixties from long-time jobs at IBM in Tucson to join Peace Corps Moldova. They'd thought they were saying goodbye to software development projects but ended up applying their programming and project development skills in new ways, notably by creating a free program to help schools manage their class schedules. Dee, who grew up in Bangkok, identified this need during her first days as an English teacher when her schedule kept changing along with everyone else's. Her director could use existing software to develop schedules but had to pay to print each version. After discussing the problem with Dee's colleagues, Brent began developing a new class-scheduling system, eventually writing more than 20,000 lines of code. He completed a prototype within three months.

The program worked so effectively that neighboring schools installed it as well. Dee and Brent then reached out to Peace Corps education volunteers throughout Moldova, many of whose schools adopted the software, which Brent and Dee kept refining. A Peace Corps staffer brought the program to the attention of friends in Moldova's education ministry. One of them recognized the program's potential to solve a long-standing national problem without incurring new costs. She embraced it and began teaching regional workshops with Brent and Dee, training administrators on how to install and use the program. The ministry piloted it in 150 schools and planned to apply it nationally until personnel changes in the ministry slowed the effort.

Brent applied his computer skills on a second project as well, helping another volunteer build an online textile library to assist the country's fashion industry. Both projects were different from what he'd been doing at IBM but deeply satisfying in their own ways. He told me, "I used to enjoy working with our customers, and, of course, the company might give me promotions or financial rewards. Here I feel like I'm really making a difference in people's lives."

Dee agreed, saying, "We're not living in poverty as Peace Corps volunteers, but we're certainly not living as multimillionaires. We're getting a heck of a lot more than money."

Dee and Brent returned home after serving in Moldova to spend time with their two adult children and four grandchildren. They then returned to the Peace Corps to serve in Armenia. "Am I just going to sit around on my couch or my porch, waiting to die?" Dee explained to me. "My experience in the Peace Corps has shown me there is so much more I can do."

Carla, another older volunteer from Arizona, first thought about joining the Peace Corps when she was in college in the 1970s. However, she got married, had children, and started a career, ending up as a librarian in Yuma. When she was fifty-five, her husband died from melanoma just a few years before they'd both planned to retire. She kept working, but her life had been upended.

"By the time I was sixty, I needed a change from my job at a library," she told me. "I'm not sure why Peace Corps came to mind again. Maybe I saw something online or in the paper. I called and found out their oldest volunteer was eighty-four — a lot older than me. So I decided to retire and apply to Peace Corps myself."

Carla applied in June, interviewed in September, and was accepted in October. She went ahead and retired in December, then headed to the Pacific Northwest to say goodbye to relatives there. She hoped to go to Japan, as well, to visit an older son, but ran out of time.

The medical clearance process was drawn-out for her, too —
"both my doctor and I felt like we had to jump through a lot of hoops,"
she said — but she felt "it turned out to be good preparation for
the scrutiny that has followed. As a volunteer, you must check in if
you leave your site overnight. You can't leave the country or change
your work partner without permission. I've also had some smaller
annoyances, such as being told to bring dressy clothes I didn't need
or confronting an excessive number of Peace Corps acronyms."

Carla found it hard to learn Romanian and discovered that
"twenty-seven months is a long time to be away from your family
and friends, and from everything you enjoy back home." She
remained connected through Skype or FaceTime and, as she
approached the end of her service, looked forward to reclaiming
her life in Yuma, where she planned to do volunteer work, update
her townhouse, play golf, and travel. "I want to drive," she told
me before she left. "I want to use a clothes dryer again. I want my
independence back."

Carla questioned whether the Peace Corps took full advantage
of her skills and life experience. "Some volunteers, especially older
ones, arrive in Moldova with impressive work experience," she told
me. "Sometimes it's under-utilized. Communities may be unsure
what to do with their volunteer and don't really understand what
having a volunteer entails. Volunteers who were lawyers back home
may end up teaching beginning English rather than working in
community development. As a volunteer, you need to be flexible
and keep a sense of humor."

Ultimately, she found her Peace Corps experience to be pretty
much what she expected, saying, "It hasn't changed my outlook on
life. I was a sociology and anthropology major in college, so I have
always been fascinated by how different people act together. My
time in Moldova has allowed me to compare their customs with

our own. As I suspected, we are more alike than different. We work, play, love our families, and carry on despite political differences."

She was glad she came, saying, "Moldova is a lovely country. I love the fields of sunflowers, corn, and grapevines, and the grazing animals. There are horse-drawn wagons, and people with faces etched with character lines. Flowers decorate every village. People are warm and welcoming but not necessarily interested in changing their lives. Sometimes, I think they view us Americans as exotic plants to tend and admire but not necessarily to keep."

I had lots of conversations with older volunteers, both in Moldova and online, through a Facebook group for current and former Peace Corps volunteers above the age of fifty.

Debbie, an attorney from Cleveland who was in the group ahead of ours, said, "Peace Corps is a challenging and difficult undertaking, and your image of service is probably very different from the reality of service. ... Having practiced law for thirty-five years and learned to deal with surprises and expect the unexpected, I think it is critically important that volunteers — especially those who are older — approach Peace Corps service with no expectations. Each volunteer's service is uniquely their own."

Donna, who'd been a professor at Howard University, found her transition "easier said than done." After she'd been in Moldova for several months, she said, "I don't think I was that honest with myself. There are just some things that I am not willing to accept when it comes to living arrangements or personal hygiene."

Similarly, my friend Tom said the "steady comfort" of his previous life as an attorney in California was "replaced by a confusing and challenging environment." He measured each day "by small victories and small defeats."

Learning Romanian and absorbing a rapid flow of information during training was tough for many of us. Our friend Jim, a former commercial real estate broker in Raleigh, described training as "a firehose of information six days a week that can be overwhelming."

Another North Carolina friend, also named Tom, told me he was "tired at the end of the day and could not study well later, so I had to adjust; I would get out of bed early in the morning and study that which I most needed to learn. Afternoons and nights were for reviewing the day's information. It took me much longer than I expected to settle on a schedule."

Sandra, who came to Moldova from Tampa, said older volunteers needed to keep reminding themselves they were making a contribution despite the problems they might face learning a new language. "Even if you never make it to the fluency level to which you aspire, you can still make a big difference in your community," she said. "As the English teacher from my village once told me, 'you only need Romanian for two years, but they are going to need English for their entire lives.'"

Lisa, who served with her husband Steve in northern Moldova, pointed out another issue: "Depending upon your country of service, you may be treated like a frail oldster (and you're visibly so not), and they will absolutely invade your bubble. Let it go. This is not a job. This is a choice. Be open-minded, patient, and flexible, and lead from behind."

Our older friends in Moldova found lots of surprises. For Jim, the biggest was "the bathroom conditions around my school. It has seven holes in the ground separated by three-foot partitions. Occasionally, the boys miss the mark, so there is urine and fecal matter right there on the floor. Even in the winter, the stench is almost unbearable."

Donna was surprised by a lack of open opinions and thought. "There is very little thinking outside the box among most Moldovans," she said. "It's almost as though if it is not written somewhere, then it is not something to think about."

Lisa didn't expect to encounter so much "defeatism and dourness."

For many of Moldova's older volunteers, though, the biggest — and most pleasant — surprise was the close friendships they formed with other volunteers of all ages, as well as with Moldovans. "It never occurred to me that joining Peace Corps would give me one of the best opportunities for new friendships and in-depth conversations with fellow Americans," said Sandra, who gained "a growing understanding and greater awareness of our own racial and cultural diversity in the U.S."

Another member of her group who came from Seattle agreed, saying, "As an older volunteer, my first concern was that I would be isolated around the younger volunteers. To my surprise, I've made many wonderful friends among both the older and younger volunteers."

Older Americans need to navigate through Social Security, Medicare, 401(k) plans, private pensions, and more. Moldovans have a state system whose pensions are tiny but easier to understand. The ones I met were mystified by our hybrid approach and had trouble understanding why an older American would voluntarily leave the comforts of family and home to serve in a developing country. "Here in Moldova, most people retire in their late fifties," Debbie told me. "They assume I was retired before I joined Peace Corps, which isn't true. When I tell them I was working until I left, they often just shake their heads."

Simultaneously, my older volunteer friends were shown deference because of their age. "It is surprising just how well Moldovans treat older people," Brent said. "They really look out for them.

Moldova is a very poor country, the poorest in Europe, but they are very friendly and share what they have. We were regularly invited to events and celebrations and given the best seats. We were also given things just because they wanted to share."

Older volunteers serving elsewhere around the world shared similar experiences on the Facebook page and on a special Peace Corps website for older applicants. "Age has high standing and respect in the culture, thus being older than the life expectancy of sixty-five in Senegal has opened many doors," said Marcee, who served in her late sixties. "If they learn that I am an attorney in the U.S., the respect doubles."

Ultimately, success depends less on someone's age than on what is in their hearts. As our friend Andrea put it: "I would say to anyone considering Peace Corps service that, in whatever manner your age impacts your work and life at home, it will be the same serving in the Peace Corps."

What was most important was to expect the unexpected and embrace it. "It's awfully hard to predict what will surprise me," said our friend Valerie, an older teacher from Alabama who came to Moldova a year after us. "It wouldn't be much of a surprise if I could predict it ahead of time."

CHAPTER 13

OUR FELLOW VOLUNTEERS

I f you think Americans sign up to become Peace Corps volunteers because they're altruistic and want to help people around the world, you're right, but not completely right. A national survey of more than 11,000 returned Peace Corps volunteers found their top three reasons for joining were "wanting to live in another culture," "wanting a better understanding of the world," and "wanting to help people build a better life." Simultaneously, the survey reported "a significant generational shift" in the importance volunteers placed on acquiring job skills and experience during their service. Volunteers who served more recently placed "a greater emphasis on career development as a motivation for joining the Peace Corps," it said. Just thirty percent of volunteers who served in the 1960s identified "wanting to develop career and leadership skills" as an important motivation." Among volunteers who served in the 2000s, sixty-eight percent cited this motivation.

A volunteer who returned from Guatemala wrote: "I'm sure that my Peace Corps service helped me gain acceptance to a selective master's degree program (because my grades as an undergraduate were disappointing, at best). Over the years, many people have told me that having the words 'Peace Corps' on my resume would only help me." Indeed, the Peace Corps touts the career benefits of service. Its recruitment materials emphasize the importance of selfless service and cultural outreach, but they also highlight medical benefits, student loan deferrals, tuition reductions, and career networking opportunities.

Back when I served as a volunteer in Nepal, we barely discussed resumes, grad school applications, and job prospects. America was the world's dominant economic power; jobs were plentiful. Years later, when I first started talking with Duke students considering the Peace Corps, I was taken aback by how many of their questions were about career paths. Would serving in the Peace Corps help them get into law school, a public health program, or the Foreign Service? I always responded with encouragement and eventually came to see how their questions reflected new economic realities, not a diminishment in sincerity.

I developed an even greater admiration for today's generation of volunteers as I served beside them. They faced a more challenging economy but still chose to devote more than two years of their lives to serving others. No doubt, doing so enhanced their resumes and career prospects, but that was also true for young people who chose to serve in Teach for America or, for that matter, in the Marines. Life was complicated, just as it was for Champa and me, who joined the Peace Corps in Moldova mainly to serve others but also to pursue adventure and jump-start our transition away from our workaday lives.

Younger volunteers could do things that got on my nerves, like waiting until the last moment to respond to an invitation, if they responded at all. Some of them drank and partied too hard, passing out or doing other things that caused the Peace Corps director to crack down on everyone. When she banned all volunteers from attending one of Chişinău's biggest cultural events, its annual wine festival, she claimed it was because of "security concerns." We all understood the real reason was her worry that some volunteers might get drunk and misbehave. Rather than deal with them individually, she denied everyone the opportunity to enjoy the event, as we and others had the previous year. The country director also locked down the new volunteers during their training and after they swore in, restricting them to their villages as long as possible in a futile attempt to prevent them from coming to the capital, which almost everyone needed occasionally.

More generally, she enforced regulations rigidly, kicking out some of our best volunteers because of violations she might have found a way to handle more flexibly, as some of her counterparts did in other Peace Corps countries and as many of us have done when handling HR challenges with valued employees. There's usually a creative solution, even in a governmental organization. Eventually, she left to take another Peace Corps post.

The former Guatemala volunteer spoke for most of us when he said that what was ultimately most important about our Peace Cops service was "doing important, unglamorous work [while] connecting with foreigners from across the globe and humanizing the U.S. for thousands upon thousands of non-Americans." What endured, he wrote, was "the culture of altruism, adventure, and patriotism that has permeated the Peace Corps since the organization's inception."

I thought he was right, perhaps almost completely right.

Whatever other's motivations were, Champa and I came to treasure our friendships with the younger volunteers. One was Haley, a member of my community organizing group who'd graduated from college a few years earlier and then worked in restaurants and with Americorps before coming to Moldova. She spoke Russian well, which is why the Peace Corps posted her to the Russian-speaking city of Comrat, where Champa and I visited her journalism class. She produced a blog with thoughtful essays and beautiful photography. She fell in love with a French volunteer while in Comrat and attended graduate school after she finished.

Among Champa's good friends was Beth, a young teacher from upstate New York with whom she regularly chatted on the phone. Beth was an admirable young woman, as were so many of the others.

Ingrid showed me through her daily example how to slow down and appreciate what she playfully called our "fellow humans."

Katie exuded gentle professionalism.

Danny was knowledgeable about the Soviet legacy and would later pursue a fellowship in Russia.

Samantha and Alexandra worked hard to help Moldovan young women to become entrepreneurs.

William did terrific writing and editing for our tourism project, along with everything else at his site.

Reggie signed up to serve again in Tonga.

These were just a few of many examples. Everyone had a story to tell, and I was lucky to have an opportunity through my communications work with Liuba to help several of them to put their experiences into words for the Peace Corps Stories website. One of my first editing jobs was with Katrina and Bartosz, two volunteers who worked with teenagers to organize recycling projects, first at their posts in northern Moldova and then across the country.

A volunteer from Colorado, Chrystal, discussed how she and others brought young people together to talk about sexual assault and harassment.

Scott, a health education volunteer from California, described his experience serving as a godparent to the child of his adult Moldovan host sister.

Hayley, an English education volunteer from Florida, shared a funny but inspiring story about coming all the way to Moldova to overcome her anxiety about singing in public.

Rebecca humorously explained how someone who grew up in American suburbs learned to live around farm animals.

Although we produced most of these stories for the Moldova section of Peace Corps Stories, many were picked up by the Peace Corps communications team in Washington to feature worldwide. As I'd told the students in the Diamond Challenge entrepreneurship competition, the best way to help an audience understand what you're doing, and to care about it, was by telling them stories, as Oprah Winfrey had done in the Golden Globes speech we analyzed. Our volunteers had great stories to share.

We met up with other volunteers at meetings or events downtown, although this became harder as the country director cracked down on people coming to the capital. At the beginning of our second year, a new group of trainees arrived and was assigned to live with host families in Ialoveni and surrounding villages. They seemed disoriented at first, as we'd been a year earlier. Along with several members of my group, I helped out with their training. I led a session about our projects at our library, followed by a walking tour of Ialoveni together with Champa. We left time at the end of our walk for everyone to visit the big market near the library so they could buy food or supplies unavailable in their villages. They looked exhausted, and I treated them all to ice cream pops. By the time they finished training several weeks later, though, most of them were speaking Romanian fairly well and were excited to begin their jobs. Shortly before they swore in, Champa and I joined a group of them in a community service project to paint a playground near Ialoveni's outdoor market.

Our own group met several times during our service to review our progress and get more language tutoring. Early in our second year, we met for a three-day "mid-service" conference at a hotel near the Nistru River, the first time we'd all come together instead of in our four program groups. Despite the differences in our ages, backgrounds, and job assignments, we shared a common experience and now felt a strong bond. Our conference included sessions on community development, helping people with disabilities, service learning, teaching life skills, and a myriad of other topics. We discussed our journeys as volunteers and how to stay healthy and resilient during the year ahead. We had a session on Moldova's history and a crash course on how to say a few expressions in Russian.

The most inspiring moment for me, though, came during our final session, when everyone in my community development group took turns describing their plans for the coming year. They spoke about dance programs, journalism clubs, robotics teams, English clubs, youth projects, women's groups, and more. Their lists were so long the session ran well past its deadline.

By then, almost everyone in M31 had formed at least a few close relationships with Moldovans. Several participated in a Facebook campaign called "Super Moldovans" that Liuba organized to call attention to our local partners. Celia, a volunteer from Ohio, posted a photo together with a science teacher from her school whose "dedication, kindness, and willingness to help" she admired. Donna posed with her school director for working "so long, with so little. She is a true inspiration to me." Michelle, from California, took a photo with a student whose "enthusiasm never ceases to amaze me." We posted these and other salutes in Romanian and English so volunteers could share them, and Moldovans could see the nice things said about their neighbors. "When I showed the Super Moldovan page to my director with a picture of the two of us, her face lit up as though I had given her a pot of gold," Donna told me later. "I swear I made her day. She began sharing it with friends and family. She recently lost her husband, and this is the first time in weeks I have seen her grin."

Some of the volunteers who came to Moldova stayed after they finished their Peace Corps assignments. They found jobs at schools, started businesses, or got married. A young woman in the group ahead of us completed her service shortly before she and her Moldovan husband had their first child.

Two recent volunteers opened their American-style barbecue joint, called Smokehouse, with a Moldovan friend. They sold barbecue sandwiches, ribs, hush puppies, and other specialties in a room decorated with U.S. state flags and a football. They also made a point of refusing to pay any Moldovan officials a bribe, organizing a group of local small business owners who insisted on transparency and honesty in their operations. Local officials tried to shut them down on various pretexts, but they resisted the pressure, calling in reporters to highlight what was happening. As I noted in an article I wrote for *WorldView*, the international magazine of the National Peace Corps Association, they were rejecting Moldova's pervasive cynicism and serving up optimism with a side of slaw. Both of the American owners thought their impact was far greater than when they'd been volunteers.

The Moldovans working for the Peace Corps made our work possible. The program staff taught us a new language, arranged our work assignments, identified our host families, and trained us before and after swearing-in. An administrative team transported us to our sites, processed our grants, replenished our bank accounts, monitored our safety, and publicized our work. The medical team vaccinated us and monitored our physical and mental health, responding to everything from sore throats to sexual assaults or heart attacks. They were supported by everyone working with the Peace Corps back in the United States to recruit and evaluate new volunteers, develop new programs, and drum up support from Congress and the White House. The staff's work was less glamorous than ours, but it undergirded everything we did. PCVs like us came and went, but the local staff remained, mastering the arcane rules of both the Moldovan government and the Peace Corps. They dealt with unreliable host families, unsettling security situations, unhappy volunteers, and more, usually with grace and effectiveness, and they rejoiced in our successes.

The chief medical officer, Dr. Iuliana, was a jewel — skillful, thorough, caring, and endlessly dedicated to keeping volunteers healthy. She knew how stressful Peace Corps service could be and never missed a chance to ask us how we were doing, always meaning it as a real question. We got our medical care for free. During our pre-service training, the medical team ran workshops on everything from water purification to traffic safety. When we moved to our posts, they gave us water filters and well-stocked medical kits. They continued to fill prescriptions and provide routine services in a clinic within the Peace Corps building. When necessary, they sent volunteers to local specialists or, occasionally, back home or elsewhere for treatment, coordinating with the Peace Corps medical office in Washington.

Champa and I both fell on the ice badly during our second winter and had a few colds and stomach issues. I got giardiasis twice. However, we were generally healthy and never had to stay overnight in

Dr. Iuliana's infirmary. When I thought back to my experience as a young Peace Corps volunteer in Nepal, where I had two bouts of pneumonia and numerous parasitic infections, I knew how lucky we were.

In another article I wrote for *WorldView*, I asked whether Peace Corps volunteers had become "over-connected," clinging to their smartphones and Wi-Fi connections as a way to avoid engaging with their host communities. I interviewed many former volunteers online and shared my own memories of working off the grid as a volunteer in Nepal, which helped me integrate with my community. I also described how I now benefitted from being online, not only to stay connected with my family and friends back home but also to help me do my job and pursue the Peace Corps goal of helping Americans learn about other countries.

Among the many responses I received was one from a former volunteer who served in Liberia and went on to pursue other developmental work in Africa. "I have worked in countries where PCVs are posted and have gotten to know them and the staff," he wrote me in a message I shared on my blog. "Many parents of PCVs these days hover too much. I know staff at PC that get calls from parents if they do not get FaceTime or chat for a few days. A week is a 3-alarm panic. Being a bit disconnected is rather difficult and unpopular these days, and it's no different in PC life. I think this has created some space for PCVs to interact less with their hosts and more with people back home in some cases. In Liberia, would I have sat under a palm tree with my local buddies drinking palm wine and chewing on kola nuts for hours if I had Facebook and chat going with my friends back home, or if I was streaming movies?

"It is not always an easy debate between old RPCVs and recent ones. It always comes down to 'we had it TOUGH because ...' Social media and the need to be connected is a sword with two blades. One keeps us more in touch with family and global events. The other may keep us from socializing with our hosts and performing the MAIN goal of PC service. That is to interact with people in host countries, so THEY get to know more about average Americans, and WE get to know more about normal people in a far-off land and bring that back home.

"When THAT interaction is achieved (forget about PC small projects that may or may not have worked), then the real purpose of PC service has been achieved. I think this is still going strong, but social media has added the risk that if a PCV is not outgoing or is too reclusive, he or she could spend two years on Facebook and never make an impact on this goal."

Many Americans seldom wonder whether today's volunteers are over-connected. They barely know that Peace Corps still exists at all. More than a half-century had passed since President Kennedy established the agency, appointing his brother-in-law, Sargent Shriver, to get it off the ground. Shriver proved to be a brilliant choice, moving volunteers into the field in a remarkably short time and defining a mission and approach that largely endured. More than 220,000 Americans had served in more than 140 countries by the time we left for Moldova, with more than sixty of the country programs currently active. Nearly half of the volunteers were serving in Africa, with the next largest contingents in Latin America, Eastern Europe, and Asia. Nearly two-thirds were women, thirty-two percent were minorities, and the large majority were single. More than sixty percent worked primarily in education or health.

"Do they come to your house, and they take you to another

country?" the late-night host Jimmy Kimmel asked former volunteer Rep. Joe Kennedy III when he appeared on the show, a segment we watched the next evening on YouTube. Kennedy answered some initial questions about his famous relatives but spent much of the segment describing the Peace Corps to Jimmy and the audience.

"No, you actually have to get on a plane," he laughed. "That's the 'volunteer' part." The Massachusetts Democrat went on to call the Peace Corps "an organization close to my heart [that] does an awful lot of good around the world" and his service as "the most impactful experience" of his life. He teased Kimmel that he should consider it as well.

Champa and I had heard Joe Kennedy speak eloquently about his Peace Corps service several years earlier at an event we attended at Arlington National Cemetery to honor the organization's fiftieth anniversary. A few weeks later, he announced his candidacy for Congress. Now, he reassured Jimmy Kimmel that the Peace Corps is "not for everybody," and Kimmel jokingly agreed. If I were Jimmy Kimmel, I wouldn't walk away either from a network talk show and a huge salary, especially with a young family. More to the point, if the thought of leaving America for two years to serve in a distant community sounded unappealing, then it wasn't a good fit for Jimmy Kimmel or anyone else. He had emerged as an important voice on health care, immigration, and other issues since Trump's election, so I was glad he didn't take the idea seriously. Maybe some of his viewers did. If it took a late-night talk show to nudge them to think about it, then so be it.

The most common question my American friends asked me after I moved to Moldova was whether I found being a Peace Corps volunteer different from when I served in Nepal four decades earlier.

My short answer was "yes, of course," but the experience still felt familiar. As before, I'd left my family and country to serve people in another country, learning their language and sharing their daily lives. After I'd been in Moldova for a while, though, several differences did stand out to me.

For starters, I was much more connected to the outside world than I was the first time. I had a smartphone, a laptop, and a Kindle, all linked to Wi-Fi. I regularly talked to my family. I could follow the U.S. election campaign and other news. I interacted online with my Moldovan partners and Peace Corps colleagues. In contrast, when I served in Nepal, I was cut off.

Another change was that safety and security had become a much bigger deal for volunteers worldwide. Neither terrorism nor street crime were serious problems in Moldova, yet our training was filled with security briefings. We were given detailed emergency action plans. I couldn't leave my post overnight without notifying the staff. I couldn't even enter the Peace Corps office without passing through a locked gate, a guard, and a metal detector — again, in a country with a low terror threat. In Nepal, I used to ride my bicycle past a front gate nominally staffed by a guard, and then stroll inside.

This new emphasis on security reflected a broader expansion in the Peace Corps infrastructure. There was so much more bureaucracy and physical stuff. My desk was piled with Romanian language workbooks, brochures on Moldovan culture, a "volunteerism action guide," and more. I had dozens of resources on a computer thumb drive the Peace Corps gave me. There were detailed protocols for everything from paying a language tutor to taking a trip. In Nepal, our training was also excellent, but we had fewer resources and a lot less red tape.

I was also serving in a different country this second time around. Moldova is in Eastern Europe, with an agricultural economy best known for its wine. Its population is almost entirely white and Orthodox Christian. Nepal is in the Himalayas and mainly Hindu, but mixed with Buddhists, Christians, and Muslims. Both countries have delicious food and fascinating customs, but they are as different as can be, except for both being landlocked.

Inevitably, the Peace Corps experience was different, too. What's more, the world had changed over four decades. When I served in Nepal, the United States was still in a Cold War with the Soviet Union, which included Moldova. China was poor. Personal computers were new. Gay people could not get married. The idea of an African American president was almost unimaginable. After four decades, the Peace Corps had evolved to reflect this changed reality, such as with programs to combat HIV/AIDS or to "let girls learn."

Most importantly, I had changed, too. When I joined the Peace Corps in Nepal, I was two years out of college, single, and eager to save the world. Now I was a father and grandfather and serving with my wife, whom I met in Nepal. I was much older and hopefully a bit wiser. In any case, I was in a different place in my life and not just geographically.

In other words, I could watch Jimmy Kimmel or a YouTube video instead of fiddling with a shortwave radio to find a signal from the BBC, but the Peace Corps still had the same beating heart. Once again, I was working alongside a wonderful group of Americans to serve others and represent our country. I felt privileged to be among them. Who knows? Perhaps there was even a new form I was supposed to fill out to confirm this.

The Peace Corps has three goals, established by President Kennedy. The first is to build the local capacity of people in interested countries and help meet their needs for trained men and women. The second is to promote a better understanding of Americans among people in other countries. The third is to increase America's awareness and knowledge of other cultures and global issues. When it comes to changing the attitudes Americans have about people in developing countries, Peace Corps volunteers are well-situated to provide facts, stories, and perspectives. Indeed, their mandate to promote cultural understanding in both directions became even more important after Trump's election.

Almost all of our training and programmatic support, however, was focused on the first goal. My "community and organizational development" (COD) group spent countless hours learning about community needs assessment, community mapping, and community surveys. Champa's English education group studied teaching techniques and pedagogy. Our overall group met together many times but never had a session devoted to the other two goals. Not even once.

When I was invited with other COD volunteers to participate in a detailed review of our program, these goals never came up until I asked about them at the end. Peace Corps Moldova did add a session on communications for incoming volunteers after I suggested it, and the training paid off with increased volunteer blogging and other activity to promote cultural understanding. But it was one session and was never followed up. A management rule is that the amount of time people and organizations spend on a topic reflects its importance to them. The tiny amount of time Peace Corps Moldova devoted to cross-cultural communications spoke for itself, although it did back Liuba's innovations and encouraged volunteers to get involved in activities such as Peace Corps Week.

Worldwide, the Peace Corps has taken some steps to give its second and third goals more prominence, such as with international contests that encourage volunteers to produce videos or blogs. It has beefed up its online and social media activities and provided training for local staff around the world. It created a "Third Goal" office that maintains a media library and assists outreach activities. Some returned volunteers also share their experiences and perspectives in various ways. All of this is good, but it was at the margins of what I saw discussed and supported while serving with Peace Corps Moldova.

To be sure, many of my fellow volunteers did amazing things at their job sites and in their communities, just like their counterparts around the world. Yet, they could have accomplished even more if the Peace Corps had made communications a real priority in its recruiting, training, program development, and assessment. I was frustrated during my service to know the Peace Corps could have been more impactful in teaching our families and friends back home about distant places they may have regarded as mysterious or dangerous. At a time when President Kennedy's latest successor was referring to developing countries as "shitholes," their voices and experiences needed to be heard more widely.

CHAPTER 14

WHAT COULD GO RIGHT

When Champa and I left the conventional workplace to pursue a life of adventure and service, and especially after we joined the Peace Corps, people pointed out all of the things that could go wrong. What if something happens to one of your children or grandchildren? What if you have a medical emergency? What if you can't learn the language? What if you're robbed? What if there's a terrorist attack? What if things just don't work out?

To be sure, we also heard, "That's awesome!" And, "I've dreamed of that!" The cautionary questions were common, though, and they illustrated why so many people who imagine making a big change in their lives never take action. I generally responded that bad things can happen in our traditional lives, too. Since Champa and I were lucky enough to have our health, finances, and family circumstances in order, we were going to listen to our hearts and take a chance.

It didn't take long after we arrived in Moldova for us to be reminded of how quickly dreams *can* end. During our training, an older woman in my group dropped out because of health problems and family issues back home. One of Champa's older friends, who had taught school for many years in the United States and other countries, also left before the end of the training. Another of her friends made it past the swearing-in process and taught success-fully at her site for several months before dropping out to return to the States, where her daughter had just given birth prematurely. My best friend in my training group worked for nearly a year at his post before returning to the States for what he thought would be a quick medical procedure. He ran into complications and never made it back.

Another older man in our group returned home for several weeks to deal with back problems. He eventually returned, although he was later kicked out because he wanted to attend his daughter's college graduation. The ceremony occurred during his final ninety days of service, when volunteers weren't allowed to leave Moldova. The country director refused to make an exception, even though the trip wouldn't have interfered with his work, and he would have paid for it. He went anyway, gave up his status as a volunteer, and then came back to Moldova on his own to rejoin his wife for an after-service trip.

Around this time, still another older volunteer had a heart scare and was rushed to England for treatment, being "medically sep-arated" just weeks before he was scheduled to finish his service. He, too, returned to Moldova on his own, so he could say a proper goodbye to his host family and travel with a friend.

Some younger volunteers had medical problems, as well. Other volunteer friends returned home because they were homesick, couldn't adjust to life in Moldova, had family responsibilities back home, or got into trouble. Several had to leave because the Peace Corps thought there were security threats in their villages. Others encountered sexual harassment, or worse. Worldwide, more than 300 people had died since 1961 while pursuing the Peace Corps mis-sion, many from motor vehicle accidents, but some were murdered.

The risks were real, in other words, as we knew before we left, and as I remembered from my two bouts with pneumonia in Nepal. Yet even though Peace Corps volunteers faced special challenges, their fatality rate was the same or lower than for Americans generally when controlled for age, marital status, and educational attainment, according to one research study.

Nonetheless, even in a place like Moldova, where living conditions were easier than in some other countries, serving as a volunteer *was* tough. It wasn't a vacation. The experience challenged us every day, forcing us to examine our lives and beliefs. It changed how we thought about the world and ourselves. We never regretted our decision, even when we were sweltering in airless minibuses in the summer. We viewed every day as a gift. Every time one of our friends left, especially the older ones, we reminded ourselves how lucky we were to have this experience. Something could go wrong for us, too, perhaps the next day. But so long as we had the opportunity, we were staying focused on what could go right.

The path we'd charted for ourselves was not for everyone. Many Americans in their fifties, sixties, and seventies *want* to be retired in a traditional sense — playing golf, gardening, or enjoying life in some other way. Others seek to remain connected to their workplace or profession. Some end up watching too much television or getting depressed. In a book published while we were in Moldova, *Too Young to Be Old: Love, Learn, Work, and Play as You Age*, sociologist Nancy K. Schlossberg described six common routes for people in the second half of life. She called them "continuers," "adventurers," "easy gliders," "involved spectators," "searchers," and "retreaters." Champa and I fit most closely into her "adventurer" category, which she described as "an opportunity to pursue an unrealized dream or try something new." In my case, there was also an element of "continuer," since I'd remained active in communications, although in a different way.

I was ready for our transition, but it still took me time to adjust. I had trouble letting go of my professional identity, which I continued to highlight on my LinkedIn profile for many months after I left Duke. Only later did I change it to emphasize my role as a volunteer and blogger. Taking extended trips across the United States and Nepal helped loosen my grip. Serving in the Peace Corps then provided me with a new identity and a well-established mission and structure. Still, the whole time we were in Moldova, I knew we would eventually return home and again face the challenge of defining "who am I?" for ourselves and others. We'd need to reaffirm our identities within our families and community back home.

The process never ended.

Schlossberg's book reminded me how other members of my generation had retirement dreams very different from our own, yet dreams that were equally valid and compelling. All of us entering this phase of our lives were sharing the challenge of finding a new blend of identity, relationships, and purpose to fit our circumstances.

What I came to understand during our three years away from home, especially while we were in the Peace Corps, is that the most important choice is to actually make a choice, to act instead of drift. We all face life transitions sooner or later. We can either resist them or embrace them, even as our destinations diverge.

Most of the changes I was experiencing weren't as big or obvious as giving up my former job title and paycheck. Before I joined the Peace Corps, for instance, I wouldn't have thought twice about eating a bowl of cereal, waving goodbye to my wife, and heading off to work in the morning.

After more than two months of training and finally moving to our permanent post in Ialoveni, though, I was excited to start going to work again every day. On my first morning, I had corn flakes for breakfast with a cup of coffee and a banana, which I savored for feeling so normal. During the previous two months, my host mother had served me breakfasts of kasha, sausages, eggs, chicken cutlets, spaghetti, or hot cereal. I enjoyed her food but yearned for cold cereal and a cup of coffee, which I could finally enjoy again after Champa and I moved to Ialoveni and bought our first three bags of groceries at a local store for $16. My coffee was instant Nescafe, and the cereal was a kind of children's corn flakes from Ukraine, but the morning was cool, ending a long hot spell without air conditioning. I noticed these simple pleasures only because I'd been living without them. I had to come halfway around the world to appreciate what I'd enjoyed routinely in America.

The Peace Corps warned us during our training that we'd need to adjust to a different pace of life. "Take your time," they told us. "Learn about your community, form relationships, and win trust. If you do that, your projects and work agenda will emerge naturally."

Their advice reflected what I'd told new communications employees at my last conventional job, to meet people and get the lay of the land before rushing off to start producing articles and websites. "You'll be busy soon enough," I told them. Soon enough, they were.

So, I should have internalized what the Peace Corps was telling me, yet I couldn't let go of old habits. I kept checking my cell phone for messages. I wouldn't go home at the end of the day until I completed every item on my "to do" list. I did try hard to meet people, attend events, and learn about my new surroundings, but I couldn't get the checklist out of my head. Champa found this amusing, reminding me that I'd named my blog "not exactly retired."

She was right, of course.

My new life wasn't as hectic as my old one, but it *was* rich and productive, as illustrated by one of my first days on the job. I had a great chat that morning with the district government's president. Then a colleague dropped by to discuss an archaeological project that needed support, leading me to spend time online exploring possible funding sources. Later that day, I received an e-mail message from a North Carolina State University expert on grapes and wine production, who responded to my request for help with Ialoveni's wine industry. I also heard back from the communications director of Dreamups, the Moldovan entrepreneurship center, and set up a meeting with her. A Peace Corps colleague contacted me, too, to answer some of my questions about an upcoming conference to discuss projects for the "Let Girls Learn" campaign.

On my way home, I went to the local telephone store to upgrade my Wi-Fi account and to the grocery store to buy food for dinner. Champa and I splurged, buying several flaky *plăcinte* — cherry-filled for breakfast and cheese-filled for lunch. The store had a plate for each kind, plus some whose Romanian name we didn't recognize. I asked the clerk whether she knew their name in English. "Halloween," she said, which we eventually figured out to mean "pumpkin."

It was a rewarding day, even before I studied Romanian after dinner, and it confirmed the advice I'd received about being patient and open to opportunities. Even so, I needed to adjust my definitions of success. I was now a Peace Corps volunteer, not a guy in a suit who earned a paycheck. Perhaps I should have written myself a reminder about this new reality with an electronic memo on my iPhone.

Learning Romanian proved far more difficult than when I'd studied Nepali four decades earlier. It was humbling to know my brain was now different from those of some younger colleagues, who seemed to remember phrases with ease. As a former science writer, I felt like shouting, "Damn you, neural plasticity!" I was so busy studying during our training that I barely had time to chat with Champa on the phone or pay attention to what was happening in the outside world.

Over the next two years, even though I followed stories such as the MeToo movement, and President Trump's confrontation with North Korea, I remained much less engaged with American news than I'd been before. American cable news stations weren't available in Moldova, where most of the content was local, Russian, or from Romania.

Champa and I didn't have a television, much less English-language newspapers or magazines. We did buy online subscriptions to *The New York Times* and *The Washington Post*, and we read other publications on our laptops. While we were cooking and eating dinner, we'd watch the previous night's comedy monologues. I couldn't believe I'd become one of those people whose main source of news was late-night comedians. This was a big change for me. When I ran a news office, I monitored the news throughout the day. It was my job and passion. My team jumped to highlight faculty experts who could discuss the latest political drama, natural disaster, or social trend. Now, just like an obese person who goes on a diet, I felt lighter and healthier. I was still curious about what was happening in the world but also grateful to no longer watch as cable stations flogged a story hour after hour while their commentators argued.

I was an active user of Facebook, Instagram, and other social media, but I struggled to stay atop the dizzying array of systems for sharing messages or speaking with someone on the phone. Our older son, back home, used Skype. His wife and my older sister preferred Facebook Messenger. My other son and his wife used FaceTime, as did my younger sister. My training group used WhatsApp. Some volunteers called home with Yolla or Google Hangouts Dialer. Our Nepali nieces in England liked Viber. Our Nepali nephew, who was studying in China, used WeChat and Sina Weibo. If I wanted to speak with an American friend in Moldova, I needed to remember whether that person preferred a phone call, an e-mail message, a text, or a specific online platform. My Moldovan friends generally preferred telephone calls, but this was changing, too.

The Peace Corps gave me a local SIM card for my iPhone when we arrived, and it paid for a monthly plan that included a generous amount of free calling minutes and internet access. I supplemented the latter with a portable router and wireless plan I purchased from a local company. Volunteers who didn't bring a phone received one from the Peace Corps, together with a SIM card. When I traveled outside Moldova, I added extra money to my phone account and activated its international roaming feature.

It was great to have all of these communications options, particularly since so many of them were free, but remembering everyone's preferences reminded me of planning a dinner party where one guest is a vegetarian, another is lactose intolerant, another keeps kosher, and another avoids gluten. Who could keep track of it all?

Things were much simpler when I served in Nepal four decades earlier. Back then, I didn't call home at all during my two years abroad. If I'd wanted to call the United States, I would have had to ride my bicycle to an office near the Kathmandu stadium and pay an exorbitant fee to sit in a booth and hope they could make a connection. I never bothered with it. Neither did most of my volunteer friends. We mailed letters instead.

I also read a lot of books in Nepal, trading them with other volunteers and looking for used books in Kathmandu's shops. I read a lot in Moldova, as well, but I downloaded almost all of them onto a Kindle. I generally got them for free through the OverDrive system offered by both the Duke and Durham libraries. Each library allowed me to borrow several books at once, for three weeks each. I read recent novels, biographies, nonfiction, and mysteries, as well as travel adventures and how-to books. I also downloaded free copies of more than a dozen classics from a site called Project Gutenberg, my favorite being Bram Stoker's *Dracula*, since we'd visit the Transylvania castle named for the famous villain. I bought some books that weren't in the OverDrive system, such as *Bessarabian Nights*, a recent novel by Stela Brinzeanu about human trafficking in Moldova. For me, an active reader living far from home with a limited budget, the ability to download books via Wi-Fi, usually for free, was a godsend, even though I missed drinking coffee in Duke's Perkins Library.

Just a few days before Donald Trump's stunning upset in the 2016 election, which left many of us in the Peace Corps wondering what we were doing in Moldova, I received a message out of the blue that confirmed what we'd heard repeatedly during our training: You never knew whose life you might touch, no matter what happened in the wider world. The message came from Signor, one of my students when I taught English at a school near Kathmandu during my second year in Nepal. He contacted me on Facebook, asking: "Hi, are you the same David Jarmul who was peace corp volunteer back in late 70 in Nepal? Remember Lab times in lab school? I was one of your student? I was looking for you since 1988."

Of course, I remembered the Lab Times, the wall newspaper I started at the school, but I didn't remember Signor — one of several hundred students I had there and in Ilam. Still, I wrote him back, and he responded quickly. "Wow, I was looking for you since I came to US as a student back in 1989," he replied, describing how he was now married, living in Maryland, and working as a software engineer for the federal government. "You used to tell a story of America and show us moon landing documentary and made me participate in play Snow White. That made me dream of America and came here. You do plant a seed on a boy who was 10 years old. Thanks for helping me. Please let me know when you visiting back to US."

Coincidentally, I'd responded just a few days earlier to another unexpected message, this one from Australia. It was from the son of a friend of mine from Ilam. Perhaps there were others, too. I didn't really know. Neither did most other Peace Corps volunteers who completed their service years earlier.

Signor's timing could hardly have been more auspicious. He was like a message in a bottle, washing ashore just when I needed to discover it in the wake of the election. It reminded me that no matter what happened in politics, we all had the power to make a difference in other people's lives, even if our impact was not revealed until years later, if ever.

That remained true for Champa and me in Moldova and for other volunteers around the world. The Peace Corps still touched lives every day, with bipartisan support from Republicans and Democrats. Even as our country struggled to heal after a bitter campaign, as it would over the next several years, Signor's message showed we all have the power to make the world a better place. Elections matter, profoundly, and I looked forward to getting engaged myself after I returned home and was free of Peace Corps restrictions against politics. But sitting there in Moldova, tempted to despair, I treasured Signor's words that we were there to plant seeds, as he had put it. We needed to keep faith that the seeds would bloom in ways we couldn't predict.

Serving previously in Nepal gave me special insight into what Champa and I were doing in Moldova. As we neared the end of our service, I shared on my blog the op-ed article I'd published in *The New York Times* shortly after I returned from Nepal in 1979. I knew I'd failed to live up to much of what I wrote then, and my perspective about the Peace Corps and life had evolved, but parts of the article still resonated with me. Let me close this chapter by sharing it here, too:

People wrote to me before I recently returned home to New York, after two years in Peace Corps, about all the changes I'd find: disco, roller skating, a new mayor, a decent Rangers team.

But nobody warned me about what's remained the same: how rich and wasteful this city is.

New York's being rich sounds strange, I know. After all, the city was staving off bankruptcy when I left in 1977. And I hear similar sacrificial moans from New Yorkers now about gas prices and inflation.

But today those cries ring hollow. After I've lived so long in a truly poor country, New York seems like Fat City. People here don't realize how lucky they have it.

My post was in Nepal. My first year was spent in a Himalayan hill bazaar, Ilam, the second in Katmandu, the capital. I taught English and writing, worked with blind students, set up several newspapers and organized a village literacy project.

The Peace Corps paid me $76 monthly, $92 in Katmandu. This was plenty. The per capita income in Nepal is less than $100 per year. Given the skewed distribution of wealth, many Nepalese live on less than 15 cents daily. Most children work. The literacy rate is below 20 percent.

One of my students in Ilam was Mardi Kumar, an untouchable. One week he didn't come to school. I went to his house to see why not. His father told me that Mardi's older brother was dying in the local hospital.

The doctor said Mardi's brother needed insulin. There was none to be had in eastern Nepal. The father pleaded with me. I was a foreigner;

didn't I have some insulin? No, I didn't. A few days later his son died.

In Katmandu, I hired a cook, Harka Bahadur. I taught him to read Nepalese and gave him room, board and $1.75 weekly. The neighbors complained that this was too much and would drive up local prices. I insisted. Harka supported his mother, wife and baby daughter on his salary. He had no money for eggs, fruit or medicines. In the winter I had to convince him to take a sweater I'd been given for the holidays.

Now I'm home. My first full day back, my folks took me to see the new shopping atrium at the Citicorp headquarters. I saw imported jams at $10 per bottle, exotic pastries, shiny furniture stores, a giant delicatessen, several chic cafes.

It was a shock. I could not believe the extravagance, the wealth.

The following morning I had an argument with my father about Mother's Day. My father wanted me to buy my mother an azalea bush. As much as I love her, I couldn't bring myself to spend the money. My mother doesn't need an azalea bush, I told him. So why waste money that others need just to survive?

My father told me that I was culture-shocked. I ought to stop converting New York prices into what they could buy abroad. Nepal was Nepal. This was New York. Why take it out on my mother?

A few days later my grandmother complained to me that she has to travel a long way from her house in Flushing to take my grandfather to the doctor to get his prescriptions filled. I sympathized, but I couldn't help reminding her how fortunate she is to have medicines available at all. After all - Mardi's brother didn't.

Then a conversation with my other grandmother: She asked what kind of furniture I plan to buy for my new apartment. I told her I will get whatever is cheapest while not squalid. She responded with a smile and reassured me that with time I will get over this "phase" and back into American life.

The point is that right now, I don't want to get back into a consumptive

American life. I don't want to jump on the bottled water bandwagon when I can just as easily drink water out of the faucet like I did before I left and give the 70 cents per bottle to somebody who really needs it.

But, as I've learned quickly, to say those things out loud, even with the excuse of being just out of Peace Corps, makes one come across like an Asianized Jeremiah. Friends ask me, quite rightly, just what it is that I expect them to do. Give up all of life's small luxuries until there are no more poor people? My instinctive reaction right now is to say yes.

That's idealistic and unworkable, I know, but I remember too vividly my Nepalese friends: Rudra Bahadur, the farmer across the street who thanked me profusely when I gave him my worn-out rugby shirt. Ram Prasad, a fellow teacher who almost burst into tears when I gave him the seven dollar calculator that I'd bought in Times Square. The Brahmin village family —I don't even know their names — who shared with me their dinner of rice, lentils and dried yams when I appeared on their doorstep one evening while hiking.

Intellectually, I recognize that if a friend here spends $20 extra on a pair of blue jeans just to sport a designer label; it isn't going to make any difference to the lives of my Nepalese friends. Not unless the friend chooses to send that $20 to Nepal and just take a pair of Levi's.

But I can't choose for others. And I also know that I must fight off this moralism. I know there are many poor New Yorkers, poor Americans. Our country can't take upon itself all of the world's suffering. We shouldn't all go through life guilt-ridden. After all: that's Nepal, this is New York.

Still, as I face my new life ahead, I keep wondering: Am I really as culture-shocked as people tell me, or is American society as profligate as it now seems to me? Will I be able to hold onto my new convictions about living modestly and helping others? Will I remember?

CHAPTER 15

TRAVELING OFF THE BEATEN PATH

We didn't spend all of our time in Moldova. While we were serving in the Peace Corps, we used our vacation time to explore several other countries near the Black Sea — Romania, Bulgaria, Armenia, Georgia, and Ukraine — as well as better-known destinations closer to the West: Vienna, Budapest, and Bratislava. We went home for nearly three weeks after our first year; and, immediately after we completed our service a year later, we traveled to northern Italy.

We also explored Moldova, such as when we joined our host family on a driving trip to the northern city of Soroca. A regional center of about 35,000 people, Soroca once had many Jews, now almost all gone, but still had a sizable Roma population living mainly in a neighborhood known as Gypsy Hill, where majestic homes mimicked St. Peter's Basilica at the Vatican, Moscow's Bolshoi Theatre, and even the U.S. Capitol. We drove there to see it for ourselves, stopping along the way for a picnic inside our van since it was too cold to eat outside. On the outskirts of Soroca, we climbed 662 steps to a monument called the Candle of Gratitude, a ninety-seven-foot tall tower honoring people who preserved Moldova's language and culture. Before we left the city, we stopped for lattes and tea at the local Andy's Pizza, where we met several Peace Corps friends posted in the area. As we drove back to Ialoveni, we stopped for a second picnic, this one featuring turkey and rabbit, cheese, stuffed cabbage, cake, and small cups of homemade wine.

A friend in the group ahead of us organized our most extensive trip in Moldova, a weekend tour of monasteries and wineries. All of us were older volunteers, happy to splurge and spend time together.

Our first monastery was Moldova's most famous tourist site, Orheiul Vechi, or "Old Orhei." Located less than an hour's drive from Chişinău, it was both a church and an archaeological complex, with caves, grottos, and religious structures that reflected different civilizations, all situated on promontories overlooking a gorgeous view. Next, we visited the Curchi Monastery, whose main structure was an imposing red baroque church dedicated to the virgin birth. A priest rang its bells when we were there, filling the air with music. Finally, we stopped along the Dniester River to see the historic Tipova Monastery and its stone cave cells, which we reached after descending a steep path. Monks have worshipped there for centuries.

We stayed overnight at one of Moldova's best wineries, Chateau Vartely, where we shared a fancy dinner with some of their wine. The next day we visited another winery, Cricova, which has the second-largest wine cellar in the world and has hosted the likes of Vladimir Putin, Angela Merkel, and John Kerry. Our tour guide drove us along underground roads named for different wines, finally stopping at a tasting room where we sampled a few bottles along with Moldovan delicacies. Champa wasn't feeling well that day, so she had the best excuse of anyone for wanting to lie down after the visit.

Our host family took us to several other sites in Moldova, including the Castle Mimi winery in Bulboaca, a restored mansion in Hînceşti, and the farmers' markets in Ungheni. We also took a long day trip with our host mother and brother across the border to

Iași, one of Romania's largest cities, where we visited a botanical garden, a "palace of culture" with four museums, a giant shopping mall, churches, gardens, a theater, and a synagogue.

Moldovans viewed Romania as their wealthier neighbor, regarding it with admiration, even envy. Americans typically viewed Romania as a developing economy, which it had been relative to ours. Yet, it had prospered since joining the European Union in 2007. It still faced many problems, including corruption, but it was doing a lot better than Moldova. Since Moldovans with family ancestry in Romania were eligible for dual citizenship, many of them sought Romanian passports, so they could work in EU countries. Every day, people lined up outside the Romanian Embassy, located down the block from the Peace Corps office, surrounded by passport photoshops, travel companies, and employment agencies. Two of the three high school students on my first Diamond Challenge entrepreneurship team left to study at universities in Romania. Several of the girls on my second team expected to study there, too. A young man from Ialoveni whom I tutored in English moved to Romania, as did many other Moldovans.

It all reminded me of Nepal, where India is the larger, wealthier, and more powerful neighbor, the one more accessible than China. A large percentage of Nepal's adult population had left to work in India or elsewhere, especially near the Persian Gulf, although there were also Indians who came to work in Nepal. When Champa and I visited her sister's small village near Nepal's border with India before we came to Moldova, we looked across the river in the evening. The bright lights in the Indian homes there contrasted with those on our side, where electricity was weak and irregular, causing us to keep candles and flashlights handy.

In Moldova, many of my colleagues at the library were earning less than $200 a month. Monthly pensions for retirees were even lower. Highly-educated employees at the local county government earned only a few hundred dollars per month. It was no wonder they and other Moldovans looked longingly at their counterparts in Romania, whose GDP per capita was $9,474 in the year we arrived, compared to $1,900 for Moldova, according to the World Bank. However, since the U.S. figure then was $57,467, the same Romanians might try to get a green card to work in the United States. Likewise for people from India and other countries whose economies looked impressive to their neighbors but remained behind our own and included wide disparities in income and opportunity.

We weren't immune from making these kinds of comparisons ourselves. When Champa and I flew home from Nepal, we stopped for several hours in oil-rich Qatar, whose Doha airport felt like a palace compared to many of ours in the United States. I was impressed, if not a little jealous, even though I was glad to leave and continue home. No matter where we come from, in other words, our sense of other people and countries starts from our own vantage point. Wealth, like beauty, is in the eye of the beholder.

Our favorite place during our two years of travel was Romania's central region of Transylvania, which many Americans associate only with Dracula. It was indeed the home of Vlad Țepeș, or "Vlad the Impaler," whose bloody reign inspired the famous vampire novel by Bram Stoker. However, as we discovered during our trip there, including a stop at the Bran Castle associated with Dracula, there was so much more to Transylvania than tacky Dracula T-shirts.

Transylvania had rolling hills, picturesque villages, and snowy mountain peaks. Its monasteries were stunning, and more than

150 fortified churches with moats and dense stone walls dotted the countryside. Braşov, Sibiu, Sighişoara, and other cities combined charm with great dining at low prices. They were also brimming with history, reflecting the German and Hungarian traditions of local people. We hired a tour guide to drive us around for a few days, staying near Braşov's central square and Sibiu's "Bridge of Lies."

Our trip reminded me of attending conferences in Prague and Budapest soon after the fall of the Soviet Union when those cities were still considered exotic by many Americans. I felt then like a pioneer who had seen something wonderful before most Americans were comfortable visiting. They'll probably "discover" Transylvania soon, as well.

We made one of our most memorable visits while driving from Braşov back to Ialoveni with our tour guide, who had always wanted to visit Moldova. He encouraged us to stop for a few hours at the Trotus salt mine, where we expected to learn about the challenges of working deep underground, as we had years earlier when touring the Lackawanna coal mine in Scranton, Pennsylvania. After we bought tickets and boarded a bus to descend into the mine shaft, we were confused to see children with scooters and families with picnic baskets. Things got stranger when we arrived and heard what sounded like a priest chanting. Sure enough, an Orthodox service was under way in what turned out to be a church honoring St. Varvara, the protector of miners. The priest was giving communion beneath a dome carved into rock salt, with icons set into the white walls.

Just past the church, we came upon kids racing small carts around salt formations. Next, we saw playgrounds, a basketball court, a badminton court, a mini-soccer field, a restaurant, a library, and even a lake and waterfall. All of this was 240 meters below ground, covering 13,000 square meters. Located near the small city where Olympic gymnast Nadia Comăneci grew up, the mine dated back to 1380. Its tourist complex was at the ninth layer of an operation that continued to produce salt for dinner tables and other purposes. Many Romanians visited to breathe the salty air to relieve respiratory problems. As we waited for the bus to drive back to the surface, we chatted with a guy who pointed out another potential benefit. "If there's a nuclear war, we can all survive down here," he said. Well, maybe, but there was no denying they'd carved out a great thing, for now, one that would forever change how I heard the expression, "Back to the salt mine!"

We didn't visit Romania's capital, Bucharest, until near the end of our service, and we liked it more than we expected. Older parts of the city reminded us of Paris, although there were also plenty of the soulless Soviet-style apartments we knew well from Moldova. We arrived in the evening at an out-of-the-way bus station where it took us several minutes to flag down a taxi. Eventually, we arrived at our hotel in Old Town, where we strolled for a late snack and view of the many clubs, where music blasted, and, in a couple of cases, scantily clad women danced in the windows.

The next morning we crossed the boulevard to Unirii Square for a two-hour walking tour that provided a great overview of the city's complicated history, which ranges from the Roman and Ottoman Empires to Vlad the Impaler, as well as the more recent Communist reign of Nicolae Ceaușescu. He was executed with his wife in 1989. Nearby was his People's Palace, the world's second-largest building after the Pentagon.

We traveled to Bucharest by bus from another European capital city, Sofia. If you can't find either of them on a map, don't feel bad. Before I began serving in Moldova, I couldn't have found them either. We visited Sofia, the capital of Bulgaria, for several days during a holiday break, using it as a base to explore western Bulgaria. Like Bucharest, Sofia had plenty of cement apartments and government buildings along with magnificent churches, lovely parks, modern hotels, excellent restaurants, and interesting places to visit, all with prices much lower than elsewhere. Together with Krakow, Poland, they were the cheapest tourist cities on the European Backpacker Index.

We toured Sofia and the surrounding area for four days, beginning with a free walking tour of the city. It was a laid-back capital that *Lonely Planet* described as "a largely modern, youthful city, with a scattering of onion-domed churches, Ottoman mosques and stubborn Red Army monuments that lend an eclectic, exotic feel." Our favorite spot was the stunning Alexander Nevski Cathedral, two blocks from where we were staying.

On our second day, we joined a group that visited the Boyana Church, a medieval Bulgarian Orthodox structure with striking frescoes on the city's outskirts. We continued on to the Rila Monastery, the largest Eastern Orthodox monastery in Bulgaria. Snow fell during our visit, making the setting even more beautiful. Next, we visited Plovdiv, an ancient city straddling seven hills, with ruins dating back to Roman times. Our last stop was Koprivshtitsa, a historic mountain town where we toured colorful houses and churches before taking a break to sample some of Bulgaria's delicious soups, salads, and breads.

I wasn't sure what to expect in Romania and Bulgaria, although "drab" and "poor" wouldn't have surprised me. As an American who grew up during the Cold War, I still associated them with run-down economies and stone-faced rulers. They turned out to be fun places to explore, filled with things to see, all undergoing lots of change. They also provided a contrast to help us make sense of Moldova's post-Soviet legacy.

This was also true in Armenia and Georgia, on the eastern side of the Black Sea, which we visited during one of Champa's school breaks. They weren't on our list initially, but we kept hearing from other volunteers that we should take a look. Like Moldova, both were small former Soviet states that declared their independence in 1991. All three shared many traditions, from Orthodox Christianity to cheese pastries, but Armenia and Georgia had their own identities. Both were more prosperous than Moldova, especially their capitals, Yerevan and Tbilisi. Their histories ranged from Armenia's genocide to Georgia's famous son, Joseph Stalin. They were Caucasian in the original sense of that word, with the Caucasus Mountains and striking landscapes.

We flew from Chișinău via Kiev to Yerevan, where we spent our first full day visiting three friends serving in Peace Corps Armenia: Brent and Dee, the Tucson couple we'd met in Moldova, and Karen Jean, a friend of mine from Duke who'd served years earlier in Peace Corps Kenya.

We toured some of the local temples and ruins, drove through the stunning countryside, and stopped by to visit the local Peace Corps office. Then, we hired a car to drive us north across the Georgian border to Tbilisi, a trip of about six hours with stops at Lake Sevan and the historic town of Dilijan. As soon as we arrived in Tbilisi, we tried some of Georgia's renowned cuisine, including *khinkali* dumplings that reminded us of Nepal's momos. The next day, we toured the capital and surrounding area, enjoying still more churches, a synagogue, outdoor markets, and a cable car ride.

Just as our friends had predicted, we loved Yerevan and Tbilisi. Both offered amazing sights and a fun travel experience at reasonable prices. We felt safe and had little trouble communicating; many people in both capitals spoke at least some English. During our tours, we met more tourists from Dubai and Abu Dhabi than from the United States, which was a shame since both Armenia and Georgia were welcoming and relatively easy to reach, without requiring visas. They seemed less likely than Transylvania to become popular soon with Americans, but Tbilisi was already gaining attention, and Yerevan seemed likely to follow.

The modest roadside cafe we saw outside the Armenian village of Sevkar lacked a sign in English, much less a website. It was hardly the place you'd expect two older Americans to stop for lunch. But we did, unexpectedly, while driving from Armenia to Georgia, and it turned out to be a highlight of our trip. It was also a reminder of why travel is most satisfying when it moves beyond plans and itineraries to embrace life's surprises.

It was before noon, and we were the only customers there. The owner led us into his kitchen, pointed to some bowls of meat, and asked which we'd like him to barbecue over his charcoal fire. Then, as the meat sizzled, he sliced bread, tomatoes, onions, and cheese onto a plate and took them outside to a wooden table, where he invited us to sit. The barbecue was delicious, as was everything else. Here along a small road in northern Armenia, we enjoyed one of the best meals of our lives. It happened only because we asked our driver to find somewhere to stop early for lunch, so we could spend our remaining Armenian money before crossing the border into Georgia. No itinerary could anticipate all of the experiences like this that make a trip memorable.

While in Armenia, we also came across an area filled with small stone cairns, which reminded us of the *mani* stones people in Nepal pile along trekking paths. Beside them were hundreds of cloth and plastic ribbons wrapped around trees and bushes, which people placed for good luck. They, too, fascinated us, even though we'd come to see the adjacent monastery, partially carved out of a mountain.

We were surprised at a Tbilisi synagogue, as well. Its caretaker gave Champa and me a private tour, opening the ark to show us some of their Torah scrolls. He told us about Tbilisi's small Jewish community and took photos for us. Nearby, we discovered wine ice cream, which we thought was a gimmick but turned out to really be wine ice cream, and tasty, too.

We also were surprised by a New Zealand woman we met at an Armenian restaurant. She had lived previously in Turkmenistan, where she'd been friends with a young American who turned out to be in our Peace Corps group. Then there was the physical therapist from the Philippines who worked in Dubai. She and her husband came to Armenia for a brief vacation while renewing their visas. They were among several foreign nationals we met who worked in the Gulf. Two of the others were Chinese air hostesses for a Gulf airline who took selfies and texted nonstop during our tour. Who knew?

It was humbling for a planner like me to see how my detailed itineraries often failed to anticipate what Champa and I would remember most. One of my goals in being "not exactly retired" had been to recognize the richness of life's surprises and make the most of them. Spreadsheets were great, but serendipity was better.

We stayed at Airbnb apartments in many of the cities we visited, including Sibiu, Sofia, and Tbilisi. All three of those places were centrally located, with kitchens, living rooms, washing machines, and comfortable beds. They cost much less than hotels, although more than local hostels. All three hosts were helpful and responsive. The woman who welcomed us to our apartment in Sofia told us about a wonderful Nepali restaurant where we ended up having a delicious meal and memorable conversation with the owner. Champa and I still used hotels, such as when we stayed in Bucharest for a couple of nights and weren't sure when we would arrive, but we came to prefer staying in Airbnbs because they provided us with extra room and a local contact to help us learn about a city. Many of our fellow volunteers used them, too, when traveling or coming to stay in Chișinău.

Some Americans are still uneasy about staying in a private home instead of a hotel, whether through Airbnb or another service. The concept may seem especially dubious to some older travelers. As one wrote on the *Senior Planet* website, "At first glance, Airbnb looked to me like a site for freewheeling hipsters." We felt the same way initially but were now among a growing number of older travelers embracing this new approach.

One of my favorite blogs, *The Senior Nomads*, described how a retired Seattle couple stayed at Airbnbs while traveling around the globe. As they explained, "we rented our house, sold our sailboat and one of our cars, and reduced our stuff until it fit in a small storage unit. We waved goodbye to our family and friends and set off to explore the world!"

When we traveled home after our first year as volunteers, Champa and I experimented with the "sharing economy" in another way, by using a car-sharing service. We rented a Toyota Camry on a site called Turo from a guy in Virginia for about half of what we would have spent with a car rental company. We had a great experience and used the service again to rent a car in Durham after we returned permanently from Moldova, giving ourselves time to buy a car. I'm not sure we would have used Airbnb or Turo if we hadn't served as volunteers. The experience opened our eyes in so many ways, and not only concerning Moldova. We became more willing to give new things a try, recognizing that our children's generation might be onto something that could work nicely for us, too.

We had to convert our dollars into local currency in all of these countries, generally using local ATM machines. We never had a problem with them. I used a Charles Schwab card I'd obtained beforehand because it allowed us to make withdrawals without paying a fee. I also had a Visa card that didn't charge me for foreign transactions. The Peace Corps paid us in Moldovan lei, and we lived comfortably within our Peace Corps budget. We rarely used our credit cards locally since Moldova largely has a cash economy. We also didn't buy much online, where transactions were generally calculated in dollars anyway, so we didn't have much reason to pay attention as the U.S. dollar rose slightly against the Moldovan currency after our arrival and then declined by more than 15 percent before we left.

It was impossible to avoid the exchange rates as I walked to and from the library every day, passing by banks and money-exchange shops that displayed their rates on big signs. In addition to their exchange rates for U.S. dollars and Euros, they typically posted rates for the Russian ruble, the Romanian leu, and the Ukrainian hryvnia — not so different from Americans paying attention to neighboring currencies such as the Mexican peso or the Canadian dollar.

For the many Moldovans who worked abroad or sent home remittances, even a small shift could make a big difference in their lives, so they paid closer attention. Peace Corps Moldova calculated its budget annually, so it wasn't affected immediately by currency shifts except in a few ways. For example, a small percentage of volunteer paychecks was designated for personal travel and pegged to exchange rates. Currency fluctuations had been more dramatic in some Peace Corps countries, causing the agency's financial planners to scramble. Someone explained to me that the dollar's slow decline in Moldova resulted from the Brexit vote in the United Kingdom, the

U.S. presidential election, Federal Reserve policy, and other things I didn't fully understand or, for that matter, care about.

I hadn't become a Peace Corps volunteer to get rich. Like others around the world, I'd come to serve and promote friendship between Americans and other people. That was the currency that mattered to me.

Another of our trips provided a new epilogue to the story of a girl from Odessa who fled with her family to America in the early 1900s to escape the pogroms that were killing and persecuting Jews in Ukraine and other parts of the Russian empire. That girl was my grandmother, Sarah. Champa and I visited the Black Sea port city to pay our respects to her memory. I was the first of Grandma Sarah's children or grandchildren to return since her family — my family — arrived with nothing at New York's Ellis Island. They sailed past the Statue of Liberty and found a new life in America.

We hired a driver to take a long day trip there with our host sister, Alisa, and her cousin Natalia. We left Ialoveni early, crossing the Moldovan-Ukrainian border at Palanca since the Peace Corps did not allow volunteers to travel through the disputed territory of Transnistria. We were lucky to arrive near Odessa's majestic opera house just before a noon performance of Tchaikovsky's *Sleeping Beauty* began. We bought the cheapest seats, less than 40 cents apiece, so we could glimpse the theater for a few minutes. It was magnificent. We then walked to another local landmark, the Odessa Steps that figure prominently in a famous scene from Sergei Eisenstein's 1925 film *Battleship Potemkin*. On one side was a plaque honoring the cinematic significance of the location; on the other was a funicular we rode to ascend after visiting the port, a major transportation hub for Ukraine.

Throughout Odessa's central area, we saw beautiful buildings, parks, shops, and statues commemorating figures such as Catherine the Great and Duke de Richelieu, the French-born governor who helped Odessa grow to become the third-largest city in the Russian empire. We thought of our two daughters-in-law when visiting the "Mother-in-Law Bridge" and ate a late lunch of traditional Ukrainian food. We ended our trip with a visit to Odessa's largest synagogue, where I left a donation in my grandmother's honor. It had taken more than a century, but one of her descendants had finally made it back to revive her memory there.

We used our remaining vacation days for something more conventional — a trip to Vienna, Budapest, and Bratislava. The first two cities are familiar to most American tourists, although our own favorite was Bratislava, the capital of Slovakia.

In each city, we found a spot we'd especially remember, beginning with the famous opera house in the heart of Vienna. Not *inside* the opera, where some tickets cost more than our monthly Peace Corps salary, but the sidewalk outside. We sat there in chairs and watched live performances on a giant screen for free. We discovered this after we arrived in Vienna and saw the ballet *Raymonda* starting as we strolled by. We enjoyed it for nearly an hour, returning the next day to catch part of Richard Wagner's opera *Die Walküre*. It was magical to sit outside on a beautiful evening and watch world-class performances in the Austrian city renowned for its music and culture.

In Budapest, our favorite spot was the Chain Bridge and adjacent funicular, which provided stunning views of the picturesque city. We'd already taken a boat ride down the Danube, sailing under bridges and past the Parliament building and other sites. As in Vienna, we toured the city atop a double-decker Big Bus. The view was spectacular from the historic bridge that spans the river between Buda and Pest, the western and eastern sides of Hungary's capital. Even better was the view from Buda Castle, which we reached by the historic funicular we boarded near the bridge.

In Bratislava, we loved St. Martin's Cathedral, and not only because it was a landmark with a stunning interior. For us, it was also the view in the window of the Airbnb we rented across the square. We admired the exterior of the three-nave Gothic structure while sipping our morning coffee.

We further upgraded our travel when we met our friends Bob and Karen in northern Italy immediately after we completed our service, but before we flew back to North Carolina. We met up in Milan, where we shared an Airbnb apartment surrounded by wonderful Italian restaurants and shops. Together, we explored the huge Duomo, or cathedral, with its memorable rooftop views, and the elegant Galleria Vittorio Emanuele II next door, along with other sites. We moved on to Lake Como, one of the most beautiful places on Earth, where we stayed in Varenna and used water taxis to explore Bellagio and other towns.

Next, we took a bus and train up to Lugano, in Switzerland, where we walked through the city, visited a mountaintop, and spent an unforgettable day hopping from one town to another along the lake. From there, we traveled all the way to Alpe di Suisi, near Italy's border with Austria, where we hiked for several days through the Dolomites, a mountain range that looked like *The Sound of Music* and was the highlight of our trip. As always, Champa started smiling as soon as she found herself in a place that reminded her of Nepal. She never stopped smiling while we were there, and neither did the rest of us, at least until we reached our final destination, Venice.

We stayed in an apartment there located a short walk from Saint Mark's Basilica and the Doge's Palace. Venice was as amazing as we'd heard, but we felt claustrophobic among the thousands of tourists, many of whom arrived on cruise ships. Even when we rode water buses to destinations outside the center city, we saw them everywhere. Especially since we'd just been hiking in the Dolomites, we wanted to escape the crowds, as we had while traveling off the beaten track during the rest of our Peace Corps travels.

One of the things for which I am most grateful for serving in the Peace Corps is how it made me less fearful about traveling to places that seem exotic or dangerous to some Americans even though they're actually safe, beautiful, fascinating, and cheap. I was reminded of this throughout our time abroad, such as when we visited Sofia and Bucharest. If we'd traveled instead to London, Rome, or Barcelona, we probably would have seen Americans on every corner, as we did in Venice. But in these two cities, we saw very few. When we took a walking tour through Bucharest's lovely Old Town, I looked at the signup list and saw Australia, Canada, Germany, India, Italy, Netherlands, Russia, and Serbia listed as home countries. The only Americans were Champa and me. When we joined twenty-three other tourists for our walking tour of Sofia, the others came from Bulgaria, Canada, Italy, Japan, Latvia, Netherlands, and Spain, plus one other American. The same was true of the other tours we took in Bulgaria. When we visited Armenia and Georgia, it was the same story. The only other American on our tours was a software engineer from Boston who came to learn about his Armenian roots. The others hailed from China, Dubai, Germany, Italy, New Zealand, the Philippines, Russia, and other countries. Mind you, all of our tours were in English, which was not the native tongue for most of these visitors.

It's possible we just happened to be in groups without Americans.

Certainly, I didn't expect to see swarms of American tourists as I might have in Cancun or Toronto. Statistics show that Americans who search for flights to Europe look first to London, Paris, and Rome, and to other familiar places such as Dublin, Madrid, and Frankfurt. Central European destinations such as Prague, Budapest, Krakow, and Dubrovnik have become popular, too. Champa and I enjoy exploring new cultures, but other travelers prefer shopping, fine dining, resorts, hiking, visiting friends, or something else. A *New York Times* article said, "nearly half of overseas travelers are from the East Coast, and they make trips within the Western Hemisphere or to Western Europe, to places that are more affordable and easier to reach (with shorter and direct flights) than those farther afield." Tourists from other countries have their favored destinations, too.

I understood why so many Americans filled the streets of Venice when we were there since we'd come to see Saint Mark's Basilica, too, just as we'd once visited Big Ben and the Eiffel Tower. Even these Americans were more adventurous than the millions who wouldn't venture further than a summer beach house. Moreover, many Americans lacked the resources to do more than dream of foreign adventures.

Champa and I were extraordinarily lucky to pursue our life-long passion for travel. Serving as older Peace Corps volunteers in Moldova only expanded our sense of what was interesting and reasonable. But, for goodness sake, it wasn't like I expected Americans to start touring North Korea. I just wished more of them would join all of the other foreign tourists we saw in experiencing some amazing countries in Eastern Europe instead of defaulting to a predictable list, like ordering only vanilla or chocolate ice cream cones in a shop offering many flavors.

Living and working in an unfamiliar culture as Peace Corps volunteers made us comfortable with these travel alternatives, but you don't need to serve abroad to expand your horizons. Many reliable companies now offer trips to "exotic" destinations, and the internet makes it easy to find reputable local travel companies and guides for almost any budget. We saw with our own eyes that there's a big world waiting beyond the American comfort zone.

CHAPTER 16

MAKING A DIFFERENCE

Our travels were a diversion from our jobs and projects. As we entered our final year, I became busier than ever with my robotics team, English conversation class, new website, videos, and everything else we were doing at the library. I also focused on my Diamond Challenge team, tourism project, and work with Liuba at the Peace Corps office, as well as on my blog and helping some younger volunteers with their graduate school applications and job letters. Of course, many Moldovans, especially women, were still busier than us. They raised families, worked in offices, sowed crops, fed animals, tended gardens, cooked meals, and helped neighbors while using vastly fewer resources than we had available.

As we moved into the second half of our service, I pursued my biggest project of all, to create a new family room at the library where kids could play and moms participate in free educational programs. When Champa and I went home during the summer after our first year, we met with the organizers of community programs for the Durham County Library, whom I asked for ideas we might bring back to Moldova. One of their best suggestions was weekly "storytimes" for families, a tradition at many libraries around the world. It was new to Moldova, although Lidia had seen it at a Romanian library.

After I got back from our trip home and told her and Valentina what I'd heard in Durham, both picked that as the idea they wanted to pursue. At my urging, they carried out a survey to assess community interest before moving ahead. Lidia brought a stack of questionnaires to a local festival and got dozens of families to fill them out. The results were encouraging, with almost everyone saying a storytime project would be good for kids and provide relief for moms who were home watching them every day. The three of us talked further about how such a project might work, what it would require, and what it would cost. We developed a plan to create a kid-friendly room with educational toys, art materials, and the like, accompanied by programs the library would organize on topics like children's health or career planning for women.

Valentina secured a small grant from the Association of Librarians in the Republic of Moldova and the National Library of Moldova, in partnership with Novateca. That was a great start but covered only a small part of the budget. We decided to request the remaining funding from the "Let Girls Learn" campaign championed by Michelle Obama. The head of the small grants program at the Peace Corps helped me polish our proposal, which Peace Corps headquarters approved and posted on a website. Some of my friends and family contributed online, with the campaign funding the remaining balance. A few months after we first discussed the idea, the Peace Corps opened an account for us with the full amount and authorized an ATM card for me to start spending the money.

I was used to the slower pace of activity in Moldova at this point, so I was startled when Lidia zoomed into action. She took me on buses around Chişinău for several days to buy the books, toys, and everything else on our budget, including a television set, a sofa, and supplies to make the room welcoming to families. We bought some of the supplies at the retail office of one of Moldova's new online stores, which delivered them a few days later. We got receipts for everything, even the bus rides, and entered the data into the Peace Corps tracking system. We ended up meeting our budget projection so closely that the Peace Corps Moldova budget analyst told me I only needed to spend fifteen cents more to hit it precisely, which I did by walking to the corner store and buying a pack of tissues to wipe the new tables.

The library's IT guy mounted the television and painted the room, which had been dingy and little-used for years. Students from the art school painted a mural featuring characters from popular Moldovan children's stories. A colorful carpet and modular shelf units brought the room to life, as did two children's tables, a slide, and a small basketball hoop. We called it Bebeteca —a combination of the Romanian words for baby and library — and launched it with a program where a local doctor discussed children's infectious diseases.

The session went well, and we got an even bigger crowd for the next one, featuring a Ialoveni native who hosted a popular Moldovan television program. Her mother worked at one of the branch libraries, which is probably why she came for free. In any case, she was delightful, and the moms had a great time while their children played with toys or sat on their laps. Bebeteca was a hit.

Valentina and Lidia were thrilled, as were the other librarians. The mayor came to see Bebeteca, as did librarians from different communities and someone from the national library. Novateca praised it. A conference invited Valentina to speak. National television did a story about it, and then the national radio station did the same, both of them interviewing me in Romanian along with my colleagues.

The project was the library's most visible effort yet to redefine itself for the modern world and become a vital community resource. Valentina posted Facebook photos regularly, showing moms and kids enjoying the new space, luring other parents who hadn't visited the library recently.

Igor, my former partner at the district government, showed up with his two young sons to see Bebeteca and, while there, borrowed some children's books. The director of Peace Corps Moldova came, too, and brought along several other members of the staff. She and I surprised Valentina and Lidia with fancy certificates that praised their accomplishments. Months later, after I'd completed my service and returned to the United States, I continued seeing Bebeteca updates regularly on the library's Facebook site. It was thriving.

The Peace Corps director came to Ialoveni that day mainly to see Champa's big project. After touring Bebeteca and our library, she and the others drove up the street to join the American ambassador and local dignitaries at Champa's school for the unveiling of more than forty new costumes for its drama program. The celebration, the highlight of Champa's service, was the culmination of many months of work by her and her partners.

Early in our second year, Champa told her school director and fellow teachers about the Peace Corps small grants program, soliciting their ideas for a proposal, just as I had at the library. In her case, she planned to apply through a Small Project Assistance (SPA) collaboration between the Peace Corps and the U.S. Agency for International Development. She expected her colleagues to suggest something similar to previous Moldovan SPA grants, such as a new classroom or playground, replacing aging windows, or updating the cafeteria. She was surprised when her friend Ana, who oversaw the school's arts activities, lobbied instead to create a costume wardrobe and prop collection for the drama program.

Champa and I were familiar with the program, having enjoyed some of its shows at the cultural center, and we'd admired the student actors. As Ana pointed out to Champa, though, there was no money to buy or create real costumes. Students had to make their own in families with little money to spare. Some didn't even try out for shows because they knew they couldn't provide the costumes needed for the parts they hoped to play. Year after year, Ana explained, she had requested money in the school budget to begin creating a costume wardrobe. Every year the request was deleted in favor of other needs. Just as in many American schools, those in charge considered the arts expendable.

A Peace Corps small grant could finally solve the problem, she believed. It was her chance to provide the costumes and props her actors deserved while performing scenes from Shakespeare or Moldovan dramas. She pleaded with Champa and the school director to pursue this unconventional proposal.

They agreed, and the director committed to providing the "community contribution" required by the Peace Corps. She would also rally the school's faculty, parents, and students to sew many of the costumes themselves as a way to stretch the budget and produce more costumes.

Ana spent several weeks working with a local designer to sketch costumes for Romeo, Juliet, kings, queens, judges, noblemen, knights, clowns, and more. For each one, the designer calculated what kind of material she would need, how many buttons and the kinds of zippers and ribbons required. She totaled all of the materials into a master list and then added up the prices. The result was one of the longest and most complex proposals ever submitted for a small grant at Peace Corps Moldova, accompanied by a detailed narrative explaining who would participate in the project, and how it would unfold.

When the Peace Corps small grants committee invited the school to present the proposal, Ana and Champa surprised them by coming with two student actors, who proceeded to act out a scene from Romeo and Juliet. The committee members, who usually listened to descriptions about how toilets would be installed, were charmed, and Ana and Champa answered all of their questions. A few days later, they learned they were among the winners, receiving the full amount of their grant proposal.

As soon as they got the money, Ana, Champa, and the designer made several trips to downtown Chişinău to buy everything. They shopped mainly on the third and fourth floors of Gemeni, a department store located next to a McDonald's on the city's main street. Gemeni was old and cramped. It had no parking, no food court, and no modern restrooms. With tiny shops and bad lighting, it was more of a bazaar than a modern department store. Its vendors, mostly women, rented stalls arranged by categories. The store, whose name means twins in Romanian, evoked its Soviet heritage. It was functional. Customers almost always paid in cash. They received their purchases in cheap plastic bags. Gemeni lacked customer service desks, fountains, or benches but offered plentiful bolts of velvet, cotton, and other fabric together with gold braid, spangles, and other supplies.

I came along to help, and soon we were all weighed down with bags, which we transported by crowded public bus to the designer's shop across town. She would sew a few of the more complicated costumes herself; however, for most of them, she cut the fabric into pieces for the students and mothers to sew in Ialoveni. The students used a couple of old sewing machines in the vocational class, and the moms worked at home, all following the designer's directions.

The costumes that emerged from this process were spectacular. Juliet's gown and cape were a vision in creme-colored satin and velvet trimmed with a white fringe. Romeo looked like he'd stepped off a Broadway stage. Ştefan cel Mare, the founder of Moldova, was draped in layers of red velvet trimmed in white and gold, with a crown atop his head and a sword in his hand.

Ana's daughter bought most of the props in Romania and brought them home during a visit, complicating our bookkeeping, but making Ana and Champa laugh with delight one afternoon as they tried on a pirate's hat, cowboy hats, Native American headdresses, and carnival masks.

As the deadline approached, the team raced to finish the remaining costumes and organize the celebration where they would show off all of them to the community. Since they'd been able to buy some of the material more cheaply than expected, they used the extra money to buy traditional Moldovan dancing boots and socks for the younger students, as well as some dresses, so they could benefit, too.

Champa coordinated with the Peace Corps director to extend an invitation to the U.S. ambassador. When he accepted, the school's director stepped up the pace of her preparations, and Ana joined with the drama teacher to organize an even more impressive event. It was the first time in recent memory an American ambassador had visited Ialoveni. The community didn't want to disappoint him. When he came with some colleagues and a security detail that Friday afternoon, he sat in the auditorium next to the Peace Corps director and the district government president.

The two of us sat behind them in our best clothes. The students and teachers were excited. The school director welcomed everyone, the lights dimmed, music started, and a parade of older students marched down the aisles, each wearing one of the new costumes and showing off the props. The spectators clapped and cheered as the students grinned and waved their props in the air. They finally assembled in the front of the room as two student hosts walked to the center of the stage to start the program, one dressed as Juliet's father and the other as a beautiful queen. The students presented short scenes from four plays, some dramatic, some funny.

Ana thanked everyone who worked on the project, especially the two of us and the Peace Corps. "Working together, thanks to the help from all of you, we have achieved something that is super," she said.

Champa came forward to give a short speech in Romanian, which she'd practiced repeatedly. She saved her deepest thanks for Ana, whom she described as "the best partner ... hard-working, dedicated, honest, and fun. Creating a project to produce drama costumes was her idea, not mine."

Then, the Peace Corps director spoke. "Thank you all so much for receiving Champa and David into your community," she said. "One of the things we say at Peace Corps is that Peace Corps service is magic. It takes certain elements for it to work well. It takes a community that's open, that's willing to receive strangers, and it takes volunteers who are prepared to put themselves out, to serve, to give, in uncertainty a lot of times. But when those two elements come together, and we see something like this, we know it's worked. Today, what I witnessed was magic."

Next, the ambassador spoke to the audience in Romanian, saying "it is great that Ialoveni has so much talent, so much potential." He urged the students to "continue to achieve great things."

The mayor spoke as well, saying, "This is not just wonderful. It's *really, really* wonderful."

After all of the big shots left, we gathered with the school director and some of the teachers in a classroom to eat snacks and toast each other with champagne from a winery down the road. Everyone was beaming, Ana most of all. She had worked hard for so many months, developing the proposal, calculating the budget, overseeing the designer, supervising the volunteers, and arranging a big celebration for the American ambassador and others. She'd never written a grant or managed a project like this before, and it had turned out better than anyone expected. She and Champa kept thanking each other. Ana and her family became some of our dearest friends in Moldova, inviting us to their Christmas dinner and then coming to our house to share Nepali food.

My colleagues from the library also came to the school's event, and they cheered along with everyone else. In the lead article in Ialoveni's monthly newspaper a few weeks later, Valentina thanked the two of us for our "diverse cultural activities at the library and in the community, for the beautiful projects they brought to Ialoveni."

As Champa and I left the school that afternoon, she clutched a bouquet of flowers as we held hands. We looked at each other and agreed we had just shared something special. This was why we had chosen to leave our family and country for so long. We had made a difference with our work. We could return home knowing we'd been right when we walked away from our conventional lives nearly three years earlier.

CHAPTER 17

_____

SAYING GOODBYE

When we'd gathered with our fellow members of M31 for the first time at our staging in Philadelphia, one of our trainers said we were meeting our "government-issued family." She was right. We'd traveled together to Moldova, learned the language, supported one another, gotten on each other's nerves, endured the country director's edicts, seen friends leave early, and cheered for each other's successes. We had transformed our lives and were still together.

Now, finally, it was time to go home.

Following a volunteer tradition, we gathered in the Peace Corps conference room for a lottery several months beforehand. Everyone's name was placed in a hat, with the three married couples each listed together. As people's names were called, they selected one of the available departure slots on a large calendar. Ours were among the first names called. We chose an early date because we needed to reoccupy our house in North Carolina soon after it was vacated by our tenants. Most of the volunteers had planned trips, like ours to Italy, although a few needed to return immediately to begin graduate school or jobs. One left a few weeks early to start working with Teach for America in Kansas City. Another started an

Air Force job in Virginia. We posed individually for funny photos next to our departure dates, then as a whole group. Finally the party moved on to Smokehouse.

I found it all bittersweet. Now that Champa and I had a date, the approaching end of our Peace Corps service was no longer an abstraction. We knew when we would reunite with our family and friends, but also when we'd have to say goodbye to our host family, our Moldovan friends, and these volunteers with whom we'd shared our journey.

Meanwhile, the volunteers who arrived a year behind us were settling into their posts and confronting the emotional lull that often occurred a few months after swearing-in, especially during a cold Moldovan winter. The staff began to focus on the group after them, which would arrive that summer. Our volunteer friends from the previous group were already fading from our Facebook pages and e-mail messages. The transitions reminded me of the rhythms I'd seen at the university — nervous freshmen arriving in minivans only to give way four years later to graduating seniors whose parents applauded as they marched into the stadium and threw their caps into the sky.

I always enjoyed Duke's graduations and missed only one during my 14 years there, when Champa and I went to the ceremonies down the road at the University of North Carolina at Chapel Hill, where our younger son was graduating. I experienced his graduation as a proud parent. It touched me personally instead of feeling routine. The staff at Peace Corps Moldova probably felt the same way about us. For our friends and us, though, it was our class getting ready to graduate. Our own countdowns had begun. For Champa and me, it was 163 days and counting.

As we looked ahead, I searched online for resources and inspiration about what we might do next. I was a regular reader of the *Next Avenue* and *Senior Planet* websites and still a fan of *Senior Nomads*, the blog by the Seattle couple staying in Airbnbs around the world. I'd enjoyed Lynne Martin describing a similar adventure with her husband in *Home Sweet Anywhere: How We Sold Our House, Created a New Life, and Saw the World*. I found lots of blogs and websites devoted to "senior travel," each with its own niche, and other sites focused on how to find short- or long-term jobs overseas.

Champa and I knew we wanted to continue providing service after the Peace Corps, so I was also intrigued by the Encore website, which promotes "second acts for the greater good," and by groups such as the Executive Service Corps and ReServe that match older Americans with positions that make good use of their skills. There was a volunteer matching site back in Durham, too. Best of all, my sister Nancy continued to write and speak about "second-act careers," so I had an expert advisor in the family.

More than anything, Champa and I were looking forward to taking a break and spending time with our family and friends after being away for so long. We missed them and weren't prepared to focus on "what's next?" until we took some time to catch our breath. Our two sons and their wives were working long hours while raising small children. We wanted nothing more than to hang out with them.

We still had several months left in Moldova, though, and I hit the gas as we entered our final lap. Instead of slowing down and starting to pack, I tackled projects I'd been wanting to pursue, like teaching the classes on writing news and opinion articles and organizing the media training session for the research faculty at the university. During my final months, I helped launch the Bebeteca room at the library, produce the music video about Ialoveni, update the library website, and organize the big event commemorating the twenty-fifth anniversary of Peace Corps Moldova.

Champa and I began filling out final reports on our projects, forms for our departure, and a detailed description of our community. We had final medical checkups, dental exams, security reports, and evaluations from Peace Corps headquarters. I helped two of my robotics students prepare a presentation for a youth conference. Both of us applied for Medicare. I corresponded with our home management company about when our tenants would leave and how we'd get the house cleaned before we returned. I arranged to have our utilities turned back on. I told our insurance agent to be ready to restore our homeowner's policy. I contacted the Durham Board of Elections to confirm our registration and Duke's HR office to activate our retiree health coverage. I also negotiated online with three car dealerships, so I could have a deal ready to sign when we got back. They were all happy to submit offers, one of which I'd accept a few days after we returned.

Before we began serving as Peace Corps volunteers, we'd spent months giving away books, clothes, and other stuff, reducing our possessions to what we could cram into our attic, a small storage room in our house, and the two suitcases we were each allowed to bring to Moldova. It was exhausting but liberating — good mental preparation for leading a simpler life. Now, we went through a similar process, sifting through boxes of language materials, teaching materials, tourist brochures, souvenirs, and other things we'd accumulated. Once again, we made three piles: "Keep," "Give Away," and "Trash," including some books and other things we needed to return to the Peace Corps. As before, "Keep" needed to fit into our suitcases, which we'd store at the Peace Corps office while we traveled to Italy after our service. Our "Give Away" pile went mainly to a Salvation Army center in Ialoveni and the "Loot Me" room in the Peace Corps volunteer lounge.

Our "Trash" pile was small since our host grandmother welcomed anything flammable to burn next winter in her fireplace.

I worked almost every day and many evenings as we neared the end, but I wasn't complaining. I viewed every remaining day of my Peace Corps service as precious, so I wanted to do as much as possible. I probably took on too much but figured there would be time to rest later. No matter how fast or slow I ran, the finish line kept getting closer.

Our group gathered for the final time at its "Close of Service" conference a couple of months before we left. We reviewed the procedures for closing our bank accounts, returning our water filters, and everything else that needed to be addressed before our return. I led a presentation about the National Peace Corps Association and other resources available to help returning volunteers.

Most importantly, people shared their plans and emotions. During one session, they wrote on flip charts what they anticipated most about returning home after two years, their answers including:

- Driving on back roads
- My dog
- Being with my family
- Access to Taco Bell at 2 a.m.
- Freedom

As for what made them the most anxious, they wrote:

- Finding housing, a car, where to live
- Seeing/hearing Trump everywhere
- Big grocery stores
- American work culture
- A different me reintegrating into a hometown that hasn't changed

And what they'd miss most about Moldova:

- My host family
- Sunflowers
- House wine
- Fresh fruit & veggies
- Waking up to fresh snow

Our three days at a rural conference center outside the capital were emotional. The conference helped us make sense of what we were feeling and what might lie ahead.

"As soon as I'm no longer a PCV," one question asked, "I can't wait to":

- Date
- Take a bath
- Hold new nieces and nephews
- Not check-in/out
- Go backpacking with my brothers

And the members of Moldova 31 also said what made them most proud of their service as Peace Corps volunteers:

- Our students' improvement
- Community impact
- Surviving rutiera (minibus) rides on hot summer days
- Language learning
- Seeing the youth gain a more positive impact on their futures
- Finishing

We took our closing language exams, posed for a group photo, and hugged each other at a farewell lunch. We traveled back to Chişinău on a bus. We were excited to leave. We dreaded saying goodbye to Moldova.

Saying Goodbye

Champa and I knew which goodbye would be the hardest for us. The most memorable person we met in Moldova was the eighty-seven-year-old grandmother, or *bunica*, of our host family. Nadejda Ciornea inspired us. She traveled almost every day from our house in Ialoveni to downtown Chișinău, where she sold handicrafts in the outdoor market in the Arts Square. She walked up a steep hill to the bus stop, and then boarded an overcrowded vehicle before finally arriving near the market. There, she sat outdoors on a folding chair in the heat of the summer and the cold of the winter. Only rain or a snowstorm kept her home. Watching this small woman shuffle on the road with her cane never ceased to amaze us. When we asked why she continued to work at her age, she smiled and wagged her finger, saying, "*la lucru*! (the work)." She said this to us almost every day, teasing us that we needed to work as hard as she did.

Every evening, I asked her how business went that day. Often she said she earned *nimic*, or nothing, usually followed by some choice words about Moldova's faltering economy. Sometimes she smiled and pointed to the small ledger she carried, where she recorded her sales. Occasionally, she shared photos or letters from customers she'd met over the years. We sometimes shared a glass of wine and a piece of cake, preceded by her toasting our good health and success. She asked about our family back home and what we did that day, always with a twinkle in her eye and a laugh.

We also became close to our host mother, Nina, her husband, Mihai, and the rest of the Bordei family. Since we were a few years older than Nina, however, it was Bunica who felt like a mother while we were in Moldova. Champa and I both lost our own mothers years earlier. We never expected to find another on this side of the world. For the rest of our lives, we knew, whenever we felt like complaining about getting old, we would remember Bunica wagging her finger and saying *la lucru!* She had shown us how to age gracefully, embracing every day with what Moldovans call a *suflet mare* — a big soul. A few weeks before we left, Bunica confided to me that she would miss the two of us a lot. We knew we would miss her much more.

We surprised the Bordeis with a photo album filled with memories of our two years together. I'd produced it online with Shutterfly and shipped it to one of the new trainees whom I'd met online. He brought it with him to Moldova and gave it to our friend Bob of the Peace Corps staff, who then gave it to me. It was a complicated journey for a special gift, which we planned to give the Bordeis at a farewell dinner we'd arranged. While we were hanging out the previous weekend, however, Alisa told us how much they'd enjoyed the photo album we'd brought with us to Moldova, showing our family and life in America. She asked whether I could send her images of its pages before we left. Champa and I looked at each other, and I asked her in Nepali whether we should go ahead and give them the new album now. She agreed. Happiness ensued.

We were so glad we made both albums. We'd shared our original book many times with Moldovan friends, who were always curious to see what our lives were like in America, especially our family. Now, our host family had its own book of memories. We titled it "Champa and David at the Chateau Bordei," based on the French-sounding name I used on our Thanksgiving menu to describe the delicious house wine they produced.

Perhaps we should have given them a certificate as well since Moldovans loved to give and receive certificates. We'd seen certificates awarded at sporting competitions, school ceremonies, and other events. A certificate was typically laminated and given the official stamp of the organization. Students began collecting them at a young age and might accumulate a thick folder by the time they graduated.

During my training in Bardar, the local librarian introduced us to some kids from the village. She asked one of them, a talented artist, to show us her certificates from painting competitions. The girl pulled out a large pile and explained them one by one. This seemed strange to me until later that evening when I recalled the many trophies and medals my two sons accumulated from their sports teams, science fairs, and other activities. Their trophies filled two large boxes when we cleaned out our house before joining the Peace Corps. I also had my own stash of certificates, diplomas, and congratulatory letters. As the walls of many American doctors' offices make clear, our traditions are not so different. Still, certificates were far more popular in Moldova, not to mention cheaper than sports trophies. Kids also sometimes received medals, like the boys on our robotics team got at one of their competitions.

I helped Champa design, print, and laminate thirty certificates to give to the teachers, students, and parents at her big celebration for the drama costumes. I also made certificates for my library partners, honoring their work with the Bebeteca project. I was able to laminate all of them with a machine at the Peace Corps office, which had undoubtedly been put to good use over the years.

Certificate ceremonies in Moldova were usually filled with pride. The speeches were heartfelt, the smiles genuine, and the certificates lovely. The moment was always captured with a *poza* — a pose for the camera. After they received a certificate, Moldovans might use it to prove their eligibility to receive a job promotion or a raise in salary, or to apply for a new position. More often, they held onto it as a souvenir of a memorable activity.

When I told Alisa what I'd noticed about certificates, she laughed and said, "I don't want a certificate. Give me some cash." She had a point, just as one could reasonably ask whether Moldova's teachers might have been better off receiving fewer flowers and bigger paychecks. As a foreign visitor, these questions were not for me to answer. I could only say I enjoyed the certificates as a distinctive part of the culture. As Champa and I began packing, we set aside space for our own stash, the laminated memories we'd take back to America.

Ialoveni's mayor presented us with two final certificates and several gifts at a ceremony the library organized for my last day, one of many ceremonies and celebrations during our closing two weeks. He and Valentina thanked us on behalf of the city. I was especially moved when two boys from our robotics team rose to speak as well. Even though it was shortly after 10 a.m., we toasted the moment with champagne and cake, reminding us anew that we'd miss Moldova.

Nina cooked a wonderful dinner, and the Bordeis surprised us with a stunning portrait of the two of us they'd commissioned from a local artist. Bunica gave us a gorgeous handmade Moldovan carpet. We received gifts from other friends, too. The members of my English conversation class and their families treated us to a farewell party at Casa della Pizza, Ialoveni's popular pizza restaurant. Champa had met there with her language tutor and then with some of the English teachers from her school. We ate there with a Peace Corps friend and again with several others.

When we said our goodbye to "Mr. Tim," a former Peace Corps volunteer who had stayed in Ialoveni to teach English, we dined on the outdoor verandah of another local restaurant, sipping beers and eating *mamaliga* and *friptura*. It was the same place he'd taken us when we first arrived. With members of Champa's Peace Corps group, our farewell party was at The Uptown Cafe, a restaurant in the capital.

We said still more goodbyes over home-cooked meals: such as one presented by Liuba and her family and cooked by her husband, Andrei, who had recently given up his career as an IT specialist to attend culinary school and pursue his dream of becoming a chef. Needless to say, it was delicious. Another night we cooked Nepali food for Ana and her family. Amid all of these get-togethers, I exchanged goodbye messages with my former Diamond Challenge students, promoted North Carolina's partnership with Moldova, and delivered presentations to the new trainees in our community and organizational development group. Champa and I began packing, too.

Each goodbye was emotional. Collectively, they were draining. However, the process helped us absorb the reality that we were leaving this place in which we'd invested so much of ourselves. We'd heard at our COS conference that we should embrace this process instead of letting our final moments drift away. We were glad we had listened. We were also glad we'd have a gym nearby when we got back home, to help us work off so many celebratory meals.

Peace Corps Moldova had a special bell marked COS outside its front door. Volunteers rang it on the day they completed their service. For us that was Tuesday, July 3, 2018, joining with several of our friends who were also in the first departing group. We posed for photos, listened to speeches, double-checked the suitcases we were storing, then slipped out of the office and walked down the street to pick up our bus back to Ialoveni. It was the last time we would travel there, for a final night with the Bordeis. We now had only our carry-on bags, which we'd be taking to Italy the next day, July 4, Independence Day. We were no longer Peace Corps volunteers. We were free to do what we wanted, independent adults once more. The next morning, Mihai drove us to the airport, stopping along the way to take photos together in a giant field of sunflowers. A few hours later we were in Milan, meeting our two friends from Maryland. Two weeks after that, we returned to Chişinău for a day to pick up our bags and do some errands. Then, more than three years after we'd walked away from our conventional lives to pursue our adventure, we finally returned home.

Champa and I had a wonderful experience in Moldova. We felt fulfilled by our work. We formed great friendships. We learned about a part of the world we'd known nothing about and shared unforgettable moments with our local partners and fellow volunteers. Our lives became deeper, richer, and more satisfying. We knew we'd made the right choice.

Every volunteer's experience is different, even within the same country, and several aspects of our service made things easier for us. Most obviously, we served together, unlike most volunteers. We were never lonely and always had our best friend nearby to share the day's events. We were also posted to Eastern Europe, specifically to a small city near Moldova's capital, where we lived in a nice house and had access to many amenities. We weren't allowed to drive, which I missed, but we did have a good internet connection and items like peanut butter and barbecue sauce in our local store. For us, the "Peace Corps experience" didn't include living in a hut.

Moreover, Champa and I came to Moldova with lots of experience outside the United States, so we had little trouble adjusting to a new culture. Nor were we distracted by family emergencies back home, at least until near the end when one of our granddaughters got sick. Thank goodness she recovered, but her illness was a reminder that our work could have ended suddenly. We were also fortunate to remain healthy ourselves, unlike some of our volunteer friends.

What ultimately mattered most was that Champa and I truly wanted to serve as Peace Corps volunteers and were willing to put up with sickness, separation from our family, and almost anything else thrown our way. We had a clear idea of what we were signing up for and were determined to succeed. The Peace Corps is hard, no matter how old you are or where you serve. If you're not fully committed, you're probably not going to make it. We joined for many reasons, but mainly because we felt we had received lots of blessings in our lives and wanted to give back. We challenged ourselves for two years, worked hard, and felt like we made a difference. Like other volunteers before us, we also ended up feeling we received more than we gave.

I would be lying if I said we liked everything about the experience. There were many more regulations than when I served as a volunteer in Nepal in the late 1970s. After living independently for so many years, I found it jarring to have to ask permission to do routine things, even to see Champa when we were separated during training. I wasn't crazy about walking on Moldova's icy roads or the dour faces on so many people. My initial job placement could have been vetted more carefully, as with many of the other members of my group. The people in charge of Peace Corps Moldova also could have been more flexible and supportive with older volunteers who wanted to share their life experience. I wish they'd been more serious about promoting two of the three Peace Corps goals, the ones about advancing cultural understanding between Americans and people in other countries.

Overall, though, we were glad we did it. We were proud of the work we did and proud to ring the bell. Champa and I didn't change the world with our service, but we did help people while changing the path of our own lives, for the better. Thirteen people started in my community and organizational development group; only four of us made it through. I was one of them.

It was time to go home.

I celebrated my sixty-fifth birthday a couple of months before we left. The event made me pause and reflect on how my childhood-self could never have predicted that I would mark this occasion in a country called Moldova with my wife from Nepal; that we'd be making a celebratory dinner of foods from our home state of North Carolina.

I'd never heard of Moldova. I'd never heard of Nepal. Even North Carolina seemed exotic to a boy growing up on Long Island in the 1950s and 1960s. For me, a big trip then was to New York City. There were no ATM machines, internet, or smartphones, much less QR codes to hop on a jet plane and fly halfway around the world. Instead of going out to some fancy American restaurant on my 65th birthday, I found myself in the former Soviet Union, nearing the end of my Peace Corps service alongside a woman from the Himalayas who became my beloved wife, giving me more happiness in my life than I'd ever deserved. I shook my head in wonder: How did I get here? How did a boy from Freeport come to celebrate a special birthday in Eastern Europe, receiving congratulatory Facebook messages in English, Romanian, and Nepali from family and friends stretching from Singapore to Seattle?

My life had gone in such unexpected directions, and I had been very lucky. Since people celebrating a birthday in Moldova are expected to arrange and pay for their own party, I organized an American-style pizza-and-cake lunch for my colleagues at the library. They surprised me with several gifts and sang the traditional "Mulţi Ani Trăiască!" in my honor. The next evening, our host family joined us for the North Carolina barbecue dinner Champa prepared. They sang both "Happy Birthday to You" and "Mulți Ani Trăiască!" when they brought out a cake and candles. I received more gifts; but, for me, the best one was learning anew that people around the world have so much more in common than the differences that separate us or make us fear one another. We can all touch each other's lives. We can touch each other's hearts. We can become friends, even families, together.

Champa and I were lucky during our time in Moldova, as well as when we drove around the United States and traveled in Nepal. We ended up with priceless new experiences and friends, putting our old life behind us and re-energizing our own sense of possibility and purpose. My sixty-fifth birthday was not what I expected, nor were the two before it, but they were more memorable than almost any I'd celebrated before. I didn't know what would happen after we returned home, but I was confident and eager to be surprised once more. I'd seen how rich life can become when you let it take you places you never predicted.

CHAPTER 18

COMING HOME

Fall 2018

Now, we're home again. We've moved back into our house in Durham. Our son and his family are less than a mile away. We've seen our other son and his family several times, along with the rest of our family. We have our dog, Bailey, again. We're sleeping in our own bed after three years. In some ways, it's like we never left.

But we did, and we're not the same people we were before.

Coming home was harder than we expected. The day after we rang the COS bell in Moldova, we flew to Italy, spending more than two weeks there before flying home on Turkish Airlines, with an overnight stop in Boston. We landed at the Raleigh-Durham airport early on a Sunday morning, meeting there with a Brazilian professor whose car we rented for several days. Then, we drove home, pulling into our driveway, unloading our four big suitcases, and unlocking the door with keys we'd packed away, wondering if we'd ever use them again. Our house looked fine, but it was empty. It had no furniture in the rooms, no food, nothing on the walls. After we'd been living for two years on the second floor of a Moldovan home, it felt enormous.

For the next several days, we slept on the inflatable bed we'd kept in our storage room. We ate on two plates. We hired a local guy and some teenagers to empty out our storage room and attic, which made us feel less like vagabonds, but we needed weeks to unpack all of the boxes and put everything back in place. We restocked our kitchen with spices, flour, and all of the basics, as well as meals for the days ahead. Our first grocery store bill was nearly $200, which would have lasted us many weeks in Ialoveni. We shopped almost every day. We opened or renewed accounts for all of our utilities. We bought a car. We bought a cell phone. We activated our retiree health coverage with Duke and our homeowners' insurance with our local agent. We got new library cards. We confirmed our voting registration. We did yard work.

While I'd been so busy during my last few months in Moldova, I kept telling myself we could rest after we got home. That didn't happen. We were a different kind of busy, but still scurrying around.

A few weeks later, our older son, Paul, and his family visited from Philadelphia. We had a wonderful time, especially with the twins, whom we still couldn't tell apart even though they were now more than three years old. The two older girls stayed behind with us for ten extra days, and we spoiled them, taking them every day to restaurants, museums, parks, and other places. Champa organized arts and crafts projects. It was heaven.

We drove back with them to Philadelphia and then continued on to our niece's wedding in Manhattan, a black-tie affair with a large band, dancing, and fabulous food. I viewed it as our exam; if we could survive a glitzy New York wedding so soon after serving in the Peace Corps, we could say we had made the transition successfully. The wedding was wonderful. Our niece was beautiful. My only problem, reminiscent of our visit to Glacier National Park, was the soles falling off the bottoms of my tuxedo shoes, which had been sitting in a hot storage room for more than two years. I bought Gorilla glue at a nearby hardware store, which held the shoes together for the rest of the evening. A few weeks later, we attended another family wedding, this one in Rhode Island. A month later, it was a family Bar Mitzvah in Atlanta. I was glad to have bought a new suit in Chişinău before we left.

Only after we returned from New York, two months after we completed our Peace Corps service, did we finally begin to slow down. No sooner did we settle in than Hurricane Florence made its slow rampage across the Carolinas, causing devastation along the coast and also knocking out power and bringing several days of rain to our part of the state. We were lucky to avoid serious damage but were a bit unnerved. All of this happened again, a few weeks later, when Hurricane Michael swept in from the Gulf Coast. The weather forced us indoors, which was fine because we needed to stop moving after three years away from home.

Now we napped. We cooked. We worked out. We binge-watched *Game of Thrones*, *Homeland*, and movies we'd missed. We put our suitcases in the storage room, at least for now.

Champa and I helped each other readjust to America. We didn't need to actually talk about Moldova and our other trips to know they were on our minds. We could sense in each other that although we were back in our house, we weren't back in our lives, at least not the way we'd known them before.

One day, we met for lunch with our friend Jim, one of the older volunteers who'd served with us in Moldova. He told us he was still working through his emotions, too. A few days later, we met with other returned volunteers at the annual picnic of the North Carolina Peace Corps Association. While eating dishes from different countries, I chatted with people who had served in Ethiopia,

Benin, Honduras, Colombia, the Philippines, Turkey, Ukraine, and other countries. I was reassured by how normal and well-adjusted they seemed.

I also distracted myself by helping the Sabin Vaccine Institute organize a workshop in Transylvania that would bring together journalists and health professionals to discuss how they might work together more effectively to improve the coverage of issues involving vaccines. I'd join the conference in early November, returning to Romania but not to Moldova. I also started writing this book, holding off any other work or volunteer jobs until I finished it, while everything remained fresh in my mind.

I'd continued buying magnets for my collection throughout our trips. Now, just like when we'd returned from our drive around the United States, I added them to the collection on our refrigerator. Moldova. Romania. Bulgaria, Armenia. Georgia. Vienna. Budapest. Bratislava. Italy. They were all there. So were Nepal and Qatar and the places we'd visited earlier. The Hare Krishna temple in West Virginia. The Badlands in South Dakota. The Redwoods in California. Chicago. Las Vegas. The Alamo. New Orleans. We'd gone to all of them.

Now they covered our refrigerator and tempted our youngest grandchildren to grab the ones near the bottom. Frankly, the magnets were a little obnoxious at this point, but I stared at them anyway, each evoking a memory. Had I really taken my sisters to the monkey temple in Kathmandu? Had Champa really taught Gagauzian girls in Moldova how to say "Namaste"? I checked Facebook, and, sure enough, Bebeteca remained active at the library. The students at Champa's school were using the drama costumes. Yes, we'd been there.

I rejoined my book club and was reunited with some of my dearest friends. One who still worked at Duke started to fill me in on the latest gossip about various people and departments. After about a minute, I realized I wasn't interested in the updates. I still loved the university and my friends there, but Duke was behind me. It wasn't my life anymore. When I'd left three years earlier, my sense of self and identity had been wrapped up in my work. No longer. Similarly, as I watched the latest political battles, such as the televised fight over Brett Kavanaugh's Supreme Court nomination, I was intensely interested in one sense yet disconnected in another. I'd just spent a long time in a place where people didn't know or care about Brett Kavanaugh or whatever else Americans were fighting about that month.

Nonetheless, it was unnerving to encounter so much rancor after we returned home. Americans were screaming at each other not only about Brett Kavanaugh but about the proposed border wall, the government shutdown, Obamacare, and other political issues. I couldn't remember people on both sides being so agitated, even during the darkest days of the Vietnam War or the Watergate crisis. This was not the America I knew when I left. I was seeing it now with new eyes and from a vantage point of having spent more than two years in a place where cynicism was pervasive.

Moldova was a cautionary example for me. Many of the people I knew there had lost faith in politics and the rule of law. They regarded their leaders as thieves. They were resigned to corruption and deceit. They were wonderful people but deeply pessimistic about the future.

When Champa and I came to Moldova with our M31 group in mid-2016, we were proud to represent the United States. Now, we were back in our country with a president who disdained international alliances, demonized refugees, and insulted developing countries.

It's possible his use of "shitholes" didn't include Moldova, but it was even worse if it didn't. As an American, was I supposed to be proud that I had served in a country where people are poor but at least are white? The new administration even tried to undercut the "Let Girls Learn" initiative that funded our grant at the library to create the Bebeteca family room. Just before we received the money, we were told to no longer refer to the initiative as "let girls learn," which was associated with Michelle Obama.

Americans are still a long way from being as hopeless as Moldovans, but it was tough to come home and find the country moving in the wrong direction. I'm not speaking here for the Peace Corps, which is non-political and has a long history of bipartisan support. I just knew we were better than this. I don't want our country to become as hopeless and cynical as my friends in Moldova or, for that matter, in many other countries around the world where strongmen pursue their own interests and lies abound. I want citizens to trust each other again and embrace the optimism that is our birthright as Americans.

A few months after we got back, I received a Facebook message from Victoria, one of the students in my English conversation class at the library. "Mr David, what happened to the American Government?" she asked me. "I see news everywhere." It was embarrassing to be asked this, but I wrote Victoria back and told her to keep watching because somehow our country will make things right. My heart told me this was true despite everything I was seeing and hearing in the country I once again called home.

Even as we've settled in, part of my heart has remained in Moldova. It will always be there, just as I will always treasure our memories of our time in Nepal and driving around America.

Champa and I are still sorting out what we will do next. We had a great experience with the Peace Corps but don't plan to sign up for another stint, as some of our fellow volunteers have. We don't want to be separated from our family again for so long, and I couldn't put up with all of the regulations, as much as I love the organization and believe in its mission. Nor am I interested in resuming my previous career with another high-stress full-time job. I want to continue working but not in another position that consumes my life and takes over my identity. I want to use my skills and experience to help others, as I did in the Peace Corps, although now I'm more interested in serving my own community and country, addressing the urgent needs we have at home. I've begun talking with various people and organizations about how we might expand the opportunities for local retirees to serve as community volunteers.

Champa is happy, for now, working in her garden, taking art classes, walking our dog, and helping to care for our grandchildren. We've given ourselves through the end of this year to finish this book, enjoy the holidays, and reclaim our American lives.

In October, we drove with my sister and her husband on a trip that took us through Asheville, N.C. We stayed overnight there at the beautiful mountain home of a couple they know who retired early and created a new life tending farm animals, participating in local politics, and enjoying time with their family. They were generous hosts, and we enjoyed sharing their lives for a day. They had made different choices than Champa and me after leaving the conventional workplace, but they were productive, satisfied, and fulfilled. For the two of them, this was their bliss. In turn, they were curious to hear what we had been doing. They were happy for us, as we were for them. Instead of drifting, each of us had chosen something new, rediscovering ourselves off the beaten path. We'd rewritten our itineraries and ended up in a better place.

Coming Home

Champa and I plan to keep traveling and serving. I look forward to revving up my blog again to share our new adventures. Maybe we'll go to the Baltics, Vietnam, or some other far-off location. We still have a list. Maybe we'll go back and spend more time in Moldova or Nepal, or I'll get involved in short-term projects like the journalism workshop in Romania. I'm not sure how or when we'll do this while also working, volunteering in Durham, and seeing more of our family, but we've learned to not worry about it.

We're not exactly retired for real now. We'll figure it out.

Our decision to walk away from our conventional lives surprised my friends at work and caused a long separation from our family.

We began our journey by driving 11,000 miles through 31 states, accompanied by our Blue Devil gnome.

We reunited with our Nepalese family and then welcomed our American family for a tour of Nepal, including an elephant ride.

We learned about Moldova during our Peace Corps training and were posted to Ialoveni, a small city near the capital.

I started a computer coding class at the Ialoveni library and coached its new robotics team.

My two Diamond Challenge entrepreneurship teams were gems, and our "Bebeteca" room at the library attracted local families.

Champa taught English at her school and the library. She got help from Ialoveni's mayor with one project outside the cultural center.

Champa worked closely with her fellow teachers on everything from a Halloween lesson to a big project to create costumes for the school's drama program.

We became dear friends with our host family, especially our beloved Bunica, or grandmother. We prepared an American-style Thanksgiving dinner for the family and another Peace Corps volunteer.

We explored Eastern Europe during our vacations. When we visited home after our first year, two of our granddaughters joined us at Philadelphia's Fourth of July parade.

When we rang the COS bell on the last day of our Peace Corps service in Moldova, we knew we had changed our lives forever.

ACKNOWLEDGEMENTS

Champa and I are grateful to everyone who helped us during the three years described in this book.

Our biggest thanks go to our sons and their families: Paul and Stephanie; Jonathan and Jamie; and our seven grandchildren, to whom I've dedicated this book. They supported our journey even as we missed too many birthday parties, Thanksgiving dinners, school plays, and soccer games. We stayed connected electronically, but it wasn't the same as actually being together. We hope our grandchildren will read this book in the future and know we were thinking of them every day.

My sister, Nancy, helped inspire our journey with her book *Second-Act Careers* and through our many conversations about older Americans finding new meaning in their lives. Nancy also monitored our mail and finances while we were in Moldova. Most important, together with my other sister, Ruth, and the rest of the extended Jarmul family, she cheered for us at every step of our journey. We especially treasured the encouraging messages we received from two older members of our family, John and Susie, and two older friends, Marv and Charlotte.

Friends across the United States welcomed us during the first part of our trip, and we thank all of them for their hospitality. In Nepal, we spent the first part of our trip with Shankar and Bindu, and later with Raju and Sanjaya, everyone in Samalbung, and Meena in Patan. Pooja and her family generously hosted a big dinner at their home for their American relatives. Thanks also to Sports Travel, which arranged everything in Nepal.

Will Shuai Liu house-sat for us while we traveled around the United States and Nepal. Heather Spell Arrington and Mark Teasley of Allenton Management ably managed our home while we were in Moldova. Our neighbors, Phyllis and Jerry Crabb, lent a big hand by accepting our packages and keeping an eye on everything. Special thanks to Jean and Linwood Sawyer for providing a loving home for our dog, Bailey, and then giving her back to us after we returned.

We are indebted to many people in Moldova — Valentina, Lidia, and everyone else at the Ialoveni library; Champa's fellow English teachers, her school director Valentina, and her partner in the costume project, Ana. We have wonderful memories of our host families during training — Vladimir and Maria Sava in Bardar and Maria Ababii in Costeşti. I loved working with my six Diamond Challenge students — Elizabet, Lucia, and Victor; Adriana, Alina, and Alisa, as well as with the members of my English conversation class, my robotics and computer coding students, and everyone else at the library. Laura Bodorin was my partner in producing "Oraşul Meu," our music video about Ialoveni, on which she sings so beautifully.

We made dear friends at Peace Corps with both fellow volunteers and the staff. Big thanks to Bob Gingrich and Joyce Hooley-Gingrich, and to Liuba Chitaev and her husband, Andrei, whose collaboration and friendship were a highlight of my service.

We were lucky that Peace Corps placed us with a host family that became our family in every sense. Mihai and Nina Bordei; their children Alisa, Andrei, and Tatiana; and especially our beloved Bunica, or grandmother, Nadeja, will remain in our hearts forever.

This book benefitted immeasurably from several people who

read and commented on earlier drafts. I am indebted to Nancy Collamer, Jim Fletcher, Bob Gingrich, Mitch Haas, Scott Huler, Camille Jackson, Keith Lawrence, Steve Olson, and Rob Waters for their insights and suggestions. I am responsible for any errors that may have slipped through.

Ryan Archer, from Archer Editing & Writing Services, copy-edited the book. Dania Zafar designed it and produced the wonderful cover. Thanks as well to everyone who took time from their busy lives to read an advance copy of the book and provide a promotional blurb for its marketing.

Marian Haley Beil of the Peace Corps Writers imprint worked for free on behalf of this book, as she has with many other returned volunteers. The entire Peace Corps community is indebted to Marian and her colleague John Coyne.

Finally, the best decision I ever made was to propose more than forty years ago to the talented teacher I met in Ilam, Nepal, where I was posted during my first stint as a Peace Corps Volunteer. Champa has brought me immeasurable happiness throughout our marriage, raising a family together, supporting each other's careers, and sharing our lives. I am now able to tell her in Nepali, Romanian, and English that I love her more than ever.

CPSIA information can be obtained
at www.ICGtesting.com
Printed in the USA
LVHW031648160720
660874LV00007B/1289